HTML5, JavaScript®, and jQuery® 24-Hour Trainer

Dane Cameron

wrox™
A Wiley Brand

HTML5, JavaScript® and jQuery®, 24-Hour Trainer

Published by
John Wiley & Sons, Inc.
10475 Crosspoint Boulevard
Indianapolis, IN 46256
www.wiley.com

Copyright © 2015 by John Wiley & Sons, Inc., Indianapolis, Indiana

Published simultaneously in Canada

ISBN: 978-1-119-00116-4
ISBN: 978-1-119-00118-8 (ebk)
ISBN: 978-1-119-00117-1 (ebk)

Manufactured in the United States of America

10 9 8 7 6 5 4 3 2 1

For general information on our other products and services please contact our Customer Care Department within the United States at (877) 762-2974, outside the United States at (317) 572-3993 or fax (317) 572-4002.

Wiley publishes in a variety of print and electronic formats and by print-on-demand. Some material included with standard print versions of this book may not be included in e-books or in print-on-demand. If this book refers to media such as a CD or DVD that is not included in the version you purchased, you may download this material at http://booksupport.wiley.com. For more information about Wiley products, visit www.wiley.com.

Library of Congress Control Number: 2014958522

ABOUT THE AUTHOR

DANE CAMERON is an author and software engineer living in Wellington, New Zealand. He has worked professionally as a software engineer for many years, developing large-scale enterprise systems, and for the last five years has specialized in the development of HTML5 web applications.

Dane has a double major in Computer Science and English Literature from the University of Otago. A Venn diagram of career prospects quickly identified technical writing as a likely option, and he has built a career based around developing interesting software and passing on what he has learned to others through his books.

Dane currently works for Fronde Systems Group in Wellington, New Zealand, and uses the technologies outlined in this book on a daily basis.

Dane enjoys reading, hiking, and taking road trips across America with his wife.

ABOUT THE TECHNICAL EDITOR

ROHAN HART is a software engineer living in Wellington, New Zealand. He has an extensive background in a variety of languages and technologies, and has worked on several large-scale HTML5 and Java projects over the last few years.

Rohan has a Bachelor of Computing and Mathematical Science, and a Master's degree in Computer Science from Waikato University. When not entranced by code and programming theory, he plays strategy games, tramps the wilderness, and tries to keep up with two sons.

CREDITS

PROJECT EDITOR
Adaobi Obi Tulton

TECHNICAL EDITORS
Rohan Hart
Bede Bignell

PRODUCTION EDITOR
Dassi Zeidel

COPY EDITOR
Nancy Rapoport

MANAGER OF CONTENT DEVELOPMENT & ASSEMBLY
Mary Beth Wakefield

MARKETING DIRECTOR
David Mayhew

MARKETING MANAGER
Carrie Sherrill

PROFESSIONAL TECHNOLOGY & STRATEGY DIRECTOR
Barry Pruett

BUSINESS MANAGER
Amy Knies

ASSOCIATE PUBLISHER
Jim Minatel

PROJECT COORDINATOR, COVER
Patrick Redmond

PROOFREADER
Josh Chase, Word One New York

INDEXER
John Sleeva

COVER DESIGNER
Wiley

COVER IMAGE
©iStock.com/Visiofutura

ACKNOWLEDGMENTS

I would like to thank Bob Elliott from Wiley who first contacted me about writing this book, and who worked with me to develop the original outline. This early feedback was invaluable, and made the writing process so much easier.

I would also like to thank the entire Wiley editorial team, especially Adaobi Obi Tulton and Nancy Rapoport, who worked tirelessly to pull the material together and offered outstanding feedback and insights. I would also like to thank the other members of the Wiley team, including Mary Beth Wakefield and Jim Minatel. The entire team made the process of delivering this book seem simple.

Additionally, I would like to thank Rohan Hart for agreeing to act as the technical editor on this book. I have worked with Rohan for around 10 years, and in all that time he has never failed to spot my mistakes and clean them up.

I would also like to thank Bede Bignell for providing the final technical proof read of the book, and catching any final issues.

I would also like to thank all the developers at Fronde, particularly those I have worked with over the last five years as we worked out the best way to use the functionality HTML5 has offered to deliver high-quality systems to our customers.

Finally, I would like to thank my wife and family for being patient and supportive while I completed this book (even when I was supposed to be on holiday) and for agreeing not to make too much noise while I worked on the screencasts.

CONTENTS

INTRODUCTION

THE BASIC TECHNOLOGIES BEHIND THE WEB are now almost a quarter of a century old. HTML dates all the way back to 1993, the same year the first popular web browser, Mosaic, appeared on the scene.

You may have thought, therefore, that the technologies behind the Web would have entered a comfortable middle-age—still improving around the edges maybe—but not innovating with the pace and excitement of their early years.

In fact, nothing could be further from the truth. The last ten years have been some of the most exciting and innovative in the history of the Web, and this pace of change is continuing to accelerate. As a result, the Web is no longer the preserve of simple "websites." It is the realm of "web applications": feature-rich applications that just happen to run inside web browsers.

A whole new class of computing devices has accentuated the pace of this change. Web browsers are no longer the preserve of desktops and laptops: They now appear on a myriad of devices from smart phones to smart TVs. The fact that web browsers are the one universal feature across these diverse devices has served to enhance the appeal of browser-based web applications: You write the web application once, and your users use it from any device they choose.

This innovation of the last decade did not happen by accident. Various standards committees have been hard at work for more than a decade devising a set of standards that have been grouped under the umbrella of "HTML5." These standards have now made their way into all the major web-browsers.

If you are familiar with HTML, the term HTML5 may simply imply a new version of the HTML markup language—which may be interesting—but not revolutionary. In fact, HTML5 is far more than a markup language; it is a set of programming APIs, implemented by browsers, that allow web pages to perform tasks that had never before been possible.

For example, it is now possible for an HTML page to store massive amounts of data in your browser, operate without a network connection, request more information from a web server as and when it needs it, and perform complex computations in the background without interfering with your browsing experience.

The goal of this book is to teach you how to write web applications. In order to achieve this, you need to understand more than HTML5. You need to understand a set of related technologies. More importantly, however, you need to understand how these technologies work together.

HTML5, for instance, is closely tied to JavaScript. In many cases, if you want to use HTML5, you need to do so through a JavaScript API. It is thus not possible to master HTML5 without also mastering JavaScript.

JavaScript is also approaching middle age, yet it too continues to evolve in tandem with HTML5. Historically considered something of an oddity, JavaScript has turned into a rich and expressive programming language, capable of much more than the simple tasks (such as form validation) that it was consigned for so many years.

A large part of the appeal of JavaScript is the myriad of enormously useful, freely available libraries that are written in the language. Chief among these is jQuery, a JavaScript library that has taken on a life of its own and come to redefine the way programmers add dynamic features to their web pages. You can write web applications without learning jQuery, but your code will lack the conciseness of expression the jQuery library affords.

Finally, in order to produce visually appealing web applications you will need to learn Cascading Style Sheets. Just like all other web technologies, CSS also continues to grow and evolve, and the newest version of CSS—called CSS3—means that web pages can achieve dazzling visual effects.

WHO THIS BOOK IS FOR

This book is for anyone who wants to learn how to build dynamic websites and web applications using standards-based technologies.

You may have experience with HTML4, although that is not required because the early lessons provide an in-depth look at all of the most important features of HTML. More experienced readers may, on the other hand, choose to skip these lessons.

This book contains many code examples based on JavaScript. It is expected that you have some programming experience before reading this book, although not necessarily with JavaScript. If you have no experience with programming, you may want to prepare with some online tutorials and exercises before beginning.

Finally, this book is for programmers who want to learn by doing.

WHAT THIS BOOK COVERS

HTML5 is a "versionless" standard. The specifications behind HTML5 continue to grow and evolve, but this evolution is not matched with "official" or versioned releases.

As such, this book does not focus on a specific version of HTML5; instead, it focuses on the aspects of HTML5 that have achieved widespread adoption in all of the most common web browsers.

The JavaScript language does contain versioned releases, but unlike most programming languages, you have no control over the version that your users will choose because this is a byproduct of the browser that they select. As a result, this book will not focus on a specific version of JavaScript: It will focus on the features that are universally available in all the major browsers.

This book will use a number of JavaScript libraries that are subject to change over time. Whenever a library is used, a specific version will be specified. In many cases, a more recent version of the library will work without issue, although the code is only guaranteed to work with the specified version.

This book is intended as a hands-on guide. Each lesson includes code and exercises that you can follow along with, and even augment if you choose. It is important that you follow along with these exercises because it is this process that will consolidate your understanding of how the technologies really work.

HOW THIS BOOK IS STRUCTURED

This book is split into five sections. The first two sections are intended to be read in order because they provide you with the foundation knowledge required to add more complex functionality. The remaining three sections can be read in any order you choose.

The first section of the book provides an introduction to HTML and CSS and looks at how to build static web pages with these technologies. By the end of this lesson, you will have a solid foundation on which to start adding more complex functionality.

In the second section, you turn your attention to JavaScript and jQuery, and look at how a static web page can be converted into a dynamic web application.

The third section of the book looks at the multimedia capabilities of web browsers and how you can harness these through technologies such as the Canvas API and CSS3.

Once you have an understanding of JavaScript, you can turn your attention to the HTML5 APIs that allow you to store data inside the browser, access data from web servers, and execute tasks on background processes. It is these features that truly turn your website into a feature-rich web application.

In the final section of the book, you will turn your attention to mobile devices and address the question of how you can convert your web application into a mobile web application that functions on any mobile device your users may choose to use.

A large portion of this book is structured around the development of a sample web application. If you choose to skip a lesson, you will therefore need to download a completed version of that lesson's web application before starting the next lesson.

WHAT YOU NEED TO USE THIS BOOK

In order to complete most of the exercises in this book, you will need nothing more than a text editor and the Chrome web browser.

If you have a favorite text editor, you can continue to use it for this book. If you do not have a text editor installed, Notepad++ (`http://notepad-plus-plus.org`) is a good option for Windows, Text Wrangler (`http://www.barebones.com/products/textwrangler`) is a good choice for Macs, and EMacs is a good choice for Linux. You may also choose to use an Integrated Development Environment (IDE) such as Eclipse.

The Chrome web browser has been chosen for this book not so much for the capabilities of the browser itself, but for the developer tools that accompany it. You can choose to use an alternative web browser if you wish, but the examples will focus on Chrome.

The Chrome web browser is subject to frequent updates, and it is assumed that you will use the latest version of the browser.

In later sections of this book, you will also need a web server. A lesson is provided to guide you through the process of installing and configuring a web server.

The source code for the samples is available for download from the Wrox website at:

```
www.wrox.com/go/html5jsjquery24hr
```

CONVENTIONS

To help you get the most from the text and keep track of what's happening, we've used a number of conventions throughout the book.

> **WARNING** *Warnings hold important, not-to-be-forgotten information that is directly relevant to the surrounding text.*

> **NOTE** *Notes indicate notes, tips, hints, tricks, or asides to the current discussion.*

As for styles in the text:

- ➤ We *highlight* new terms and important words when we introduce them.
- ➤ We show keyboard strokes like this: Ctrl+A.
- ➤ We show filenames, URLs, and code within the text like so: persistence.properties.
- ➤ We present code in two different ways:

```
We use a monofont type with no highlighting for most code examples.
```

```
We use bold to emphasize code that is particularly important in the present
context or to show changes from a previous code snippet.
```

SOURCE CODE

As you work through the examples in this book, you may choose either to type in all the code manually or to use the source code files that accompany the book. All the source code used in this book is available for download at www.wrox.com. For this book, the code download is on the Download Code tab at:

```
www.wrox.com/go/html5jsjquery24hr
```

You can also search for the book at www.wrox.com by ISBN (the ISBN for this book is 978-1-1190-0116-4) to find the code. A complete list of code downloads for all current Wrox books is available at www.wrox.com/dynamic/books/download.aspx.

Most of the code on www.wrox.com is compressed in a .ZIP or .RAR archive, or a similar archive format appropriate to the platform. Once you download the code, just decompress it with an appropriate compression tool.

ERRATA

We make every effort to ensure that there are no errors in the text or in the code. However, no one is perfect, and mistakes do occur. If you find an error in one of our books, such as a spelling mistake or faulty piece of code, we would be very grateful for your feedback. By sending in errata, you may save another reader hours of frustration, and at the same time, you will be helping us provide even higher quality information.

To find the errata page for this book, go to

> www.wrox.com/go/html5jsjquery24hr

and click the Errata link. On this page you can view all errata that has been submitted for this book and posted by Wrox editors.

If you don't spot "your" error on the Book Errata page, go to www.wrox.com/contact/techsupport.shtml and complete the form there to send us the error you have found. We'll check the information and, if appropriate, post a message to the book's errata page and fix the problem in subsequent editions of the book.

P2P.WROX.COM

For author and peer discussion, join the P2P forums at http://p2p.wrox.com. The forums are a Web-based system for you to post messages relating to Wrox books and related technologies and interact with other readers and technology users. The forums offer a subscription feature to email you topics of interest of your choosing when new posts are made to the forums. Wrox authors, editors, other industry experts, and your fellow readers are present on these forums.

At http://p2p.wrox.com, you will find a number of different forums that will help you, not only as you read this book, but also as you develop your own applications. To join the forums, just follow these steps:

1. Go to http://p2p.wrox.com and click the Register link.

2. Read the terms of use and click Agree.

3. Complete the required information to join, as well as any optional information you wish to provide, and click Submit.

4. You will receive an email with information describing how to verify your account and complete the joining process.

> **NOTE** *You can read messages in the forums without joining P2P, but in order to post your own messages, you must join.*

Once you join, you can post new messages and respond to messages other users post. You can read messages at any time on the Web. If you would like to have new messages from a particular forum emailed to you, click the Subscribe to this Forum icon by the forum name in the forum listing.

For more information about how to use the Wrox P2P, be sure to read the P2P FAQs for answers to questions about how the forum software works, as well as many common questions specific to P2P and Wrox books. To read the FAQs, click the FAQ link on any P2P page.

PART I
HTML and CSS

Introduction to HTML5

This lesson is an introduction to the HTML5 markup language. The HTML5 markup language is a language for structuring and expressing the content of a web page in a manner that can be consistently interpreted by a web browser.

If you are already familiar with HTML, much of this chapter will look very familiar. It is still important that you read through this lesson, however, because there are a number of important changes in HTML5, and many of these are very subtle.

If you are not familiar with HTML, or have only a passing familiarity, this lesson will provide you with the background you need to understand the basics of an HTML web page. This lesson is only an introduction, however; the material in this lesson will be enhanced in the remainder of this section.

WHAT IS A MARKUP LANGUAGE?

A markup language is a language for annotating a document with a set of tags. These tags are used to provide additional meaning and structure to the text of the document, or provide instructions on the manner in which it should be displayed to the reader.

For instance, a tag may state that one portion of the text is a header, while another portion is a paragraph of text. Consider the following document fragment:

```
<h1>This is a heading</h1>
<p>This is a paragraph of text</p>
```

In this example, the tags can be clearly differentiated from the content of the document by the angle brackets. The following represents the start of a heading:

```
<h1>
```

while this represents the end of the heading:

```
</h1>
```

> **NOTE** *HTML defines six categories of header from h1 to h6. The lower the number, the more important the header is.*

The entire `h1` structure—including the start tag, the end tag, and its textual content—is referred to as an element.

The HTML5 markup language specifies the tags that can be used in an HTML document, how they should be used, and what additional information (called attributes) they can contain.

In the early days of HTML, many of the tags included in the markup language instructed the browser how to present information. For instance, tags were used to dictate font size and color.

The HTML markup language is no longer responsible for dictating the presentation of a document, and in HTML5 most of the remaining presentation tags have been removed. Presentation is now the sole preserve of another technology called *Cascading Style Sheets*, which will be examined later in this section.

Instead, the HTML5 markup language is responsible for conveying the meaning of the various components of the document and how they interact with other components.

> **NOTE** *Browsers can still provide their own default styles for tags, however, and this is why an `h1` element will appear in large, bold text.*

HTML5 greatly enhances the expressiveness of earlier version of HTML, however, and allows sections of the document to be marked as, amongst other things, headers, footers, and asides.

Earlier versions of HTML were based on a technology called SGML, which is a language for expressing markup languages. As of HTML5, the HTML markup language is not based on any other technology. This has removed a number of restrictions from the language; therefore, if you are familiar with HTML, you will notice in the sections that follow that a number of the old rules no longer apply.

THE SIMPLEST HTML PAGE POSSIBLE

When learning any technology, it's always a good idea to start out with the simplest implementation possible. In HTML5, the simplest page you can possibly write is as follows:

```
<!DOCTYPE html>
hello world!!!
```

Open your favorite text editor, enter this text, and save the document as `hello.html`.

Now, open Chrome, and select Ctrl-O in Windows or ⌘-O on a Mac, navigate to the file you have just saved, and select "Open". This should look like Figure 1-1 when loaded in the web browser.

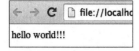

FIGURE 1-1

This may not look like a web page; after all, there are no tags in the page except the strange looking tag on the first line of the document.

With the page open in Chrome, now select to open the developer tools:

➤ Command+Option+I on OS X

➤ F12 or Ctrl+Shift+I on Windows

This should open the window shown in Figure 1-2 below the web page.

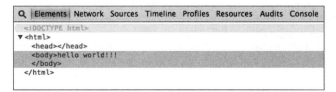

FIGURE 1-2

This is the web-browser's internal representation of the web page. As you can see, this has normalized the structure of the document, and does provide a set of tags nested inside one another. On the outermost level is the html element, and inside this are two elements: head and body. The content of the body element is the text you wrote in the text editor.

The document has been normalized to conform to the rules of the Document Object Model (DOM). The DOM will turn out to be enormously important throughout this book because much of the power of modern web pages comes from their ability to manipulate the DOM after the page has loaded.

The manner in which a Document Object Model should be constructed from an HTML page has been a contentious issue since HTML first appeared. Historically, different browsers would generate different models for the same HTML, and this made it very difficult to write cross-browser web pages.

In order to counteract cross-browser issues, the World Wide Web Consortium (W3C), which is the standards body behind web standards such as HTML, decided to recommend a set of standards placing the onus on the web page developer. These standards, called HTML Strict and XHTML, forced the web page developer to create a normalized web page, and therefore made it easy for web browsers to render pages consistently.

This approach did not work very well. The real power behind HTML is not the standards bodies, but the browser vendors because they ultimately decide what is a valid web page. They did not want to enforce this strictness on web pages because failing to load web pages would only serve to make their browser look deficient.

As the W3C continued on with their strict standards, a rival group called WHATWG started work on a rival standard that would eventually become HTML5. The members of this group were made up of participants from the main browser vendors, and their goals were far more pragmatic. Rather than creating a whole new set of standards, this group first looked at what browsers were already doing and, where possible, formed standards from this.

W3C eventually abandoned their efforts for strictness and joined WHATWG's efforts, and the two groups each publish a version of the HTML5 standard.

A large part of the HTML5 standard describes how browser vendors should create a normalized DOM from a non-normalized HTML document. This is why Chrome created the DOM that it did in the preceding example, and why Firefox, IE, and Safari would create exactly the same structures.

AN HTML TEMPLATE

In the previous section, you wrote the simplest web page you could write. In this section, you will write a web page following a basic template that is intended to represent the simplest HTML structure you should write.

I will first present the template, and then I will walk you through it line by line. Open a new document in your text editor, and save the following as `template.html`:

```
<!DOCTYPE html>
<html lang="en">
<head>
    <meta charset="utf-8">
</head>
<body>
        This is the body of the document.
</body>
</html>
```

If you open this in Chrome, and then view the DOM in the developer tools, it will look like the example in Figure 1-3.

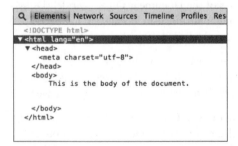

FIGURE 1-3

As you can see, in this case there is far closer alignment between the content you provided in the HTML file and the normalized structure generated by the browser.

Let's now walk through each line in the document and examine its purpose.

The first line in the document is as follows:

```
<!DOCTYPE html>
```

This line defines the document type of the page. Because there have been many different HTML standards over the years, the browser uses this line to understand which of these standards the page is using, and then uses the rules applicable for this standard to interpret the content of the page and render it accordingly.

This is the HTML5 document type definition, and comes as a pleasant surprise for developers who may be accustomed to copying and pasting DOCTYPE declarations such as:

```
<!DOCTYPE HTML PUBLIC "-//W3C//DTD HTML 4.01//EN" "http://www.w3.org/TR/html4/
strict.dtd">
```

The other main surprise about this document type definition is that it does not include a version number: The document type is simply `html`.

Although the specification is referred to as HTML5, it defines a "living-standard" that will be subject to incremental change as and when browser vendors implement, and agree on, new features. Put another way, there will never be another version of HTML, but HTML will always continue to evolve.

The next line contains the opening `html` tag, which encapsulates the remainder of the document:

```
<html lang="en">
```

This tag contains an attribute called `lang`, which has been given the value `en`. Attributes provide a mechanism for providing extra meaning to tags. This particular attribute is stating that the language of the document is English.

> **NOTE** *The ISO standard 639-1 defines the set of two-letter codes that can be used for languages. These can also be paired with a country code, for instance en-US. Country codes are defined in the ISO standard 3166.*

As with many aspects of HTML5, although the specification defines the attributes and their expected values, it is up to the browser to decide what to do with this information. The browser may use this information to suggest a translation to a non-English speaker, or it may do absolutely nothing with this information.

The next element in the document is the `head` element. This is the section of the document where you can provide important metadata about the document, along with links to other files needed by the document. The `head` section never contains any visual components of the web page. In this particular case, the `head` contains one important piece of metadata:

```
<meta charset="utf-8" />
```

This specifies that the character encoding of the document is UTF-8. I will not cover character encodings in this section, but the specification recommends setting this.

There is one other element that is commonly added to the `head` element: the `title` element. This is the text that the browser will display in the title bar when the web page is loaded. Therefore, add the following inside the `head` section:

```
<title>Basic template</title>
```

and then view the page in Chrome; the tab header will appear as follows:

FIGURE 1-4

Next you come to the body element. This is where all the visual elements of the page will be described. In this particular example, the body consists of a single text string, but it is this area of the document that you will enhance in the chapters ahead to create interesting web pages.

UNDERSTANDING ELEMENTS AND ATTRIBUTES

Even though the examples you have created are very simple, you can already see that elements can be nested inside one another, and as a result, create a tree-like structure.

Every HTML document has a single top-level element, which is always the html element (the document type element is not part of the document as such).

In addition, every element in the document can have zero or more children. The html element has two children: head and body. The head element in turn has a child of its own: the meta element.

Every element in the document (except the html element) has one (and only one) parent. The parent of the head element is the html element. The parent of the meta element is the head element.

As you will see, the structure of pages will become considerably more complex, and the degrees of nesting will increase enormously. No matter how complex the pages become, however, all the elements will follow these simple rules.

You have examined how elements consist of an opening and closing tag; for instance the opening of the head tag is <head> while the closing is an identically named tag preceded by a forward slash </head>.

Some elements do not require any content: The tag and its attributes provide all the information that is required. In this case, the start and the end tag can be combined into the following construct:

```
<meta charset="utf-8" />
```

The forward slash before the end of the tag indicates that the tag is being closed. This is the direct equivalent of the following:

```
<meta charset="utf-8"></meta>
```

You should always ensure that all tags are closed in the reverse order they are opened. For example, you should never write markup as follows:

```
<p><strong>Hello</p></strong>
```

In this case, the strong element is supposed to be the child of the p element, but the p element ends before the strong element.

> **NOTE** The strong *tag is used to indicate that a piece of text is important. Although this is often confused with the now deprecated* bold *tag, it is, in fact, still a valid HTML5 tag. This tag is not considered a presentation tag because it indicates that text is important, not how this text should be styled. You may decide that* strong *elements are colored red rather than with a bold font.*

If you add this to your `template.html` file before the ending `body` tag, and then view the normalized structure in Chrome, you will notice that the browser has rearranged these tags, as you can see in Figure 1-5.

Although the HTML5 specification does have rules for fixing up your mistakes, it is generally best not to make mistakes in the first place because the rules of the HTML5 specification may not be what you intended.

FIGURE 1-5

I generally find it best to write tags in lowercase. As it turns out, tag names are entirely case insensitive because they are automatically converted to lowercase in the DOM. The following is therefore valid, but should be avoided for obvious readability reasons:

```
<HEADER>this is a header</header>
```

The final feature I will cover in this lesson is attributes. You have already seen two examples of attributes, on the `html` tag and on the `meta` tag. Many other tags also support attributes, and you will examine these throughout the book.

Attributes often consist of a name/value pair. When an attribute has a value, the value can either be included in single or double quotes. The following are equivalent:

```
<meta charset="utf-8" />
<meta charset='utf-8' />
```

A tag can contain more than one attribute, in which case they are simply separated by white space:

```
<p id="firstParagraph" class="bold">
```

Additionally, some attributes do not have a value. These are referred to as Boolean attributes. The presence of the attribute is all that is required. For instance:

```
<input read-only/>
```

In this case, the attribute is called `read-only`, but the presence of the attribute is enough to indicate that the element is read-only. It is still possible to add a value to a Boolean attribute, but it has no meaning. For instance, the following input field is still read-only:

```
<input read-only="false"/>
```

Attribute names should also be written in lowercase (because this is how they will be represented in the DOM). Generally attribute names will also use hyphens if they contain more than one word.

TRY IT

In this Try It, you will duplicate the template html page outlined in the lesson. You may choose to skip this portion if you are familiar with HTML, but the simple act of typing code word for word enhances your understanding.

If you get stuck in this example, you can refer back to the example earlier in the lesson, or use the screencast to guide you though the process.

Lesson Requirements

You will need a text editor and a web browser.

Step-by-Step

1. Open your text editor and create a new document.

2. Add the HTML5 `doctype` to the document.

3. Add an `html` element (both the opening and closing tags) below the document type.

4. Indicate the language of the document using an attribute on the `html` tag.

5. Add a `head` element inside the `html` element. You will need both an opening and a closing tag.

6. Add a `title` inside the head element, and give the document a name. Remember that this needs to be a child of the `head` element.

7. Add a `body` element inside the `html` element just below the closing `head` tag.

8. Add a `meta` element to the `head` indicating that the charset is UTF-8.

9. Add any text you like to the `body` of the document. Any text that you add should be displayed back to you when you open the web page in Chrome.

10. Save the document with a `.html` extension.

11. Open the document in Chrome and inspect the Document Object Model in the developer tools.

When you open this in Chrome, and then open the development tools to inspect the elements, the markup should look like Figure 1-6.

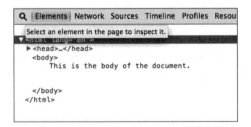

FIGURE 1-6

There is also a complete example in the Lesson 1 folder on the book's website called `tryit.html`.

> **REFERENCE** *Please select the video for Lesson 1 online at www.wrox.com/go/ html5jsjquery24hr. You will also be able to download the code and resources for this lesson from the website.*

Basic HTML

This lesson provides a basic introduction to the most common HTML tags. If you are already familiar with HTML and are reading this book primarily to learn about HTML5, you could choose to skip the next two lessons, although each lesson does include material that is specific to HTML5.

In the previous lesson, you created an HTML template. In this lesson, you will start adding content to the body of this template using some of the most common HTML tags.

STRUCTURING TEXT

You will begin by examining the ways you can structure text in a web page. HTML originally started life as a means of sharing research papers; thus, text formatting has always been an important part of HTML.

Begin by opening the `template.html` file created in the previous chapter. Replace the `body` of the web page, as shown in the following markup:

```
<!DOCTYPE html>
<html lang="en">
<head>
    <meta charset="utf-8">
</head>
<body>
    <h1>This is a top level heading</h1>
    <h2>This is a second level heading</h2>
    <h3>This is a third level heading</h3>
</body>
</html>
```

The `body` now contains three separate header elements. If you open this in Chrome, it should look like Figure 2-1.

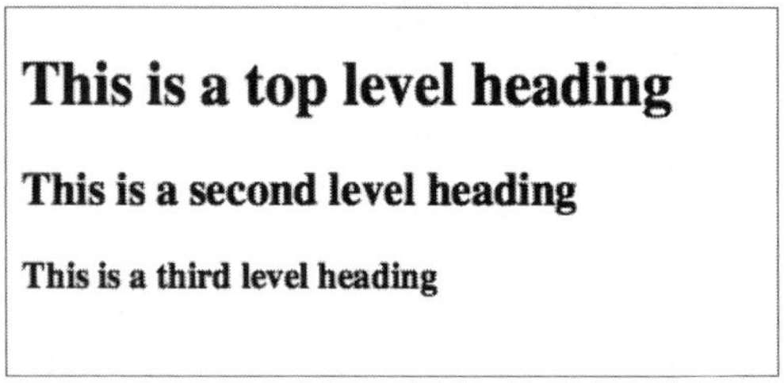

This is a top level heading

This is a second level heading

This is a third level heading

FIGURE 2-1

Notice that the `h1` element's text is displayed in a larger font than the `h2` element. As it happens, this has nothing to do with the HTML specification; this is simply the default style provided by the web browser, just as the font is the default font of the browser. In Lesson 4, you will see how this can be overridden with Cascading Style Sheets (CSS).

You will also notice that each heading is displayed on a new line. This is not because the elements are placed on new lines in the HTML file; in fact, white space is mostly ignored in HTML. In order to prove this, change the `h1` tag as follows:

```
<h1>This is     a     top
       level heading</h1>

     <h2>This is a second level heading</h2>
```

If you reload the web page, you will see that this change makes no difference to the way the headings display. Although a single whitespace character is displayed as a space inside an element, a sequence of whitespace characters, even if it contains new-line characters, is collapsed down to a single white space character.

HTML does provide a special character sequence, ` `, for adding extra whitespace characters, but new lines should be created using the tags introduced shortly.

> **NOTE** *The ampersand character, followed by a sequence of characters and terminated by a semicolon, indicates that this is a special character sequence.*
>
> *There are a number of special character sequences in HTML. Perhaps the most common ones you will encounter are* `&lt;` *and* `&gt;`*, which are used for the less than (<) and greater than (>) characters respectively. These are required because the < and > characters have special meaning in HTML. In case you were wondering,* `nbsp` *stands for "non-breaking space."*

So what did generate the new lines after each heading? These appear because the elements `h1` through `h6` are `block` elements. All visual HTML elements have a display type, the most common of which are `block` and `inline`. Whenever a `block` element ends, the next element automatically begins on a new line.

Next, you can continue by adding some paragraphs to the `body`:

```
<p>This is the first paragraph</p>
<p>This is the second paragraph</p>
```

If you refresh the web page, it will look like what you see in Figure 2-2.

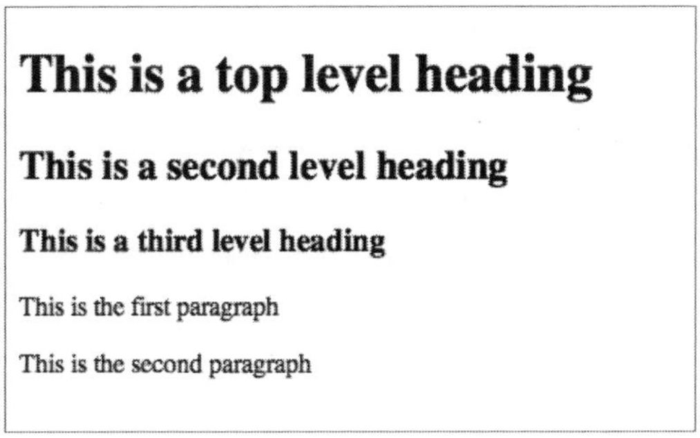

This is a top level heading

This is a second level heading

This is a third level heading

This is the first paragraph

This is the second paragraph

FIGURE 2-2

Each paragraph appears on a new line, and there is a space between each paragraph.

It is actually possible to omit the ending tag from a `p` tag. In fact, there are many cases where the ending tag can be omitted because the next tag in the document implies it. I usually find it easier to add the ending tag in these cases, but the specification makes this entirely optional. You will see throughout the examples that I sometimes omit the closing tag and sometimes include it.

WHAT ABOUT XHTML?

If you are already familiar with HTML, you may be aware of XHTML, which is an XML-based version of HTML. HTML5 extends and replaces XHTML as well as HTML. In order to serialize an HTML5 page to XML, all tags must be closed, and the document as a whole must be well-formed. In addition, the `html` tag should be declared as follows:

```
<html xmlns="http://www.w3.org/1999/xhtml">
```

and the content type of the document should be set to `application/xhtml+xml` rather than `text/html` when it is served to the browser.

If you are not already familiar with XHTML, you can ignore it for the duration of this book: It is typically only used if you have a need to process an HTML page with XML parsers and tools.

The text in a paragraph will automatically wrap if it reaches the far right side of the browser. Additionally, if the user resizes their browser, the text will automatically be adjusted: This process is referred to as a browser reflow.

Sometimes the browser will break your paragraphs in an inconvenient place, especially if it contains very large words. In order to give you more control over line breaks, HTML5 has introduced a tag called wbr that can be added anywhere inside a paragraph as a hint to the browser that this would be a good place to add a line break.

If you would like a line break within a paragraph, you can use the br tag. This is also a self-closing tag so it can be used as follows:

```
<p>This is a paragraph<br>that spans two lines</p>
```

HTML supports several other tags for encapsulating blocks of text. The final one you will look at in this section is the blockquote element, which can be used to capture quoted text, optionally with a citation:

```
<blockquote>Tell me and I forget. Teach me and I remember. Involve me and I learn.
    <cite>Benjamin Franklin</cite>
</blockquote>
```

This structure is slightly more complex: The blockquote tag contains the quote, while cite, which is an optional child tag, captures the source of the quote. Figure 2-3 shows an example of this tag in Chrome.

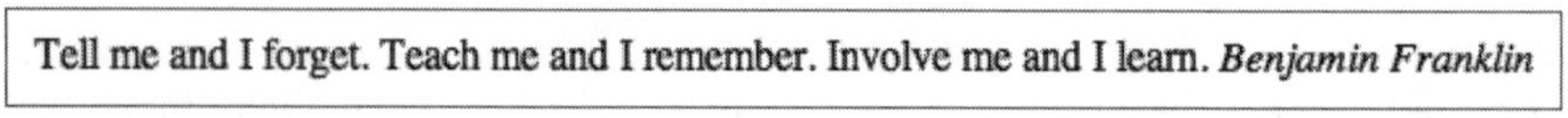

Tell me and I forget. Teach me and I remember. Involve me and I learn. *Benjamin Franklin*

FIGURE 2-3

Notice that the blockquote is indented and that the cite element displays in italics. Again, these are browser defaults rather than part of the HTML5 specification.

Finally, as your web pages become more complex, you may find cases where you would like to add comments to remind you what the markup means. Comments can be added as follows, and will not display to the user:

```
<!-- This is a comment -->
```

LINKS AND IMAGES

HTML pages naturally consist of far more than text. This section will introduce two of the most fundamental tags found in most web pages: hyperlinks and images.

I will assume you know what hyperlinks are: They are a mechanism for referencing another HTML document and can be clicked to allow the user to navigate to that document.

Start by creating a new page in the same folder as the page you developed in the previous section, but call this one page2.html. Add some contents to this page so that you can distinguish it when it loads.

Now, in the original HTML file, add the following paragraph:

```
<p>Please click <a href="page2.html">here</a> to view page 2</p>
```

If you reload the page, this HTML will generate the text found in Figure 2-4.

> Please click here to view page 2

FIGURE 2-4

Notice that the text displayed to the user is derived from the content of the a tag, while the page that is loaded when the link is clicked can be found in the `href` attribute.

This particular URL is referred to as a relative URL because it does not start with a forward slash or a domain name. The browser will attempt to find `page2.html` in a location relative to the page currently being displayed.

If you had created `page2.html` in a subfolder called sub, the URL would be represented as follows:

```
<p>Please click <a href="sub/page2.html">here</a> to view page 2</p>
```

When running a website inside a web server, it is also possible to use absolute URLs. These begin with a leading / and require the full path for the file to be specified.

It is also possible to add URLs to other websites. For example:

```
<a href="http://www.google.com">Link to Google</a>
```

You will also notice that the a tag does not cause an implicit new line to be generated in the document. This is because, unlike most of the other tags you have examined, it has a display type of `inline`.

Hyperlinks can be surprisingly complex. As you progress through the book you will see more interesting features of hyperlinks, such as the manner in which they can encode parameters, but for now a basic understanding is sufficient.

Images can be inserted into an HTML page with the `img` tag. I seldom use the `img` tag anymore: I typically use CSS to embed images as the background of other tags because this provides greater control for positioning the image, but it is important to understand how this tag works.

You can either find an image you would like to use or download `photo1.jpg` from the Lesson 2 files at the book's website.

Now, add the following to the HTML page:

```
<p>This is a photo I took in Cambridge
<img src="photo1.jpg"
title="Cambridge, England" width="200"></p>
```

If you view this in Chrome, it will display in much the same way as you see in Figure 2-5.

FIGURE 2-5

This is the first tag you have examined with multiple attributes.

> ➤ The `src` attribute is used to specify the location of the file. Just like hyperlinks, this can be an absolute or a relative URL, or it can even reference an image on another website.

> ➤ The `title` attribute is used to specify a tooltip that will be displayed to the reader when the reader hovers over the image with her mouse cursor, and to describe the image to screen readers.

> ➤ The `width` attribute is used to specify the width of the image in pixels. It is also possible to specify a `height`, but if just `width` or `height` is specified, the image will be scaled appropriately.

Browsers support many different image types, but by far the most common are PNG, GIF, and JPEG images.

The `img` tag previously supported a number of other presentation-orientated attributes. These are deprecated in HTML5, and CSS properties should be used instead.

> **NOTE** *When a feature is deprecated, it is still available to use, and will probably still work, but it is strongly suggested that you find an alternative because support may be removed entirely in the future.*

TRY IT

This Try It is an opportunity to experiment with the tags that have been discussed in this lesson. You do not necessarily need to follow this lesson exactly; just try to create an interesting web page from the tags that have been introduced.

Lesson Requirements

You will need the `template.html` file from Lesson 1, a text editor, and a web browser.

Step-by-Step

1. Open the `template.html` page in your text editor.

2. Add an `h1` element to the page and include some header text.

3. Add some paragraphs to the web page using the `p` tag, and split some paragraphs across multiple lines with the `br` tag.

4. Add a quote to the page along with a citation, using the `blockquote` and `cite` tags.

5. Find an image you would like to include in the page, and add it at the bottom. Make the image a fixed width, and allow the browser to determine the correct height.

6. Add a hyperlink to your page to point to another page in a subfolder of the current page.

7. Add a hyperlink to an external website such as Google.

8. Although I have not covered it, attempt to turn the image into a hyperlink so that it loads another page when it is clicked. Hint: The image will need to be a child element of the hyperlink.

My example can be found in the Lesson 2 resources on the `tryit.html` website.

> **REFERENCE** *Please select the video for Lesson 2 online at www.wrox.com/go/*
> *html5jsjquery24hr. You will also be able to download the code and resources*
> *for this lesson from the website.*

3

Lists and Tables

In this lesson, you will look at two important ways content can be structured in web pages: lists and tables.

LISTS

Lists are common to anyone who has worked with word processing tools such as Microsoft Word: They are the bulleted and numbered lists that are used for capturing a sequence of points. HTML lists are very similar to these lists. In this section, I introduce the three types of list provided by HTML.

Unordered lists

Unordered lists are used to create the familiar set of bullet points seen in Word documents. In order to create an unordered list, a set of li elements is placed inside an ul element. li stands for "list item," while ul stands for "unordered list."

The following is an example:

```
<!DOCTYPE html>
<html lang="en">
    <head>
        <meta charset="utf-8">
    </head>
    <body>
        <ul>
            <li>This is the first point
            <li>This is the second point
            <li>This is the third point
        </ul>
    </body>
</html>
```

If you save this in an HTML file and open it in Chrome, it will display like the example in Figure 3-1.

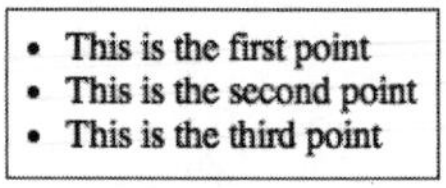

The li tag is self-closing, so I have omitted the ending tag. Obviously, this could have been included without affecting the display of the list.

- This is the first point
- This is the second point
- This is the third point

FIGURE 3-1

Although unordered lists are simple, once they are combined with CSS, they can become very powerful. Whenever you see a horizontal list of navigation links at the top of a web page, there is a good chance that they were created from an unordered list.

Ordered Lists

Ordered lists are identical to unordered lists, except they use the ol tag rather than the ul tag. The only visual difference between the two lists is that ordered lists are numbered:

```
<ol>
    <li>This is the first point
    <li>This is the second point
    <li>This is the third point
</ol>
```

Figure 3-2 illustrates how this displays.

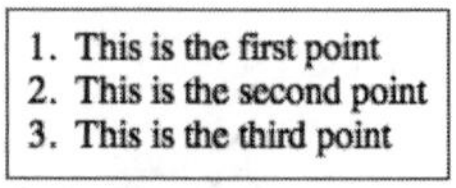

Any element can be used as the content for an li tag; thus, it is possible to nest lists within lists. The following example lists an unordered list inside an ordered list:

1. This is the first point
2. This is the second point
3. This is the third point

FIGURE 3-2

```
<ol>
    <li>point 1
        <ul>
            <li>sub point 1</li>
            <li>sub point 2</li>
        </ul>
    </li>
    <li>point 2
        <ul>
            <li>sub point 1</li>
            <li>sub point 2</li>
        </ul>
    </li>
    <li>point without sub points</li>
</ol>
```

The result of this can be seen in Figure 3-3.

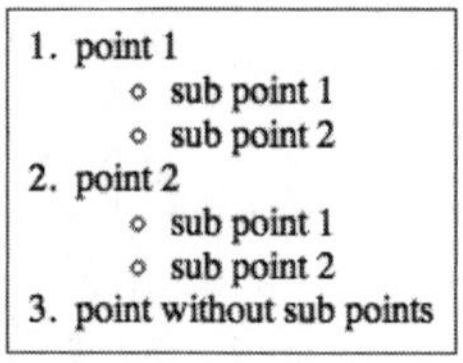

1. point 1
   o sub point 1
   o sub point 2
2. point 2
   o sub point 1
   o sub point 2
3. point without sub points

FIGURE 3-3

Description Lists

Description lists are probably the least used type of list. They are a type of list where each entry captures a name-value group. Each group in turn consists of one or more names, followed by one or more definitions. Consider the following list, which captures information about the drinks served by a cafe:

```
<dl>
    <dt>Coffee</dt>
        <dd>Cappuccino</dd>
```

```
        <dd>Espresso</dd>
        <dd>Mocha</dd>
    <dt>Tea</dt>
        <dd>Earl grey</dd>
        <dd>Green tea</dd>
        <dd>Chai tea</dd>
</dl>
```

This list contains two groups: coffee and tea. Each group then consists of a set of beverages relating to that group. You can see the result of this in Figure 3-4.

Definition lists were originally specified purely in terms of terms and definitions. The HTML5 standard broadens the suggested uses of definition lists and encourages you to think in terms of groups with names and values.

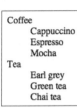

FIGURE 3-4

TABLES

Tables are a more complex structure than lists and support the familiar notion of rows and columns.

Throughout the course of this book, you will write a web application from scratch, and this web application will utilize a table. The web application will perform basic Customer Relationship Management (CRM) capabilities; in particular, it will keep track of a set of contacts and the last date they were contacted.

In order to start this web application, create a folder somewhere on your file system called CRM. This will hold all the files needed by the web application.

Next, add a file called `contacts.html` to this folder, and populate it with the basic HTML5 template outlined in Lesson 1.

You will now create a table in the `body` of the web page for capturing the following information:

➤ Contact name

➤ Phone number

➤ Email address

➤ Contact's company

➤ Date last contacted

To start, begin by creating an opening and closing `table` tag in the `body` of the web page:

```
<table>
</table>
```

HTML tables are row orientated: You add one row at a time using the `tr` (table row) element and provide values for all the relevant columns. The rows can either be added to the header, body or footer of the table. Add the following inside the `table` element:

```
<thead>
    <tr>
        <th>Contact name</th>
        <th>Phone number</th>
```

```
            <th>Email address</th>
            <th>Company name</th>
            <th>Last contacted</th>
        </tr>
    </thead>
```

The row in the `thead` element contains five children of its own: These `th` (table heading) elements are the individual cells in the row of the table.

Next, you will add two rows to the body of the table. The body of the table is encapsulated in a `tbody` element. The individual cells in the body use the `td` (table datum) element rather than the `th` element. Add the following after the end of the `thead` element:

```
<tbody>
    <tr>
        <td>William Smith</td>
        <td>555-642-7371</td>
        <td>william@testing.com</td>
        <td>ACME Industries</td>
        <td>2014-10-21</td>
    </tr>
    <tr>
        <td>Bob Morris</td>
        <td>555-999-2991</td>
        <td>bob@testing.com</td>
        <td>ABC Corp</td>
        <td>2014-09-12</td>
    </tr>
</tbody>
```

Next, you will add a footer row to the table. The footer will simply state how many rows are in the `table`; thus, it only needs to occupy a single cell. This presents a dilemma because you want all the rows in the able to have the same number of columns. The solution to this is to utilize the `colspan` attribute with the `td` element to specify that a single `td` spans multiple columns. Add the following after the end of the `tbody` element:

```
<tfoot>
    <tr>
        <td colspan="5">2 contacts displayed</td>
    </tr>
</tfoot>
```

Finally, you will add a caption for the table. This can be added anywhere in the table, provided it is a direct child of the `table` element itself:

```
<caption>Sales leads</caption>
```

The complete web page should now look as follows:

```
<table>
    <thead>
        <tr>
            <th>Contact name</th>
            <th>Phone number</th>
```

```
            <th>Email address</th>
            <th>Company name</th>
            <th>Last contacted</th>
        </tr>
    </thead>
    <tbody>
        <tr>
            <td>William Smith</td>
            <td>555-642-7371</td>
            <td>william@testing.com</td>
            <td>ACME Industries</td>
            <td>2014-10-21</td>
        </tr>
        <tr>
            <td>Bob Morris</td>
            <td>555-999-2991</td>
            <td>bob@testing.com</td>
            <td>ABC Corp</td>
            <td>2014-09-12</td>
        </tr>
    </tbody>
    <tfoot>
        <tr>
            <td colspan="5">2 contacts displayed</td>
        </tr>
    </tfoot>
    <caption>Sales leads</caption>
</table>
```

If you open the page in Chrome, it should display as you see in Figure 3-5.

		Sales leads		
Contact name	**Phone number**	**Email address**	**Company name**	**Last contacted**
William Smith	555-642-7371	william@testing.com	ACME Industries	2014-10-21
Bob Morris	555-999-2991	bob@testing.com	ABC Corp	2014-09-12
2 contacts displayed				

FIGURE 3-5

You will notice that the columns in the table have sized themselves according to the data that has been added to them, but the last row in the table spans column boundaries.

Technically, you could have avoided using the thead, tbody, and tfoot tags, and just wrapped every row in a tr element directly within the table element. There are, however, a number of reasons why it is worth adding the extra structure to the table that these tags afford:

➤ It will help you style the different components of the table differently. Usually, the header and footer rows will be styled differently from the rows in the body of the table.

➤ You can add extra functionality to the table such as sorting and filtering. In this case, you would not want to sort or filter the header and footer rows.

Prior to HTML5, the `table` tag supported a number of attributes for controlling the presentation of the table such as the border size, the width of the table, the background color of the table, and the padding that should surround each cell. These have all been removed in HTML5, and you should not use them.

> **NOTE** *In the early days of website development, it was common to use tables as a layout mechanism. This is now strongly discouraged because CSS provides more than enough power to lay out complex web pages by itself. Tables should only be used for data where data needs to be stored in columns and rows.*

TRY IT

In this Try It, you will experiment with lists and tables. As with the previous lesson, you do not need to follow this lesson implicitly, the most important thing is to experiment with the tags and discover for yourself the way they can be combined to create interesting web pages.

Lesson Requirements

You will need the `template.html` file from Lesson 1, a text editor, and a web browser.

Step-by-Step

1. Open the `template.html` page in your text editor.

2. Start by creating a simple numbered list of all the tags that you have learned about in this lesson—for instance `table`, `tfoot`, and `thead`.

3. Now, imagine that you want to categorize these based on whether they are relevant to tables or lists. Try to convert the numbered list into a description list. Each category should be captured in a `dt` element, while the tag names should be placed in `dd` elements. The goal is to create a structure that looks like Figure 3-6.

FIGURE 3-6

4.   Now you will add a table to the web page to present the same information in the same way. Create a table with the following columns:

➤   Tag name

➤   Category (for example, list, table)

➤   Description

Ensure that the table utilizes the `thead` and the `tbody` elements.

Provide a caption for the table.

The first few rows of the table may look like Figure 3-7.

Tags in lesson 3		
Tag name	**Category**	**Description**
ul	List	creates an unordered list
ol	List	creates an ordered list
li	List	creates a list item
dl	List	creates a description list

FIGURE 3-7

> **REFERENCE** *Please select the video for Lesson 3 online at* www.wrox.com/go/ `html5jsjquery24hr`. *You will also be able to download the code and resources for this lesson from the website.*

Introduction to CSS

The first three lessons of the book introduced you to a large number of tags, but it has so far not been possible to style the presentation of these tags when they appear onscreen. As mentioned, HTML5 has removed most of the remaining presentation-based tags and attributes, and presentation and style are instead the responsibility of another technology called Cascading Style Sheets (CSS).

The main reason for this is a concept called "separation of concerns." The HTML markup language is responsible for providing the content of the page, while CSS is responsible for the presentation and styling of this content. This means it is possible to change either without affecting the other.

For instance, it is usually possible to completely restyle an existing web page without changing the HTML at all. Additionally, it is possible to change the content of a web page without needing to change the CSS at all.

This lesson will introduce the fundamentals of CSS, and will mainly focus on the way individual elements can be styled. In the next lesson, you will consolidate this knowledge, and also look at how CSS behaves when elements interact with one another.

The HTML5 specification includes a companion specification called CSS3—version 3 of Cascading Style Sheets—that greatly enhances the power of CSS. You will look in-depth at CSS3 later in the book, but for the next two lessons you will focus on the fundamentals of CSS.

> **NOTE** *The capabilities of CSS are truly astounding, so this lesson will not intro-duce you to everything CSS can do. The aim of this lesson is instead to provide you with a sound understanding of the fundamentals: once these are understood it is easy to find information about specific features.*

CSS SELECTORS

In this section, you will get started with CSS by styling the web page developed in Lesson 2. This page utilized header and paragraph elements to format text, and also included images and hyperlinks. Ensure you have the following HTML available to work with in this section:

```
<!DOCTYPE html>
<html lang="en">
<head>
    <meta charset="utf-8">
</head>
<body>
    <h1>This is a top level heading</h1>
    <h2>This is a second level heading</h2>
    <h3>This is a third level heading</h3>
    <p>This is the first paragraph</p>
    <p>This is the second paragraph</p>
<blockquote>
        Tell me and I forget. Teach me and I remember. Involve me and I learn.
        <cite>Benjamin Franklin</cite>
    </blockquote>
<p>Please click <a href="page2.html">here</a> to view page 2</p>
<p>This is a photo I took in Cambridge
<img src="photo1.jpg" title="Cambridge, England" width="200"></p>

</body>
</html>
```

As you will see, CSS can be included in a web page in three different ways. This section will focus on a single approach: adding CSS within a `style` element in the `head` of the web page.

In order to apply a style to an element, you first need a way of selecting the elements that you wish to style. CSS provides four key selection mechanisms, the most simple of which is to select the elements based on their tag name. For instance, if you wanted to select all the `h1` elements in the document and display them in a red font, you could add the following to the `head` section:

```
<style>
    h1 {
        color: red;
    }
</style>
```

If you refresh the web page, the top header will display in red.

> **NOTE** *A number of colors can be referenced directly by name, but it is more common to represent colors as a string such as #FF0000. This is a hash, followed by three sets of hexadecimal numbers specifying the ratio of red, green, and blue respectively. There are many resources online for finding colors using this format, and you will see many examples throughout this book.*

This simple example demonstrates most of what you need to know about the syntax of CSS. You start by specifying the selector: h1 in this case. Next, you place a set of stylistic properties between curly brackets where each stylistic property is in the form of a name/value pair. In this case, the name of the property is color (technically this is foreground color), while the value is red. A colon separates the name and value, and the whole construct is concluded with a semicolon. I will refer to this entire construct as a CSS rule.

It is possible to add multiple stylistic properties to the same selection. The following rule also specifies the font-family and the fact that the text should be underlined.

```
<style>
    h1 {
        color: red;
        text-decoration:underline;
        font-family: Arial, Helvetica, sans-serif;
    }
</style>
```

Figure 4-1 shows the result.

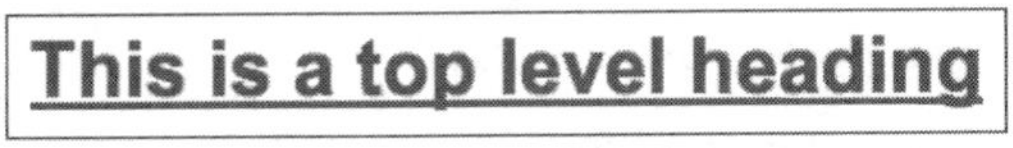

This is a top level heading

FIGURE 4-1

The font-family property has a more interesting value than color. Many fonts are proprietary; therefore, you cannot be sure which fonts the user's browser will provide. The value of the property therefore contains a list of fonts in priority order. In this case, the value states:

➤   Try to use Arial if it is available.

➤   If that is not available use Helvetica.

➤   If that is not available use any sans-serif font.

Imagine now that you want this style to apply to all the headings in the web page. Obviously, you could duplicate this rule three times and select h1, h2 and h3 in three separate rules. You always want to avoid duplication if you can, however, because it leads to maintenance issues.

There are, in fact, two ways you can achieve this without duplication. The first is by specifying the three different tags separated by a comma:

```
h1, h2, h3 {
    color: red;
    text-decoration:underline;
    font: Arial, Helvetica, sans-serif;
}
```

A more elegant solution, however, is to use classes. Any element can be assigned one or more classes with the class attribute. A class is just an arbitrary name you choose and usually describes some aspect that a set of elements have in common. For example:

```
<h1 class="redHeader">This is a top level heading</h1>
<h2 class="redHeader">This is a second level heading</h2>
<h3 class="redHeader">This is a third level heading</h3>
```

In this case, `redHeader` is the class name. It is then possible to style all elements with this `class` using the following selector:

```
.redHeader {
    color: red;
    text-decoration:underline;
    font: Arial, Helvetica, sans-serif;
}
```

Notice the dot at the start of the selector: This always implies that you are selecting elements by a `class`. If you redisplay the web page, all three headers will display with the specified properties.

If you want to assign two classes to an element, the class names are separated by a space. For example:

```
<h1 class="redHeader pageHeading">This is a top level heading</h1>
```

You can then select elements based on either of these classes.

Another common way to select elements is by their `id`. Any element can be given an `id`, but, unlike classes, IDs must be unique within a document. The following is an example of a paragraph with an `id`:

```
<p id="firstParagraph">This is the first paragraph</p>
```

It is then possible to create a CSS rule that selects this element as follows:

```
#firstParagraph {
    font-weight: bold;
}
```

Notice that the selector begins with a # to indicate it is based on `id`. This particular example will display the paragraph with the matching `id` in `bold`.

The final common way to select elements is via pseudo-classes. These allow you to select elements based on features that cannot be expressed by the other selectors, for instance, every even numbered row in a table.

If you consider the `firstParagraph` example, you may notice that there is a potential issue lurking here. If a new paragraph is added before the current first paragraph, you would need to remember to swap the `id` onto this element—which would be easy to forget. A better option is to state that you want the first paragraph to be in bold, without specifying which paragraph is the first in the document. This can be achieved as follows:

```
p:first-of-type {
    font-weight: bold;
}
```

This selector first selects all the p elements, and then limits this selection to just the first element found of its type. Because all the elements returned have the type of p, the `first-of-type` selector will return the first p element in the document. Pseudo-class selectors always begin with a single or double colon.

Pseudo-classes are also useful for providing styles to elements based on their state. For instance, if you wanted links to turn green when the user hovered over them, you could use the following selector:

```
a:hover {
    color: green;
}
```

There is no way to perform this selection without pseudo-classes.

> **NOTE** CSS *actually supports two related, but technically distinct, mechanisms: pseudo-classes and pseudo-elements. Technically, the selectors you have looked at are pseudo-classes because they select elements that you could not select via other selectors. CSS also supports pseudo-elements: These allow a portion of an element to be selected, such as the first letter in a paragraph, or the first line in a paragraph.*
>
> *Pseudo-element selectors are supposed to use a double colon rather than a single colon, but some browsers do not support the double colon syntax, so the single colon syntax is regularly used for both types of selector.*

When selecting the first paragraph in the document, you are actually combining two types of selector: an element selector and a pseudo-class selector. It turns out that you can combine selectors in many interesting ways.

For example, if I wanted to select all the `h1` elements that had the class `redParagraph`, I could use the following selector:

```
h1.redHeader {
    text-align: center;
}
```

Notice that there is no space between the element selector and the class selector. Alternatively, if I wanted to select all `h1` elements that had both the `redHeader` and `pageHeader` classes, I could use the following:

```
h1.redHeader.pageHeader {
    text-align: center;
}
```

Alternatively, you can select elements only when they are children of elements returned by other selections. For instance, you can specify that the `cite` element should be capitalized, but only when it is a child of a `blockquote` element (which, as it happens, it always is):

```
blockquote cite {
    text-transform: uppercase;
}
```

Notice in this case there is a space between the two selections. This will match `cite` elements if they are a descendant of a `blockquote` element, even if `blockquote` is not their immediate parent. Another way to think about this is two distinct selections. CSS first selects all the `blockquote` elements, and then it searches for any `cite` elements that are descendants.

With the > operator, it is possible to specify that the selection should only occur if the element is an immediate child of the first selection:

```
blockquote > cite {
    text-transform: uppercase;
}
```

CSS FILES AND INLINE STYLES

So far, you have used the `style` element to add CSS to a web page. Although this is an easy way of adding CSS, it has the disadvantage that you cannot use the same CSS across multiple pages.

It is therefore far more common to place all the CSS in a file with a `.css` extension and link it to each web page that needs to use it. In order to try this out, save the styles you have added so far in a file called `examples.css`. Place this in the same folder as the HTML page, but do not include the `style` element.

Now, remove the whole `style` element from the `head` of the document, and replace it with the following:

```
<link rel="stylesheet" type="text/css" href="examples.css">
```

Again, the `href` attribute is using a relative URL to load the style sheet, but it could also use an absolute URL. If you reload the web page it should display the same as before.

An alternative way of specifying CSS properties is via the `style` attribute on individual elements. Although this approach is generally discouraged, it can be useful when a style is unique to a single element. As you will also see, these styles have a higher precedence, so it can be a useful approach for overriding global styles. The following is an example:

```
<blockquote style="color: #888888;font-size:12px;">
```

Notice that the inline styles use the same basic syntax: Colons separate names and properties, and semicolons separate styles. Obviously, they do not include a selector because they are applied to the element they are declared on.

SPECIFICITY

The same element may match multiple CSS rules. When this occurs, all the properties defined in all the rules are applied to the element. You have already seen an example of this with the `h1` element.

Imagine, however, if you had the following in your style sheet:

```
h1 {
    color: blue;
}

h1.redHeader {
    color: green;
}

.redHeader {
    color: pink;
}
```

All three of these styles match the first header in the document; therefore, what `color` should it be assigned? The answer to this lies in a concept called *specificity*. In order to determine the style to use, CSS assigns points to each rule that matches an element based on its selector:

➤ If the selector matches on an element or pseudo-element 1 point is assigned.

➤ If it matches on class or pseudo-class, 10 points are assigned.

➤ If it matches based on `id`, 100 points are assigned.

➤ If the style is contained in a `style` attribute on the element, 1,000 points are assigned—which usually ensures it automatically wins.

You can therefore determine which of these three rules should be used:

➤ Rule 1 matches on an element so it receives 1 point.

➤ Rule 2 matches on an element and a class so it receives 11 points.

➤ Rule 3 matches on a class so it receives 10 points.

As a result, the color of the header should be green.

It is, of course, possible that two styles will have the same specificity. In this case, the rule defined last will have precedence. If the two rules are in the same external style sheet, the rule that occurs closest to the end will win. If they are in separate style sheets, the last style sheet declared in the web page will win.

There is one important exception to this rule. If a style is so important that you never want it to be overwritten by a rule with a higher specificity, you can assign it a tag called `important`. For instance, if the following two rules were defined:

```
h1 {
    color: blue;
    text-align: center !important;
}

h1.redHeader {
    color: green;
    text-align: left
}
```

the color will be green because of specificity, but the text will be aligned in the center because it is marked as `important`. It is best not to overuse this approach, but it works well in an emergency.

INHERITANCE

Obviously, it is annoying to need to style every single element. There are many cases where you want many elements to share the same style, and therefore it would be convenient to specify that the style applies to an element and all its descendants. This concept is called *inheritance* because styles are inherited from a parent.

CSS supports this concept for many, but not all, styles. For instance, you may want all the text in the document to use the same font family. You could therefore specify the following:

```
body {
    font-family: Arial, Helvetica, sans-serif;
}
```

Because all the visual elements in the document have the `body` element as a parent (even if not a direct parent), all the elements in the document will inherit this style. Likewise, if you were to specify the following:

```
blockquote {
    text-decoration: underline;
}
```

the text for both the `blockquote` and `cite` elements will be underlined.

Inheritance does not always make sense, however. Imagine that you used the `border` property to add a 1-pixel solid black border around the `blockquote`.

```
blockquote {
    border: 1px solid black;

}
```

Should a separate border be drawn around the `cite` element? I think you can probably agree that borders should not be inherited, and, in fact, they are not.

If you would like to inherit a non-inherited style, you can do so by using the following syntax:

```
cite {
    border: inherit;
}
```

BROWSER DEFAULTS

All browsers have a set of default styles that they apply to elements. These defaults include font types and sizes, the space between lines and paragraphs and the weight of the fonts on table headers. Browser defaults are only used when you do not provide your own style for an element.

One problem with browser defaults is that they tend to vary between browser vendors. This may mean your web page looks perfect in Chrome but looks terrible in IE because it is picking up a default.

Because of these issues, it is common to completely remove the browser defaults. This is typically performed using a separate style sheet called `reset.css` (you will find examples on the Internet), which is then the first style sheet that is loaded on each page.

CHROME SCRATCH PAD

When experimenting with CSS, it can be an annoyance to make changes to the style sheet, save the changes, and reload the web page. Fortunately, Chrome makes it easy to experiment with styles directly in the browser. In order to demonstrate this, right-click on the first `h1` element and choose Inspect Element.

On the left-hand side of the console, you will see the control shown in Figure 4-2.

```
Styles  Computed  Event Listeners  »
element.style {                  + ⸬
}
h1.redHeader {          example.html:12
    color: ■green;
    text-align: left;
}
h1.redHeader {          examples.css:7
    text-align: center;
}
.redHeader {            example.html:17
    color: ▢pink;
}
.redHeader {            examples.css:1
    color: ■red;
    text-decoration: ▶underline;
}
h1 {                    example.html:7
    color: ■blue;
    text-align: center !important;
}
h1 {            user agent stylesheet
    display: block;
    font-size: 2em;
    -webkit-margin-before: 0.67em;
    -webkit-margin-after: 0.67em;
    -webkit-margin-start: 0px;
    -webkit-margin-end: 0px;
    font-weight: bold;
}
Inherited from body
body {                  example.html:30
    font-family: Arial, Helvetica,
        sans-serif;
}
```

FIGURE 4-2

This is telling you all the rules that match the element, from the most specific at the top, to the least specific at the bottom. Any time that a style is not used because of specificity, a line is drawn through it.

At the bottom of this panel, you can see the styles inherited from the browser defaults (called "user agent stylesheet") and those inherited from other elements (for instance, body).

This can be very useful for determining why certain styles are used. For instance, have a look at the example in Figure 4-2 and determine which rule provided the text-align property and why.

You can also change styles, or add styles to any of these rules: These changes will be reflected in the web page in real time. You can also eliminate any styles you want by clearing the checkbox that appears next to them when you hover over them.

Additionally, if you click on the very first rule called element.style, you can add new rules just for this element. For instance, you could make the color of the header blue by adding the property demonstrated in Figure 4-3.

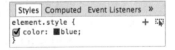

FIGURE 4-3

TRY IT

In this Try It, you will style the table that you created in Lesson 4 to hold contact information.

Lesson Requirements

You will need the `contacts.html` file from Lesson 4, a text editor, and a web browser.

Step by Step

1. Start by creating a file called `contacts.css` in the same folder as `contacts.html`.

2. Add a link in the head section of `contacts.html` to the CSS file following the instructions earlier in the lesson.

3. Set the font family for the entire document to use `Arial, Helvetica, sans-serif`. Remember that you will need a rule that matches the `body` element.

4. Add a 1-pixel solid black border to the elements `table`, `th`, and `td`. You will find an example of a border style earlier in this lesson.

5. Load the page in Chrome. You will notice that there is a double border around cells (see Figure 4-4) because each cell has its own border, and there is a gap between these. To fix this, add a new style to this rule with the property `border-collapse`, and a value of `collapse`. This will collapse the duplicate borders into a single border.

Sales leads

Contact name	Phone number	Email address	Company name	Last contacted
William Smith	555-642-7371	william@testing.com	ACME Industries	2014-10-21
Bob Morris	555-999-2991	bob@testing.com	ABC Corp	2014-09-12
2 contacts displayed				

FIGURE 4-4

6. Add some space between the content and the border of each cell (`td` element). Add a property called `padding`, and set this to `5px`.

7. Add a style for the `thead` element. Set the `background` to the color `#3056A0`, and set the `color` to `white`.

8. Set the `caption` for the table to display in `bold`, but ensure this is only applied if `caption` is a child of a `table` element.

9. Set the `font` of the `tfoot` element to be three-quarters the size of the font used elsewhere. Hint: Setting the font to `2em` would double the size of the font (you will look at this setting further in the next lesson). In addition, set the text alignment to be on the right-hand side of the table.

10. Every second row of the table body should be given a background color of #E6E6F5. In order to select every second row, use the pseudo-class selector `tr:nth-child(even)`, but ensure this is only applied to children of `tbody` because `thead` and `tbody` also have `tr` elements.

When complete, the table should look like the screenshot in Figure 4-5.

Sales leads				
Contact name	**Phone number**	**Email address**	**Company name**	**Last contacted**
William Smith	555-642-7371	william@testing.com	ACME Industries	2014-10-21
Bob Morris	555-999-2991	bob@testing.com	ABC Corp	2014-09-12
				2 contacts displayed

FIGURE 4-5

> **REFERENCE** *Please select the video for Lesson 4 online at www.wrox.com/go/html5jsjquery24hr. You will also be able to download the code and resources for this lesson from the website.*

5

Structuring Pages with CSS

In the previous lesson, you looked at how individual elements could be styled with CSS. This lesson builds on this knowledge and looks at how elements come to occupy the screen position that they do, how this can be manipulated, and how this impacts other elements around them.

THE BOX MODEL

The box model is one of the most important CSS concepts and dictates the width and height each element will occupy onscreen. The box model starts from the observation that all elements in the document occupy rectangular boxes, but the rules for calculating their height and width are not as straightforward as you may think.

For a start, the height and width occupied by an element is greater than the height and width required for the content of the element for several reasons. For instance, the element may have a border that occupies additional space. In the previous lesson, you created borders that were 1 pixel in size. Thus, these borders added 2 pixels to the height and width required for the element.

Padding may also be added between the content and the border, as with the table cells in the previous lesson. Finally, it may also be necessary to add additional margin between the element and its neighboring elements.

The total space occupied by the element's box can therefore be visualized in Figure 5-1.

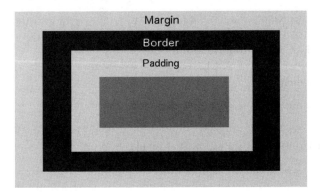

FIGURE 5-1

In order to see this in action, create a web page as follows:

```
<!DOCTYPE html>
<html lang="en">
    <head>
        <meta charset="utf-8">
        <style>
            h1 {
                width:400px;
                height:30px;
                padding:10px;
                border:2px solid #999999;
                background:#dddddd;
                margin: 10px 20px 20px 10px;
            }
        </style>
    </head>
<body>
    <h1>This is a header</h1>
</body>
</html>
```

This code declares an `h1` element with the following sizes (working from the inside of the box to the outside):

➤ A `width` of 400 pixels and a `height` of 30 pixels. If these were omitted, the element would have a default height and width calculated from the content of the element.

➤ Ten pixels of padding between the content and the border. When specifying a single value, the value is automatically applied to the top, right, left, and right of the box.

➤ A 2-pixel border.

➤ A margin between itself and its neighbors, but this has different values on each side. Therefore, four values are provided. You can remember which side these apply to with the acronym TRouBLe (Top, Right, Bottom, Left). For instance, in this case the left margin is 10 pixels.

It is also possible to specify the border, padding, or margin for any side individually by using properties such as `margin-left`, `border-top`, and `padding-right`.

Open this web page and view it in Chrome. Right-click on the h1 element, and select Inspect Element. Ensure the element is selected in the Elements tab, and then take a look to the bottom right of the console. It should show a box like the one in Figure 5-2, which is a visualization of the box model for the element.

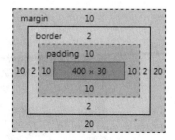

FIGURE 5-2

You can therefore use this to determine how much height and width the element will need onscreen:

➤ The width will need 10 + 2 + 10 + 400 + 10 + 2 + 20 = 454 pixels.

➤ The height will need 10 + 2 + 10 + 30 + 10 + 2 + 20 = 74 pixels.

One other interesting aspect you may notice about the box model is the scope of the background color. The background color fills the content and the padding, but not the margin or border.

If you add two more h1 elements to the document and then refresh the web page, you will notice that there is a margin between the elements, as shown in Figure 5-3.

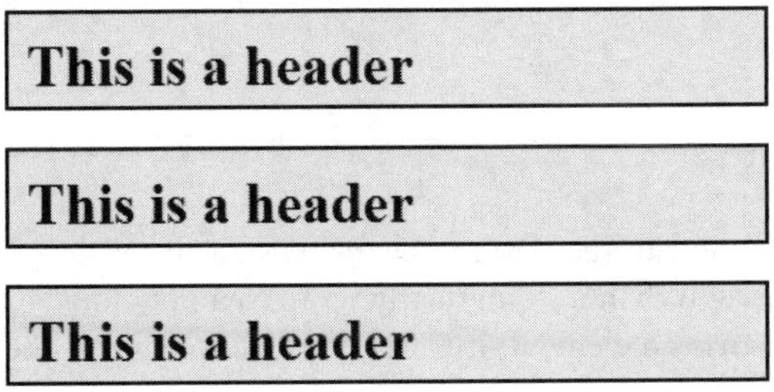

This is a header

This is a header

This is a header

FIGURE 5-3

You may notice something unusual here however. Each of the headers has a top margin of 10 pixels and a bottom margin of 20 pixels. You might therefore expect that there would be 30 pixels between each element.

If you select the top element in Chrome, however, you will notice that the bottom margin is only 20 pixels (as demonstrated by the fact the space taken by the element extends down to the top of the next element). You can see this in Figure 5-4. The top margin for the second header has been ignored.

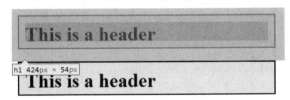

FIGURE 5-4

This is referred to as *collapsed margins.* The top and bottom margin of block elements are collapsed into a single margin that is calculated as the greatest of the top and bottom margin: 20 pixels in this case. Working around collapsing margins can be a headache; therefore, it is often better to rely on only top or bottom margins, not both.

DISPLAY TYPE

I have alluded to display types several times already in this book, but now is the time to look at this property in more depth. Every element has a display type and is initially defaulted to the appropriate type for each tag. There are quite a number of display types, but you really need to understand only four of them.

By default, h1 elements have a display type of block. As mentioned previously, block elements insert a break in the document meaning the next element will appear below the previous element. It is possible to control both the height and width of a block element, as you saw in the previous section.

The next most widely used block type is inline. Add the following rule to the style section and refresh the web page:

```
h1 {
    display: inline;
}
```

This will now display as you see in Figure 5-5. As you can see, inline elements sit alongside one another. If they exceed the width of the page, they will then automatically wrap to a new line. Although it is possible to control the width of an inline element, it is not possible to control their height: This is automatically calculated.

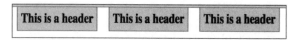

FIGURE 5-5

Additionally, it is only possible to add margin and padding to the left and right of the element, not to the top and bottom. As you can see, the elements are positioned at the very top of the web page, without any margin between the headers and the address bar.

The third major category of display type is inline-block. When elements are assigned this display type, they sit alongside one another, just like inline elements, but it is possible to specify their height, and add margin and padding to all four sides.

The final display type to understand is none. When an element is assigned this display type the element is hidden from the viewer but remains in the document. Change the second header as follows and then refresh the web page:

```
<h1 style="display:none">This is a header that is hidden</h1>
```

If you reload the page, you will see that there is no sign of this element: It does not even leave an empty space for the position it would hold if it had visibility. It is common to dynamically hide and show content with JavaScript by manipulating the display type, as you will see later in this book.

POSITIONING ELEMENTS

Now that you understand the box model, it is possible to start looking at how different elements interact.

Imagine that you want to create a web page split into five sections:

➤ A 100-pixel high header that spans the width of the page

➤ A 50-pixel high footer that spans the width of the page

➤ A content section broken into three sections:

➤ An area to the left where menus can be positioned: This should occupy 20 percent of the width and have a minimum height of 500 pixels.

➤ An area on the right for advertising material: This will also occupy 20 percent of the width and have a height of 500 pixels.

➤ A main content section in the middle occupying as much of the remaining space as it requires.

The screen therefore consists of the five boxes seen in Figure 5-6. The first question you might want to ask yourself is: What type of element is each of these boxes? Essentially, they are just containers for other elements, and you may want to encapsulate many different elements inside each of these containers.

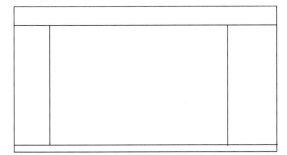

FIGURE 5-6

HTML supports a tag I have not discussed so far called a `div`. This is potentially the most widely used tag in HTML: It is a `block` element with no default presentation itself; it is simply used as a container to group other elements together.

HTML supports a second related tag called a `span` (perhaps the second most widely used tag in HTML). This is the same as a `div`, except it is an `inline` element rather than a `block` element.

You will start by creating a page called `structure.html` with the following `body`:

```
<body>
    <div id="header">This is the header</div>
    <div id="sidebar">This is the sidebar</div>
    <div id="content">This is the main content</div>
    <div id="advertising">These are adverts</div>
    <div id="footer">This is the footer</div>
</body>
```

Because these are block elements, you will notice that the five elements simply sit on top of each other for now. I have added `id` attributes to the elements to allow them to be styled individually in CSS.

In order to style the header element, add a `style` element with the following value:

```
#header {
    height:100px;
    background:pink;
}
```

When I am laying out a web page, I find it convenient to give every element a distinctive background color to start—this allows me to see exactly how much space has been allocated to each element.

If you view this web page in Chrome, you will see that the header has a white margin around it. This is the result of a style inherited from the `body` element; therefore, you should also add the following to the styles section to remove this:

```
body {
    margin: 0;
}
```

Now, add the following for the `sidebar` element:

```
#sidebar {
    width:20%;
    background:orange;
    height:500px;
    float:left;
}
```

Notice that the `width` element uses a percent for the unit rather than pixels: This means it will utilize 20 percent of the space potentially available to it, which for a top-level element like this is the entire width of the screen. Sizes are also commonly expressed in the following formats:

➤ `mm`: Millimeters

➤ `in`: Inches

➤ `em`: 1 em is the equivalent size of the current font; this measurement therefore allows elements to be sized in relation to the standard font size.

This element also declares a `height`. This property ensures that the element occupies 500 pixels of vertical space.

The most interesting property here, however, is the `float` property. Because you need three `block` elements to sit alongside each other, you need to control how they interact with each other horizontally. The `float` property can be used to position block elements to either the left or the right of the area available to them, and in addition, this suppresses the break that would normally accompany block elements in the left-to-right flow.

Although using the `float` property is similar to declaring the display type as `inline-block`, it has the additional benefit that it is possible to position elements to the left or the right of their available space. By comparison, `inline-block` elements always float to the left of the available space.

Next, you will add style for the `content` element. You will leave this without any style, except you will specify that it should float to the left of its available space, which will position the element directly to the right of the `sidebar` element. Add the following to the styles:

```
#content {
    float:left;
}
```

With this in place, you want to place the element with the `id` of `advertising` on the right side of the screen. The style for this element is therefore virtually identical to `sidebar`, except you will request that it floats `right`:

```
#advertising {
    width:20%;
    background:blue;
    height:500px;
    float:right;
}
```

Notice that this is not sitting directly up against the content element; instead, it is being positioned directly against the right of the screen.

Finally, you come to the footer. It may seem that you can simply add the following:

```
#footer {
    height:50px;
    background:pink;
}
```

If you try loading this page, however, you will see that the footer div sits beside the content div. You need to request that this element drops below the floated elements preceding it with the following property:

```
clear: both;
```

In this case, both refers to the fact that this element should drop below both left and right floated elements.

If you load the page, you will see that it looks exactly as expected (see Figure 5-7). Once the page structure is in place, you can then start adding content to each of the divs.

FIGURE 5-7

CONTROLLING POSITIONS

Up until this point, the position elements that have been placed onscreen have been a product of the elements that appear before them in the DOM and the properties of the element itself. Elements are simply laid out in the order they appear in the web page and take up as much space as they need. This then impacts the position assigned to elements that appear after them in the DOM.

This is technically called static positioning, but it is only one of several ways of positioning elements. This section will briefly look at three other ways of positioning elements.

In order to demonstrate positioning, start by creating the following web page, which consists of three boxes. These three boxes are sufficient to demonstrate the various approaches to positioning:

```
<!DOCTYPE html>
<html lang="en">
<head>
    <meta charset="utf-8">
    <style>
        .box {
            height:200px;
            width:200px;
            display:inline-block
        }
    </style>
</head>
<body>
    <div class="box" style="background:red"></div>
    <div id="middleBox" class="box" style="background:green"></div>
    <div id="lastBox" class="box" style="background:blue"></div>
</body>
</html>
```

If you view the web page, you will see that it consists of three boxes sitting alongside one another (see Figure 5-8).

FIGURE 5-8

Imagine that that we want to move the second box (with the id of `middleBox`) 50 pixels to the right and 50 pixels down without impacting the third box at all. This is not possible with static positioning because adding 50 pixels of width to the second element would push the third element 50 pixels right.

In order to achieve this, add the following rule to the `style` section:

```
#middleBox {
    position: relative;
    top:50px;
    left: 50px;
}
```

This starts by setting the `position` of the `middleBox` element to `relative`. This means that you want to set its position relative to the default position it would be given on the page.

Once the `position` property has been set, you can start using the `left`, `right`, `top`, and `bottom` properties to move the element to a different position on the screen. In this case, you then want to specify that you want 50 pixels of space added to the `left` and 50 pixels of space added to the `top`. If you view this, you will see the screen displayed in Figure 5-9.

FIGURE 5-9

Notice that the elements now overlap one another: The third box is simply given the position it would have held if you had not moved the second element to the right.

It is also possible to use a `position` of `absolute` to position an element relative its parent. Try changing the preceding style as follows:

```
#middleBox {
    position: absolute;
    top: 150px;
    left: 150px;
}
```

Because the parent of `middleBox` is the `body` element itself, you are effectively positioning the element relative to the browser window. If you view the page now, it should look like what you see in Figure 5-10.

Using absolute positioning removes the element from the flow of the page, and therefore the position of the third box is also impacted.

You can also control which of these elements sits in the foreground and which are relegated to the background. This is controlled by a CSS property called `z-index`.

FIGURE 5-10

The element with the highest `z-index` will be placed in the foreground. Therefore, if you add the following to the style of `middleBox`, it will be relegated to the background:

```
z-index:-1;
```

The final main type of positioning is `fixed`. This is similar to `absolute` positioning, except elements are positioned relative to the browser window. In the preceding example, `fixed` and `absolute` positioning would achieve the same result.

TRY IT

In this step-by-step, you will pick up the CRM application from the previous lesson and add more structure to the overall web page. This will include adding a header, a footer, and an area for adding new contacts (although we will not populate this until the next lesson).

Lesson Requirements

You will need the CRM application as it stood at the end of Lesson 4. You will also need a text editor and the Chrome web browser.

Step-by-Step

1. Open the `contacts.html` page and add a `div` immediately after the opening body tag. In the body of the tag, enter **Contacts**. Assign the `id` of `header` to this tag.

2. Wrap a `div` tag around the table, and give this the `id` of `contactList`. The opening tag should be immediately before the opening `table` tag, while the closing tag should be immediately after the closing `table` tag.

3. Add another `div` immediately before the closing body tag and give this the `id` of `footer`. Add a copyright statement to this `div`.

4. Add one final `div` immediately after the header `div`, and give this the `id` of `contactDetails`. This is where you will eventually place a new form for adding contacts. Add an `h2` element to this with the text **Contact Details**.

5. Open `contacts.css`. Start by adding a `margin: 0` property to the `body` rule to ensure you remove white space from around the header.

6. Create a rule for the `div` with the `id` of `header`. This should specify that the `background` and `color` are the same as for the `thead` element rule from the last lesson. Additionally, add a `text-align` property with a value of center, and a `line-height` property with a value of 70px.

   `line-height` is similar to height, but it will ensure that the text is vertically aligned. If you had simply specified `height`, the text would be positioned near the top of the `div`. Also add a `font-size` of 3em: three times larger than the standard font.

7. `contactDetails` and `contactList` need to share a number of properties, so create a rule that matches both of these elements. Add a `border` with a 1px solid line and a color of `#999999`. Also add `margin` and `padding` of 15px around all sides.

8. Add a style for the footer `div`. This should be the same as the header, except the `line-height` should be 40, and the `font-size` should be `0.8em`.

9. Black font can be quite overpowering, so set the `color` property of the body to `color: #333333`, which is a very dark grey.

If you open the page, it should look like the example in Figure 5-11. If you need assistance, the finished version can be downloaded from the Lesson 5 resources, or you can watch the screencast online.

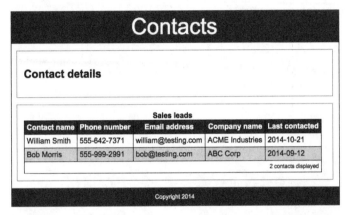

FIGURE 5-11

> **REFERENCE** *Please select the video for Lesson 5 online at www.wrox.com/go/ html5jsjquery24hr. You will also be able to download the code and resources for this lesson from the website.*

HTML Forms

The HTML tags examined up until this point have all been used to display content to the user. This lesson examines HTML forms, which allow the user to submit data back to the web server. Any time you enter data into text fields, or select values from drop-down lists, you are using HTML forms.

This lesson will provide an introduction to HTML forms, but will also look at some of the interesting changes that have occurred to forms in HTML5. These changes were originally called Web Forms 2.0, but have since been integrated into the HTML5 standard. Therefore, even if you are familiar with HTML forms, this lesson is recommended.

WHAT IS A FORM?

A form is a set of input fields, grouped together inside a single element, with the purpose of obtaining a set of information from the user. Forms have historically consisted primarily of the following fields:

➤ Text fields

➤ Select lists

➤ Text boxes (multiline text fields)

➤ Checkboxes

➤ Radio buttons

➤ Password fields

As you will see shortly, this list has been greatly enhanced with HTML5.

In addition, fields contain a Submit button that causes their contents to be posted to a specified URL on the server. The server can then process this data as required and return a new web page as a result.

In this book, you will make extensive use of forms but will not post their contents to a server. You will instead extract and process their data using JavaScript. In this chapter, I will present a more conventional view of forms but will not provide server-side code for processing the form information because this would require me to introduce a whole new set of technologies.

This section of the lesson introduces a very simple form and examines its component parts. You will then create a more complicated form for the Contacts web page.

Create a new page called `simpleform.html` and add the following `body` to it:

```
<body>
    <form action="submit.html" method="post">
        <label for="firstName">First Name</label>:
         <input id="firstName" name="firstName" type="text"/>
        <p>
        <label for="lastName">Last Name</label>:
        <input id="lastName " name="lastName" type="text"/>
        <p>
        <input type="submit" value="Submit">
    </form>
</body>
```

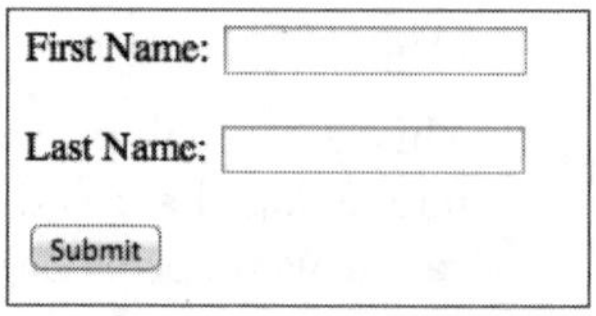

If you open this in Chrome, it will look like Figure 6-1.

Notice that all the input fields are nested inside a `form` element. All of the input fields within a form should represent a related set of data that is processed together.

FIGURE 6-1

The `form` element contains two important attributes. The `action` attribute is the address on the web server that the contents of the form will be posted to when the form is submitted. It is assumed that this address will be capable of processing the contents of the form and redirecting the user to a new web page as a result.

The `method` attribute refers to the HTTP method that will be used to send the data to the server. When you simply type an address in a browser address bar, you are using an HTTP method called GET. This is a simple mechanism for requesting a web page, although it can contain data if required.

When you send form data to the server, you typically have a large quantity of data that needs to be sent; therefore, you use the HTTP POST method. With this method, all the input fields and their values are included in the body of the HTTP request rather than encoded in the URL. You do not need to understand HTTP methods to progress through the book, although you will look at them in slightly more detail when AJAX is introduced.

In this particular case, the form consists of two labels and two input fields.

Obviously, labels do not allow the user to provide input; thus, you may be wondering why you need to use them rather than just adding text to the form. Labels have the following benefits:

➤ Clicking on the label puts the cursor focus in the input field. This relies on the fact that the value of the `for` attribute is the `id` of the input field that it relates to.

➤ Labels provide more structure to the document because they make it obvious that the label is associated with a specific input field.

HTML uses an element called `input` for many, but not all, input fields. For this reason, an attribute is added to the element specifying the `type` of input it accepts. In this particular case, you have specified that the type is `text` (which is the default).

Finally, a button is added to the form allowing it to be submitted. Notice that this is also an `input` element, but because it is given a `type` of `submit`, it displays as a button rather than an input field.

When the submit button is clicked, the fields are serialized into a textual string of name/value pairs. The `name` attribute for each input field is used as the name, and the current value of the field is used as the value. The textual string is then placed in the body of an HTTP request and posted to the server.

If I enter `Dane` and `Cameron` into the two fields, and then press the submit button, it will post an HTTP request to the server, as shown in Figure 6-2 (this was captured from the Network tab of Chrome's developer tools after first clicking the Preserve Log option).

```
▼ Request Headers CAUTION: Provisional headers are shown.
  Content-Type: application/x-www-form-urlencoded
  Origin: null
  Referer:
  User-Agent: Mozilla/5.0 (Macintosh; Intel Mac OS X 10_8_5) App
▼ Form Data      view source      view URL encoded
  firstName: Dane
  lastName: Cameron
```

FIGURE 6-2

ADDING FIELDS TO A FORM

In this section, you create the form for capturing information about a person in your Contacts web application.

To complete this section, open the `contacts.html` file as it stood at the end of Lesson 5, or download it from the book's website.

Start by adding the following content to the `contactDetails` div:

```html
<div id="contactDetails"><h2>Contact details</h2>
    <form method="post">
        <div class="formRow">
            <label for="contactName">Contact name</label>
            <input name="contactName" id="contactName" type="text"/>
        </div>
    </form>
</div>
```

This adds a `form` with a single input field. The `label` and `input` elements have been placed in a `div` with a class of `formRow`, which ensures that each pair will be placed on a row of its own.

Because you want all your labels and fields to have a consistent size, add the following to
`contacts.css`:

```
label {
    width:150px;
    display: inline-block;
    vertical-align: top;
}

input {
    width:200px;
}
```

Notice that you need to change the display type of the `label` in order to set its width.

You can now add input fields for the email address and phone number fields:

```
<div class="formRow">
    <label for="phoneNumber">Phone number</label>
    <input name="phoneNumber" id="phoneNumber" type="text"/>
</div>
<div class="formRow">
    <label for="emailAddress">Email address</label>
    <input name="emailAddress" id="emailAddress" type="text"/>
</div>
```

Because you also want some space between each row, add the following to the style sheet. Figure 6-3
shows what the form should look like.

```
.formRow {
    margin-bottom:10px;
}
```

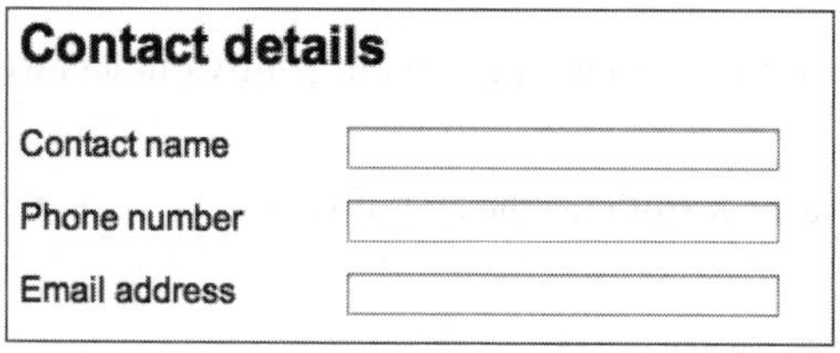

Contact details

Contact name	
Phone number	
Email address	

FIGURE 6-3

Next you will add a field for capturing the company of the contact. In this case, you may want the
user to select from a list of companies that have already been added into the system. This can be
achieved with a different input type called a *select list*. Start by adding this to the form:

```
<div class="formRow">
    <label for="companyName">Company name</label>
    <select name="companyName" id="companyName">
        <option value="-1">Please select</option>
        <option value="1">ABC Incorporated</option>
```

```
            <option value="2">XZY Ltd</option>
            <option value="3">ACME iInternational</option>
        </select>
    </div>
```

Notice that the select list is encapsulated inside an element called `select`. Within this, you have a series of `option` elements providing the various possibilities. Each `option` consists of two values: The text between the opening and closing `option` tag is the text that will be presented to the user. Each `option` tag also has a `value` attribute, however, and this is the value that will be assigned to the field when the form is submitted.

It is possible for the `text` and the `value` to carry the same value, but it is also common for them to differ. For instance, in this case the `value` may represent a unique code for each company, as assigned by an accounting system.

By default, a select list selects the first option, although it is possible to add a selected attribute to any other option to make it the default. This is a Boolean attribute; thus, it does not require a value. For example:

```
    <option value="3" selected>ACME iInternational</option>
```

You will now add one more field for capturing notes about the contact. This will be slightly different from the other text-based fields because you want to provide space for a large amount of text to be captured. You will notice that the input fields you have used up until now do not even allow line breaks, so they are not appropriate for capturing large quantities of text.

You therefore want to add a different input type called a `textarea`:

```
    <div class="formRow">
        <label for="notes">Notes</label>
        <textarea cols="40" rows="6" name="notes" ></textarea>
    </div>
```

Notice that the text area allows you to specify the number of columns and rows that the `textarea` contains. Although these dictate the size of the element, and therefore are semi-presentational, they are still valid attributes in HTML5.

With this in place, the form should now look like Figure 6-4.

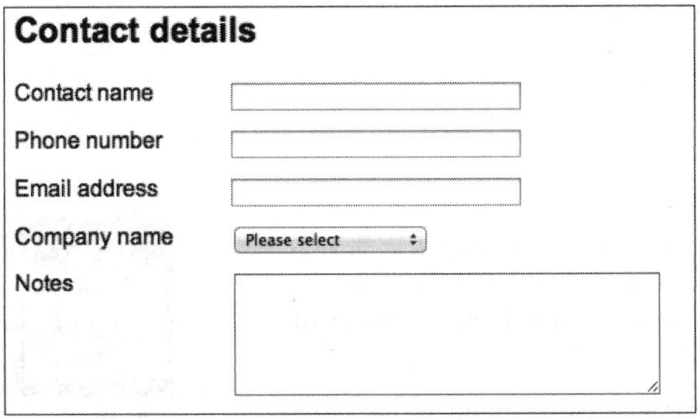

FIGURE 6-4

Finally, add a submit button to the bottom of the form. Because you want this to be smaller than other input fields, you will use an inline style.

```
<div class="formRow">
    <input style="width:70px" type="submit" value="Save"/>
</div>
```

HTML5 INPUT FIELDS

There is one final field you should add: You want to capture the date that the contact was last spoken to or emailed by your staff. Users generally expect to provide this information by selecting a date from a calendar.

Up until the release of HTML5, you needed to resort to JavaScript libraries in order to achieve this. One of the great enhancements in HTML5 is the introduction of a whole set of new input types, including a date input type. This allows browsers to provide native support for selecting dates.

In order to see this in action, add the following row to the form, before the row with the submit button:

```
<div class="formRow">
    <label for="lastContacted">Last contacted</label>
    <input name="lastContacted" id="lastContacted" type="date"/>
</div>
```

Notice that the only difference between this and other input fields is that the type has been specified as date. If you open this in Chrome, however, you will see that a date picker has been provided for you, as shown in Figure 6-5.

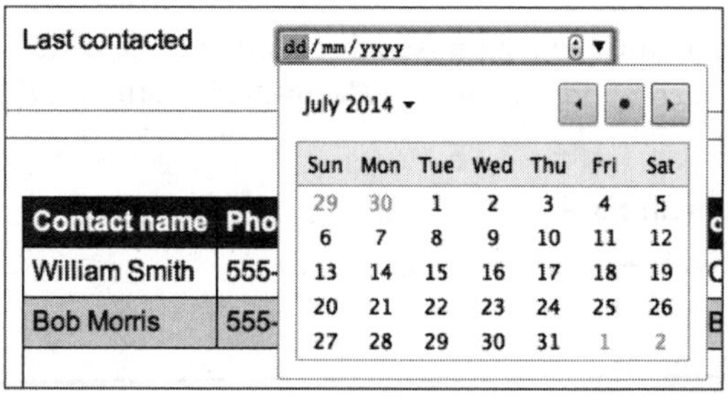

FIGURE 6-5

The great thing about native support for calendars is that different browsers can implement them in the most appropriate way they see fit. For instance, if you viewed this page on an iPad, the date picker would look like the example in Figure 6-6.

As you can see, this has been optimized for a touch-based operating system.

FIGURE 6-6

The main problem with the date input type is that all browsers do not support it. This means that, for now, you will probably need to rely on a technique called polyfills, as outlined later in Lesson 10.

HTML5 actually specifies many additional input types. As with the date input type, the specification does not tell browsers how they should implement each type, and in fact, many are not widely supported, but the following are some of the input types that have been included in the specification:

➤ `email`: Allows the user to capture an email address.

➤ `color`: Allows the user to capture a color, presumably from a color picker.

➤ `number`: Limits the user to entering a number in an input field, and allows the user to increase or decrease the value by a step amount.

➤ `range`: Lets the user specify a number from a possible range of numbers. This will also be introduced in Lesson 10.

➤ `tel`: Lets the user capture a telephone number.

➤ `url`: This lets the user capture a URL.

➤ `datetime`: This is similar to `date`, but allows the user to select time as well as date information.

➤ `time`: This is also similar to `date`, but limits the selection to the time of day.

In order to see what these elements do, change the email address and phone number fields to use `email` and `tel` respectively. If you now reload the page, you probably will not notice any difference.

As you will see in Lesson 8, this is not entirely true; HTML5 provides native support to validate fields based on their type. In addition, although Chrome on a desktop does not treat these types any differently from `text` fields, this may not be true of other browsers.

For instance, if you were to click on either of these fields in a mobile phone or tablet browser, you can envisage that the software-based keyboard would change to reflect the keys needed by the input type. The same would be true if the input type was set to `number`.

It is worth reiterating that one of the key strengths with the HTML5 specification is that it does not second-guess how browsers should implement features. A browser on a phone may therefore attempt to auto-complete phone numbers based on the user's phone book if it determines this is useful to the user.

Datalist Element

HTML5 also contains a new input type called a `datalist`. This is similar to a `select` list, but it does not limit the user to the values in the list: It allows the user to type his or her own value if required. The following is an example:

```
<input list="companies" name="companyName">
<datalist id="companies">
    <option value="ABC Incorporated">
    <option value="XZY Ltd">
    <option value="ACME iInternational">
</datalist>
```

As you can see, this element is made up of two distinct tags. The first is an input field, which, because its type is not specified, defaults to a `text` input field. This specifies a special attribute called `list`.

The next element is a `datalist`, which has the same `id` as the `list` specified on the input field. This then provides a default list for the user to select from, and also allows the value to be autocompleted as the user types.

Although you will not use this in the contacts web page, if you were to add it, it would display as you see Figure 6-7.

Form Attributes

FIGURE 6-7

In addition to new input types, HTML5 provides a number of new attributes for existing input types. You will look at several of these in Lesson 8 when you look at HTML5 validation, but it is worth mentioning a number of them in this lesson.

The `placeholder` attribute allows you to provide a hint to users to help them enter a value. For instance, if you changed the telephone input field as follows:

```
<input placeholder="Include area code" name="phoneNumber" type="tel"/>
```

the field would display as you see in Figure 6-8. Notice the gray text in the field. This will disappear as soon as the user starts typing in the field.

Phone number	Include area code
Email address	

FIGURE 6-8

The `autocomplete` attribute can be used to specify whether the browser should attempt to autocomplete text entered by the user based on values that they have provided before. The following is an example that turns `autocomplete` off on the contact name field:

```
<input autocomplete="off" name="contactName" type="text"/>
```

The `autocomplete` attribute can also be used on the form as a whole.

The `autofocus` attribute is used to automatically set the cursor in a specific field when the page loads. It has always been possible to do this with JavaScript, but this attribute makes it far simpler. For instance, if you added the following to contact name field, you will notice that the cursor is in this field when the page loads:

```
<input autofocus autocomplete="off" name="contactName" type="text"/>
```

Finally, the `form` attribute can be used to specify that an input field is part of a form, even if it is not nested inside of it. If this attribute is given a value corresponding to the `id` of a form, it will be included in the post to the server when the form is submitted, regardless of where it is placed in the page.

This can be useful if you have a field that is located in a completely different area of the screen from other fields.

TRY IT

In this Try It, you will experiment with the various form elements and input fields introduced in this lesson. This Try It also covers the few remaining form elements not covered so far in the lesson.

You are encouraged to experiment here; the goal is to gain an understanding of how the form elements work. If you get stuck, my version is available on the book's website in a file called `tryit.html`, or you can watch the screencast online.

Lesson Requirements

You will also need a text editor and a web browser.

Step-by-Step

1.   Start by creating a simple HTML5 web page that you can use to add the elements outlined in this lesson.

2.   Begin by adding a `form` element to the web page and adding a `method` of `post` to this. Because you will not submit this form, you do not need to add an `action`.

3.   Start by adding a simple text input field with the name of `fullName`. Use the `placeholder` attribute to provide a hint to the user, and request that this field receives focus when the page loads.

4.   Add a `label` for this field, and use the `for` attribute to specify the `id` of the field that this relates to.

5.   You want to add radio buttons to specify whether the person is male or female. Add the following markup to the web page:

```
<label for="male">Male</label>
<input checked type="radio" name="gender" id="male" value="male">
<label for="female">Female</label>
<input type="radio" name="gender" id="female" value="female">
```

     Notice in this example that both input types are given the same name. This is how the browser knows that the two radio buttons are connected, and ensures that only one can be selected. When the form is submitted, the field will be given the `value` of the radio button currently selected.

6.   Add a checkbox to the form asking if the user wants to subscribe to your newsletter. A checkbox is identical to a radio button, but the `type` of the input field is `checkbox`. In addition, you do not need to specify a value with checkboxes: The value of the field will be set to either `on` or `off`.

7. Add a `textarea` for capturing notes. This should be sized to capture 5 rows and 30 columns.

8. Add a "Date of birth" input field that uses an input type of `date`.

9. Add a salary field to the form. Specify this as type `number`, and define a `step` attribute with a value of 500.

10. Add a submit button to the bottom of the form to allow the contents to be submitted.

11. Ensure that you have added a `<br>` before each `label` to make sure the inputs are placed on separate lines.

The finished result should look something like the screenshot in Figure 6-9, but you are encouraged to experiment, and try out the other features outlined in this lesson.

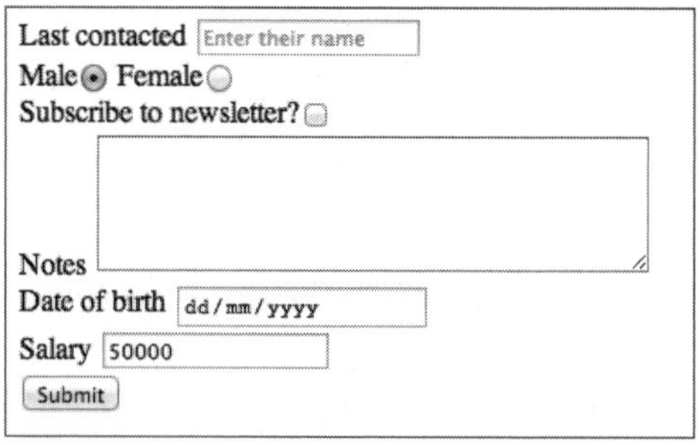

FIGURE 6-9

You should notice one new feature on this form: if you enter a value into the salary field, Chrome provides up and down arrows for increasing and decreasing this value by the step amount. This also ensures that the value is rounded down to a multiple of the step amount.

> **REFERENCE** *Please select the video for Lesson 6 online at www.wrox.com/go/ html5jsjquery24hr. You will also be able to download the code and resources for this lesson from the website.*

Semantic Tags

Most of the tags you have encountered up until this point will be familiar to anyone who has worked with earlier versions of HTML. In this lesson, you will explore a new set of tags defined in HTML5 called *semantic tags*.

If you consider the lessons you have looked at so far, thanks to the power of CSS, it is possible to create the body of even complex web pages entirely from span and div tags. In fact, many web pages are created exactly like this.

Each element that appears on a page—from a header banner, to a table cell, to an image—is responsible for providing the presentation for a rectangular area of the screen, and therefore a div or span can fulfill this role.

Although this approach works from a presentation perspective, the individual tags do not contain any meaning about their purpose in the web page: They are therefore said to lack semantic meaning. Not only that, it would be very difficult to deduce from the markup what role each element played in the web page.

> **NOTE** *The "semantic web" was a term coined by the inventor of the World Wide Web, Tim Berners-Lee. He envisaged a web of data that could be processed by machines as well as people. Although Tim's vision remains largely unfulfilled, the tags you will look at in this chapter are one step along the line to achieving this.*

Let's look at a concrete example. A header section for a web page could be defined as follows:

```
<div class="header">This is the header</div>
```

You will notice that the class name does describe the purpose of the div, but is just an arbitrary name: I could just as easily have called this class headSection or head.

In many ways, it would be better if there were a semantic tag called header, and everyone used this to indicate the header of their pages.

The rationale for semantic tags comes from the observation that if the browser knows this is a header, it may be able to provide additional services or features to the reader based on this fact:

➤ It may decide to render the information differently on different devices. For instance, on a small screen device such as a phone, it may only show the header when the user taps near the top of the page.

➤ It may support different modes. For instance, a user may indicate that he or she wants to read the content of the page without any distractions (similar to the Reader mode in Safari); therefore, the header could be temporarily removed.

➤ It may provide support for alternative browsers, such as screen readers for the visually impaired. For instance, it would help the screen reader understand that this is the title section of the page and should be read first.

In addition to these benefits, there are clear benefits to the web page developer. Pages consisting of heavily nested `div` tags can become very difficult to maintain. Not only is it easy to miss an ending tag, but it becomes difficult to determine which tag needs which style applied to it.

In order to support these benefits, there needs to be a way to definitively mark an element as the header. Therefore, the HTML5 specification defines a set of semantic tags, including the following:

```
<header>This is the header</ header >
```

This lesson will walk you through the most important semantic tags and look at how you can structure a web page with these tags.

As it happens, few of these tags do currently provide any of the potential benefits outlined. Still, I recommend that you take advantage of these tags because they will make your code easier to read and comprehend, and they may offer advantages in the future.

GROUPING AND SEGMENTING CONTENT

Many of the semantic tags are used for building the core structure of a web page—for instance, the header, the footer, sections of content, and asides. The example that follows contains a number of semantic tags: Start by reading through this example. you will then look at the meaning of each tag:

```
<body>
    <header>This is the header</header>
    <main>
        <aside>This is where the advertising goes</aside>
        <section>This is the first section in the page</section>
        <section>This is the second section in the page</section>
    </main>
    <footer>This is the footer</footer>
</body>
```

As you can see, this example is taking advantage of a number of tags that you have not encountered so far. The next sections will describe these tags and explain where they should be used. It will also cover a number of other tags not found in this example.

Header

The `header` tag is used to group introductory information such as the title of the page and any relevant header imagery. The `header` should also contain the main navigation links for the page.

There can, in fact, be more than one `header` on a page: Each `section` may have its own `header` element, while the page as a whole may have its own `header` element.

Footer

The `footer` tag is used to group information that should appear at the bottom of a web page or section. For instance, this may contain copyright information or contact information.

As with `headers`, it is possible to have multiple `footers` in a page, and `footers` do not need to be paired with `headers`.

Main

The `main` tag should surround the content that forms the central functionality or content of the web page. There should only be one `main` tag on a page, and it cannot be nested inside other elements such as `header`, `section`, or `footer`.

I have not placed the `headers` and `footers` inside the main element, but this is a choice I have made. The HTML5 specification leaves you a wide degree of discretion over how and where you use the tags, and how they interact with other tags. It would therefore also be perfectly valid to nest the `header` and `footer` inside the `main` element.

Section

`Sections` are used to capture discreet subdivisions of a document. For example, in the web page you have been developing, the editable portion of the screen may be considered a `section`, and the list of contacts may be considered another `section`.

In order to determine if a portion of the web page is a `section`, consider whether you could pick up this whole area of the page and reposition it elsewhere within the web page. If so, it is a good candidate to be tagged as a `section`.

Aside

`Asides` are used for content that is loosely associated with other content around it, but which could be considered separate. It may also be used for advertising material or other unrelated information. An `aside` will often be visually separated from the content around it with a border or font.

Article

An `article` is similar to a `section` in that it contains self-contained information, but it is generally used for segregating textual content, such as blog posts or reviews, rather than just generic sections of the document.

Some people prefer to see the `article` tag not as a magazine article, but instead like an article of clothing: something that exists in its own right, but can be mixed and matched with other articles.

I personally prefer to use `article` only for self-composed text blocks that could be extracted from one web page and embedded in another. For this reason, `article` is not appropriate for the contacts web page because this page does not contain self-contained text blocks.

Nav

A `nav` element provides a container for the main navigation links on the page. This allows them to be located by alternative browsers such as screen readers.

This is an easy element to overuse: The specification does not expect all navigation links to be encapsulated in a `nav` element, only the primary navigation options for the page.

Address

The `address` tag is not new at all, but it does fit in with the other semantic tags, and is part of the HTML5 specification. This element is used to define the address or contact details of the maintainer of the page.

STYLING SEMANTIC TAGS WITH CSS

If you save the markup from the previous section in a file called `semantic.html` and then open it in Chrome, you may be disappointed with the results (see Figure 7-1).

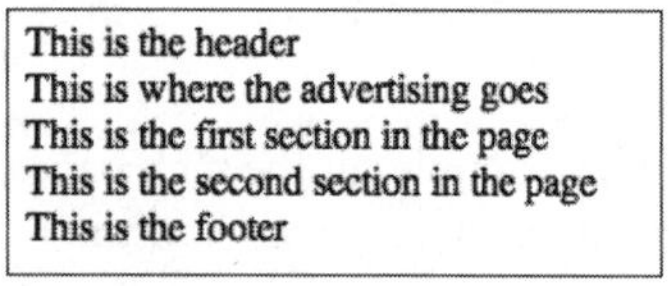

This is the header
This is where the advertising goes
This is the first section in the page
This is the second section in the page
This is the footer

FIGURE 7-1

Although the semantic tags imply presentation information in their names, browsers typically do not style them differently from regular `div` elements: They are simple `block` components. For instance, the `header` tag tells the browser the content of the element contains header information; it does not tell it what to do with this.

Semantic elements need to be styled with CSS, just like regular elements. In addition, you can style these tags any way you like—there is nothing (except common sense) to stop you from placing the `footer` at the top of the page and the `header` at the bottom of the page.

In order to style these tags, place the following in a `style` section in the `head` of the page:

```
header, footer {
    padding: 30px 0 30px 0;
    width:100%;
    background:#B3B2CF;
    text-align:center;
}
```

```
header {
    font-size:22px;

}
section {
    float: left;
    padding: 10px;
    margin:20px;
    width:70%;
    border: 1px solid black;
}
aside {
    position:relative;
    float:right;
    padding: 10px;
    margin:20px;
    width:150px;
    height:200px;
    border: 1px solid black;
}
footer {
    clear: both;
    margin-top: 50px;
    font-size:18px;
}
```

If you now refresh the page the various elements will be displayed in an appropriate style for their names.

MICROFORMATS

So far you have examined the way semantic tags can be used for encapsulating a portion of a page, and labeling it according to its role in the page. Semantic tags can, however, also exist on a micro scale.

Consider the elements in the contacts web page displaying date information. Currently, these are placed in `td` elements, but HTML5 provides a new element called `time` for encapsulating date and time information in a more meaningful way. This element allows the date and time information to be provided in a human-readable and machine-readable manner simultaneously. For instance

```
<time datetime="2014-08-20">20th August 2014</time>
```

This could also have been written:

```
<time datetime="2014-08-20">August 2014</time>
```

Notice that in each case, the same information is provided twice. The first version of the date is presented in an attribute and conforms to the ISO standards for dates (and times if required). The second version appears between the tags and is the version that will be displayed to the user.

Although dates and times, in all their myriad of formats, are very easy for a human to read and comprehend, they can be notoriously difficult for a computer to process. By allowing tags to always provide an ISO-compliant version of the date, it suddenly becomes trivial for a computer to process the element and comprehend its meaning.

Features such as this are referred to as *microformats* and are widely used in computing to provide semantic meaning to search engines and other automated clients, while providing human-friendly versions of the same data to humans.

Microformats have not been officially included in the HTML5 specification at this point, although the time element is an example of a microformat. There are several standards for additional microformats, and it is likely that HTML5 will be expanded to support these in the future.

SUMMING UP

It would be overly optimistic to think that semantic tags are going to revolutionize your approach to web page development. They are, in many ways, one of the least interesting features of HTML5 because they do not provide any visual or functional capabilities that could not be achieved with HTML4.

They do, however, have an important role to play in enhancing the readability of your code, and may provide other benefits in the future once browsers begin incorporating features that rely on semantic tags. In many ways, it is not until web page developers start using these tags consistently, and en masse, that browser vendors will begin to provide functional support for them.

As a final note, it is also important not to overuse the semantic tags. There is still nothing wrong with using div and span elements for structuring sections of a page: Save the semantic tags for the main building blocks of the web page.

TRY IT

In this Try It, you will take the web application from Lesson 6 and add semantic tags in the appropriate places.

Lesson Requirements

You will need the files from the end of Lesson 6, a text editor, and a web browser.

Step-by-Step

1. Open the contacts.html page in your text editor.

2. Locate the div with the class header and convert this into a header element without a class.

3. Locate the div with the class footer and convert this into a footer element without a class.

4. Convert the div with the id= "contactDetails" into a section.

5. Convert the div with the id= "contactList" into a section.

6. Surround the two sections with a main element and give this an attribute id= "contactScreen".

7. Find the td elements containing dates and convert these to time elements with both a human readable and machine-readable form.

8. Save `contacts.html`.

9. Open `contacts.css` and change the selector for the header class from an `id` selector to an element selector.

10. Also change the selector for the `footer` from an `id` selector to an element selector.

11. Save `contacts.css`.

12. Open `contacts.html` in Chrome. The page should not look any different.

13. Right-click the header element and choose "Inspect Element."

14. Confirm that this has the element type `header`.

> **REFERENCE** *Please select the video for Lesson 7 online at* www.wrox.com/go/ html5jsjquery24hr. *You will also be able to download the code and resources for this lesson from the website.*

HTML5 Validation

When the user submits a form, it is common to perform validation of the data the user has entered within the browser. This allows any issues, such as missing data, to be resolved before the form is sent to the server, and generally provides a superior user experience.

Form validation has traditionally been performed with JavaScript: In fact, until recently this was the most common use of JavaScript within web pages. HTML5 provides built-in form validation, and allows fields to be validated based on attributes added directly to the fields themselves. This lesson will look at how you can enable validation on the form created in Lesson 6.

The HTML5 form validation specification is not perfect—it lacks some of the rules you would expect in a complete validation framework. It does, however, have the advantage of being a native solution and is very easy to use. It is therefore necessary to decide at the outset of a project whether HTML5 validation is sufficient, or whether you will use one of the many JavaScript libraries available—for instance, jQuery validation.

ADDING VALIDATION RULES

This section will add form validation to the `contacts.html` web page as it stood at the end of Lesson 7. If you would like to follow along, open this file now, or download it from the book's website.

The most common form of validation is specifying that a field is mandatory. You can indicate that the user is required to provide a value for a field by simply adding the `required` attribute to it. This is a Boolean attribute, so it does not require a value:

```
<input required autofocus autocomplete="off"
name="contactName" id="contactName" type="text" />
```

If you open this page in Chrome, you will not initially notice any difference. If you now press Enter in the Contact name field without first providing a value, however, you will receive the message shown in Figure 8-1.

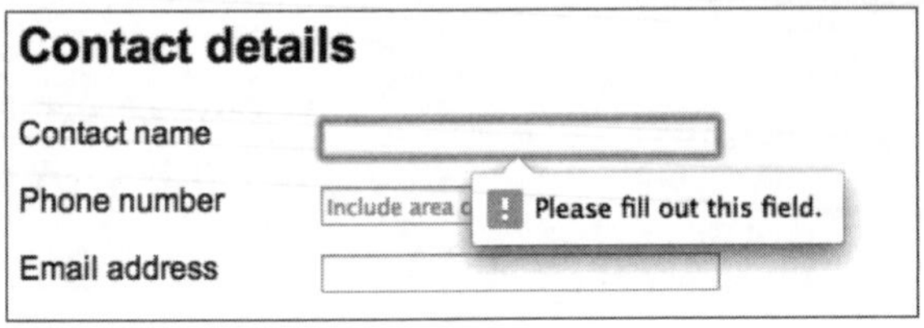

FIGURE 8-1

Unfortunately, you only receive this error when you press Enter in the field, or press the Submit button without providing a value for the field. Tabbing out of the field is not enough to trigger the validation message.

With field validation, it is generally better to provide immediate feedback to the user when a field is invalid. Users can become frustrated when told a number of fields are invalid when they submit the form because they need to locate each of these individually and provide values.

One way to provide immediate feedback to a user is via a pair of CSS pseudo-classes called `valid` and `invalid`. In order to demonstrate these, add the following to the `contacts.css`:

```
.validated:invalid {
    background:#FAC3C9;
}

.validated:valid {
    background:#BDF0A8;
}
```

These rules will set the background color of an element a shade of pink if it is invalid or a shade of green if it is valid.

Notice that you have specified that these rules only apply if the element is tagged with the `validated` class. Technically, all input fields can be valid or invalid, even ones with no rules applied to them, such as submit buttons. Rather than have these appear green, you will explicitly add a class when you want an element to use these styles. Therefore, add the `validated` class to the input field:

```
<input required autofocus autocomplete="off"
name="contactName" id="contactName" class="validated" type="text" />
```

If you reload the web page it should initially display with the pink background, as shown in Figure 8-2.

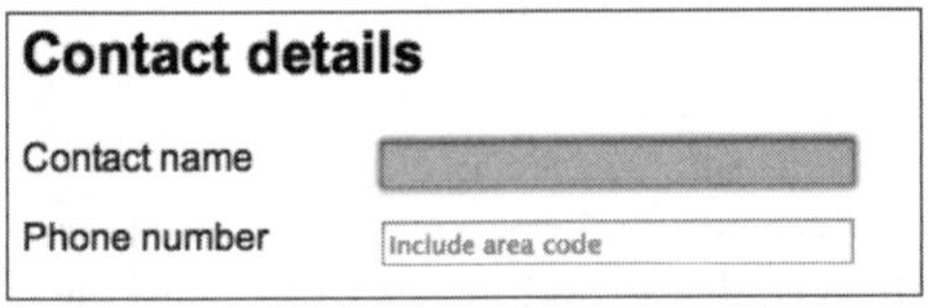

FIGURE 8-2

If you now type some text into the field, you will notice that it immediately turns green.

Another common validation rule for a field relates to the number of characters it can contain. It is common to specify both a minimum and a maximum number of characters for a field.

The HTML5 specification specifies two new attributes called `min` and `max` that look promising in this respect. Unfortunately these are only useful for validating that a number is between a minimum and maximum value; they are of no use at all for textual data.

The specification does provide an attribute called `maxlength` that can be used to control the maximum number of characters that can be added to a field. This works by physically preventing the user from typing into the field when this limit is reached. The only way to perform validation for a minimum length, however, is to use the `pattern` attribute. This accepts a regular expression. For example:

```
<input required autofocus autocomplete="off" name="contactName"
    type="text" class="validated" id="contactName" pattern=".{5,100}"/>
```

> **NOTE** *Regular expressions are a formal language for expressing textual patterns and checking if a string of text matches this pattern. In this particular case the "." matches any single character, while the two numbers in curly brackets specify that this must occur between 5 and 100 times. I will not explain regular expressions in any more detail in this book, but there are many online resources available for learning more.*

If you reload the web page and start typing into it, you will notice that the background does not turn green until you type the fifth character. Additionally, if you type more than 100 characters, it will turn pink again.

You can add similar validation to the phone number field:

```
<input required pattern=" [0-9() ]{5,15}" placeholder="Include area code"
name="phoneNumber" type="tel" id="phoneNumber" class="validated"/>
```

In this case, you ensure that the number of characters is between five and fifteen, and you are limiting the characters the field will accept to numbers, brackets, and spaces.

When you come to the email address field, things become slightly more interesting. If you simply add the `required` attribute, you may be pleasantly surprised by the resulting behavior:

```
<input required name="emailAddress" id="emailAddress" type="email"
class="validated" />
```

If you start typing into the field, you will notice that it does not turn green until you enter the @ symbol. Because the `type` has been specified as `email`, the browser automatically checks that the value adheres to the rules for email addresses.

For the select box, you also want to ensure that the user selects a genuine value, not the first entry from the list. You can achieve this as follows:

```
<select required name="companyName" id="companyName" class="validated">
    <option value="">Please select</option>
    <option value="1">ABC Incorporated</option>
    <option value="2">XZY Ltd</option>
    <option value="3">ACME iInternational</option>
</select>
```

Notice that, in addition to setting the select box to `required`, you have also specified that the value of the first option is an empty string. This does not count as a value; therefore, the `select` will turn green only if the user selects another value from the list of options.

Finally, for the `notes` field, you will simply specify a maximum number of characters that can be entered because this field is not mandatory.

```
<textarea cols="40" rows="6" name="notes" id="notes" class="validated"
    maxlength="1000"></textarea>
```

This means that the field will appear green when the screen first loads because even an empty value is valid.

> **NOTE** *The* `textarea` *element does not support the* `pattern` *attribute. This means there is no straightforward way to ensure a* `textarea` *contains a minimum quantity of text.*

You do not need to add any information to the last contacted field. This field is not mandatory, and Chrome has provided an input mask to ensure that the user cannot enter an invalid date.

CUSTOMIZING VALIDATION

The browser itself has generated all the validation messages that have been displayed up until this point. This brings some benefits; for instance, the messages are automatically localized based on the user's location and operating system settings.

If you look at the error that is generated when the contact name is less than five characters, however, it will appear as in the example in Figure 8-3.

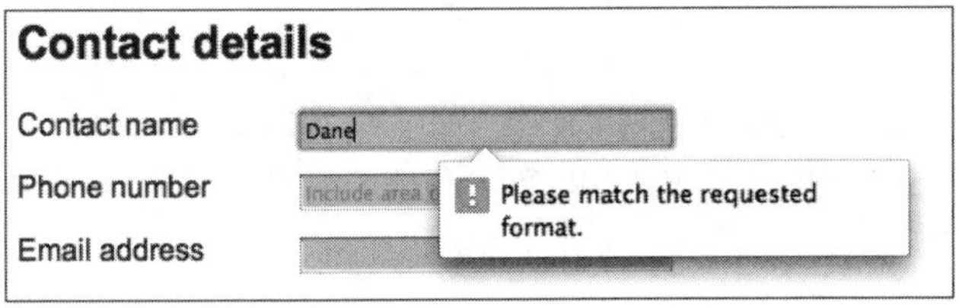

Contact details

Contact name: Dane

Phone number: Include area [...] ⚠ Please match the requested format.

Email address:

FIGURE 8-3

This does not tell the user what the pattern should be; therefore, it is unlikely they would know how to resolve the issue.

It is possible to control the validation messages displayed to users, but unfortunately it is not as straightforward as you might expect and needs to be accomplished with JavaScript.

> **NOTE** *The next example contains relatively simple JavaScript. You may, however, decide to return to this example after reading Lesson 11.*

In order to customize the contact name message, add the following immediately before the closing html tag.

```
<script>
    var contactName = document.getElementById('contactName')
    contactName.oninvalid = function(e) {
        e.target.setCustomValidity("");
        if (!e.target.validity.valid) {
            if (e.target.value.length == 0) {
                e.target.setCustomValidity("Contact name is required.");
            } else if (e.target.value.length < 5) {
                e.target.setCustomValidity("Contact name must be at least 5
characters.");
            }
        }
    };
</script>
```

> **NOTE** *This needs to be placed at the bottom of the page because it attempts to access the* contactName *field when it executes. If it were added to the* head *tag the field would not have been present when this code executed. Although placing JavaScript at the end of the page is an acceptable solution to this problem, you will look at a more elegant solution later in the book.*

If you enter four characters in the field, it should now display the message you have specified (see Figure 8-4).

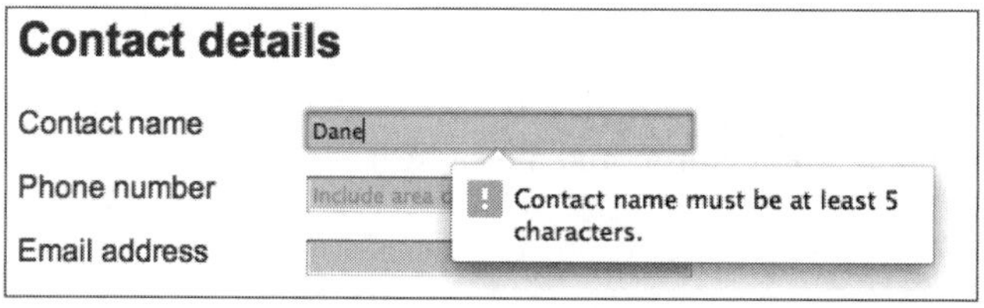

Contact details

Contact name `Dane`
Phone number ⚠ Contact name must be at least 5 characters.
Email address

FIGURE 8-4

In this code, you add an event listener to the `contactName` field, after retrieving it with the native DOM API. You then request that the browser sends you an event every time its validity status changes. When you receive that event, you first determine whether the field is invalid by accessing property on the field itself.

If the field is invalid, you can determine the current value of the field, and therefore determine which of the validation rules has been breached and create the appropriate message.

Once you determine the message you want to display to the user, you can call the `setCustom Validity` function on the field to set this value.

DISABLING VALIDATION

HTML5 provides a number of additional attributes for controlling validation.

A `novalidate` attribute can be added to the form in order to disable validation. If this is added, fields are still marked as valid and invalid, so the CSS styling you added to the web page will still work, but error messages will not be displayed to the user, and it is possible for the user to submit the web page, even if it is invalid.

Because HTML5 validation is enabled by default, this option is sometimes useful. For instance, any time a field is marked as type `email`, validation will be automatically added, even if you did not want it.

It is also possible to mark individual fields with the attribute `formnovalidate` to disable validation. It is common to add this attribute dynamically to fields when specific circumstances are met: For instance, some fields do not need to be validated if specific data is entered elsewhere in the form. This is a form of cross-field validation.

This can also be used to disable the default validation on a field—for instance, to allow an `email` field to contain an invalid email address.

TRY IT

In this Try It, you will add validation to the form you created in the Try It for Lesson 6. You can download this from the book's website or use the version you created in Lesson 6.

The book's website contains a completed version of this exercise under the name `tryit.html`. You can also view the screencast if you need additional help.

Lesson Requirements

You will need the `tryit.html` from Lesson 6, a text editor, and a browser.

Step-by-Step

1.   Open the `tryit.html` file in your text editor.

2. Add attributes to the `fullName` field so that it is mandatory for the user to enter a value, and the minimum length of 7 characters, and a maximum length of 50 characters.

3. For the `notes` field, make the field mandatory and add a pattern that ensures the field contains no more than 500 characters of text.

4. Change the salary field to define a minimum salary of $20,000, and a maximum salary of $200,000. Although this was not shown in the lesson, it can be achieved with the `min` and `max` attributes, but make sure not to include commas or the dollar sign in the numbers.

5. Add a style to the web page so that any invalid `input` field or `textarea` displays with a red border. Although it may not seem like it, the line around an `input` field or `textarea` is just a simple border and can therefore be modified with CSS.

The finished version of the form should display as you see in Figure 8-5 when a validation error occurs.

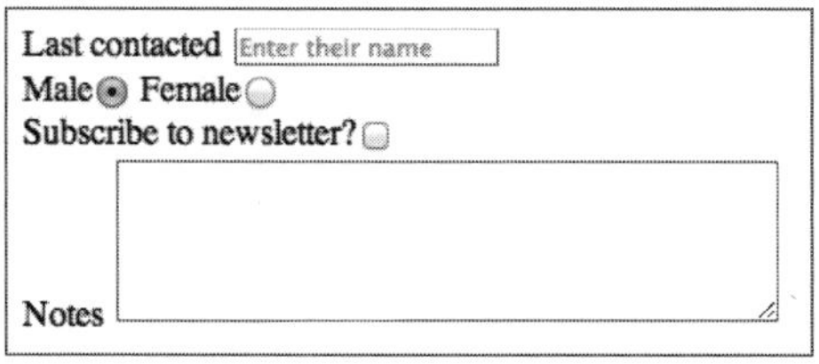

FIGURE 8-5

> **REFERENCE** *Please select the video for Lesson 8 online at* www.wrox.com/go/ html5jsjquery24hr. *You will also be able to download the code and resources for this lesson from the website.*

Drag and Drop

Drag and drop has been a common paradigm in user interface design for decades. What is less known is that drag and drop has been supported by web browsers for well over a decade and first appeared in IE5 in 1999.

The implementation of drag and drop that has been standardized in HTML5 is largely the same version from IE5. Where possible, HTML5 standards are based on existing implementations. This is both a strength and a weakness of HTML5. A drag and drop standard developed from the ground up would have significantly improved and streamlined the API outline in this lesson, but it would have taken longer for browsers to adopt.

Drag and drop is a technique allowing elements to be dragged from their original location on the screen, and dropped in a different area of the screen. Drag and drop follows the following process:

➤ The drag processes begins with a mouse down event. This selects the element that will be the source of the event.

➤ While holding the mouse button down, the user can move the element around the screen with his or her mouse.

➤ The process ends when the user releases the mouse button. The element that the mouse is over at the time becomes the target of the drag-and-drop event.

Drag and drop can therefore be seen as an approach for connecting two different elements that are related in some way.

> **NOTE** *Before beginning, it is worth mentioning that this lesson will use simple JavaScript. Although this should be easy to follow if you have some programming experience, you may opt to return to this lesson after reading Lesson 11.*

UNDERSTANDING EVENTS

The drag-and-drop API relies heavily on events. Nodes within the DOM generate events when the user performs various operations on them. For example:

➤ Clicking the mouse

➤ Typing text into them

➤ Hovering over them with the mouse

Dynamic web applications are largely based on writing JavaScript code to respond to these events and performing some operation as a result. This is often referred to as "event-driven programming".

Responding to events involves the following process:

➤ A JavaScript function is registered with a node in the DOM for a specific type of event.

➤ When the event occurs, the browser automatically calls this JavaScript function, and passes it an `Event` object. This object contains context about the event that has occurred—for instance, the element that generated it.

➤ The JavaScript function can respond to the event in any way it needs, including manipulating the DOM.

In this lesson you will use native DOM events. In the next section, you will start using jQuery to listen to events. Therefore, this lesson will not look in-depth at how event handling works.

DRAG AND DROP EXAMPLE

In this section, you will write a simple drag-and-drop example, consisting of a screen that looks like Figure 9-1.

FIGURE 9-1

You will then implement the following drag-and-drop functionality:

➤   The user can drag any of the colored boxes on the top line to any of the white boxes on the second line.

➤   If the user drops a colored box on a white box, it will adopt the color for itself.

➤   When a colored box is dragged, its color should appear lighter to indicate it is the source of the event.

➤   When a colored box is over the top of a white box, the white box's border should be enhanced to show it is the target for a drop.

Although simple, this example is sufficient to demonstrate all the important drag-and-drop events.

Start by creating a web page called boxes.html with the following content:

```
<!DOCTYPE html>
<html lang="en">
<head>
    <meta charset="utf-8">
    <style>
        .box {
            height:200px;
            width:200px;
            display:inline-block;
            border: 2px solid black;
        }
    </style>
    </head>
    <body>
        <div class="box" style="background:red"></div>
        <div class="box" style="background:green"></div>
        <div class="box" style="background:blue"></div>
        <p>
        <div class="box"></div>
        <div class="box"></div>
        <div class="box"></div>
    </body>
</html>
```

Most visual elements can be marked as draggable to make them available to be the source of a drag-and-drop operation; therefore, add the following attribute to each of the boxes on the top row:

```
<div draggable="true" class="box" style="background:red"></div>
```

Next, you want the browser to invoke a JavaScript function when the user starts to drag a box. Within this function, you will extract the color of the element being dragged and store it away for later in the drag-and-drop process. This will ensure that the color is available to the target element when the drop event occurs.

Start by adding the following to each of the boxes on the top row:

```
<div ondragstart="startDragging(event)" draggable="true" class="box"
    style="background:red"></div>
```

ondragstart is triggered when the mouse is clicked on a draggable element. When this occurs, the startDragging JavaScript function will be invoked (you will write this function shortly). This is an arbitrary name for the function; you could call it anything you wanted.

When the function is called, you want to pass information about the event to it (providing context about the event). Thus, you place event between brackets to indicate it will be passed as a parameter to the function. The event object will be created and populated by the browser itself; your code simply needs to pass it on.

In this lesson, you will embed JavaScript directly in the head section of the web page. JavaScript can be added by simply including it within a script element. Therefore, add the following just below the end of the style element:

```
<script>
function startDragging(evt) {
    evt.dataTransfer.setData("Color", evt.target.style.background);
    evt.target.style.opacity = 0.3;
}
</script>
```

> **NOTE** *Functions that are invoked when events occur are commonly called "callback functions." You are responsible for implementing these functions, but you then ask the event handling framework to invoke them at the appropriate time.*

The event object contains a wide variety of information about the event that has occurred, but most importantly, it allows you to access the element that has caused the event by invoking evt.target.

A JavaScript object represents each node in the DOM. Once you have access to the object, you can start inspecting it and interacting with it. For instance, you can access the current CSS styles of the element with the code evt.target.style.

Additionally, the event object provides a dataTransfer object that enables you to store information for the duration of the drag-and-drop operation. You are storing an arbitrary parameter called Color, which is given the value of the background color for the source element.

On the second line of the function, you are manipulating the style of the element that caused the event using the native DOM API to set the opacity level of the element.

> **NOTE** *Opacity describes the transparency of an element. If an element has opacity of 1.0, it has no transparency. As the value moves toward 0, the element becomes more transparent, which in this example, will make the color appear faded.*

Next, you want to provide functionality to the boxes on the second line of the web page: These are the boxes that will act as the targets for the drag-and-drop operation.

To start, you will add the functionality so that the `border` of the box is set to 4 pixels in size if the user hovers over it with the mouse down, and then is set back to normal if the user's mouse leaves the box. Remember, the user may move her mouse over the element without releasing the mouse button.

Add the following to the three boxes on the second row:

```
<div ondragenter="setBorderSize(event, '4px')" ondragleave="setBorderSize(event,
'2px')" class="box"></div>
```

This registers the same JavaScript function with two different events, `ondragenter` and `ondragleave`, but passes a different parameter to the function in each case. This is simply a design decision on my part to reduce the number of functions that I needed to write. I could have just as easily implemented this with two JavaScript functions.

The implementation of the function is as follows:

```
function setBorderSize(evt, size) {
    evt.currentTarget.style.border =  size + " solid black";
}
```

This implementation should look familiar now; the only interesting aspect is that I am using the `size` parameter passed in to set the size of the border but assuming it is still `solid` and `black`.

In order to drop the source onto the target you need to add two additional event listeners:

```
<div ondrop="drop(event)" ondragover="allowDrop(event)"
    ondragenter="setBorderSize(event, '4px')"
    ondragleave="setBorderSize(event, '2px')" class="box"></div>
```

First, you need to listen for an `ondragover` event. This event will be called to determine whether or not the element the mouse is hovering over is a valid target for the drop event.

You may be wondering why I did not change the border in the `ondragover` event. This event is called every time the mouse moves by event one pixel; therefore, it is potentially called hundreds or thousands of times as the mouse hovers over the element. As a result, you want to make sure that the function called by this event does as little as possible.

By default, elements are not targets for drop events; therefore, all the function needs to do is prevent this default behavior. This can be achieved by calling a special function on the event itself, as shown here:

```
function allowDrop(evt) {
    evt.preventDefault();
}
```

Next, you need to add the `ondrop` event listener. This is the event that occurs when the user releases the mouse button while hovering above the element. The implementation of the `drop` function is as follows:

```
function drop(evt) {
    var color = evt.dataTransfer.getData("Color");
    evt.currentTarget.style.background = color;
    setBorderSize(evt, '2px');
}
```

On the first line of this function, you access the value of the `Color` property you set previously and store it in a local variable called `color`.

Next, you set the `background` color of the target element to this color. Notice that the `target` of the event is now the element that is the target rather than the source of the operation.

Finally, because the `ondragleave` event will not be fired in this case, you need to manually set the `border` of the target back to the normal size by invoking `setBorderSize`. Notice that you can pass the `event` object to other functions if required.

You still have one more feature to implement: You need to change the `opacity` of the source element back to 1.0. This can be achieved by adding another event listener to the boxes on the top row:

```
<div ondragend="dragEnded(event)" ondragstart="startDragging(event)"
    draggable="true" class="box" style="background:red"></div>
```

The event listener should then be implemented as follows:

```
function dragEnded(evt) {
    evt.target.style.opacity = 1.0;
}
```

The target of the event is the source of the drag-and-drop operation rather than the target; thus, you can simply change its `opacity` style.

A finished version of this web page is also available on the book's web site called `boxes.html`.

Although this is a simple example, it has introduced you to the six key events that are commonly used with the API. In some cases, it is not necessary to listen for all six events because, for instance, you may not need to perform any action when the mouse leaves an element.

You should now be able to open the web page and try out the functionality. Figure 9-2 shows a drag operation in progress.

TRY IT

In this Try It, you will use the techniques outlined in this chapter to create a very simple web page.

You will create a web page with a single drop zone. When any element is dropped onto this, it will display the text from this element.

There is a finished version of this Try It on the book's website under the name `simpledragand-drop_finished.html`.

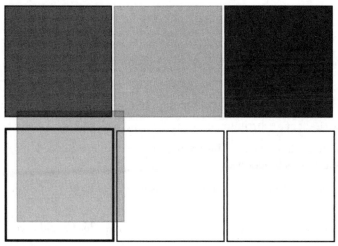

FIGURE 9-2

Lesson Requirements

You can use the file `simpledraganddrop.html` from the Lesson 9 resources on the website as the basis for this Try It. You will also need a text editor and a web browser.

If you like, you can create the web page yourself as follows:

```
<!DOCTYPE html>
<html lang="en">
<head>
    <meta charset="utf-8">
    <style>
        .box {
            height:200px;
            width:400px;
            display:inline-block;
            text-align:center;
            border: 2px dashed black;
            line-height: 200px;
            margin: 50px;
        }
    </style>

</head>
<body>
    <div class="box">Drag something onto me</div>
```

```
            <h1>I am a header 1 tag</h1>
            <h3>I am a header 3 tag</h3>
            <p>I am a p tag</p>
      </body>
  </html>
```

Step-by-Step

1. Open the `simpledraganddrop.html` file in your text editor, or create it from the markup in the previous section.

2. Start by adding the `draggable="true"` attribute to the h1, h3, and p elements.

3. Add an `ondragstart` attribute to these events. This should invoke a function called `start-Dragging` and pass the `event` to this function.

4. Add a `script` block to the `head` section of the web page. This is where all the JavaScript functions will be located.

5. Create a JavaScript function in the script block called `startDragging`. This should accept a parameter called `evt`.

6. The body of the function should set a property called `Text` on `evt.dataTransfer` using the technique outlined earlier in this lesson. In order to extract the text from the element being dragged, use the call `evt.target.textContent`.

    The text of an element is actually contained in a child node of the element in the DOM, and therefore it can be accessed with `firstChild`. The text can then be extracted with `textContent`.

7. Ensure that the `div` element allows other elements to be dropped on it by using the `ondragover` event. This should invoke a JavaScript function that prevents the default behavior of the event, as outlined earlier in this lesson.

8. Provide functionality to support the drop operation. Start by adding an `ondrop` attribute to the `div` and have this invoke a function called `drop`.

9. The `drop` JavaScript function that is fired during the `ondrop` event first needs to extract the value of the `Text` property from the `dataTransfer` object on the `event`.

10. The function also needs to set this text on the `div`. This can be achieved by providing a value for `evt.target.textContent`.

11. You should now be able to open the web page and start dragging elements onto the `div`. Every time you drop an element onto the `div`, its text will be updated to reflect the element that was dropped on it.

> **REFERENCE** *Please select the video for Lesson 9 online at* www.wrox.com/go/ html5jsjquery24hr. *You will also be able to download the code and resources for this lesson from the website.*

10
Dynamic Elements

This lesson is based around four additional features added in HTML5 that provide dynamic components: a native progress bar, a meter element, a range control, and a set of tags that allow the user to expand a summary to view its details.

These differ from many other tags you have examined because browser support is not consistent. Therefore, you will also look at a concept called *polyfills* that enables you to upgrade the functionality of a browser when a feature is missing.

SUMMARY AND DETAILS TAGS

One of the most frequent pieces of JavaScript I find myself writing is code to show extra information to a user when he or she chooses based on a summary.

Because this is such common functionality, the HTML5 specification defines two tags that combine to provide native support for this functionality. In order to see this in action, create the following web page:

```
<!DOCTYPE html>
<html lang="en">
    <head>
        <meta charset="utf-8">
    </head>
    <body>
        <header>This page provides an example of the summary and details
tags</header>
        <details>
            <summary>Table of contents</summary>
            <ul><li>Lesson 1</li>
            <li>Lesson 2</li>
            <li>Lesson 3</li>
            <li>Lesson 4</li>
            <li>Lesson 5</li></ul>
        </details>
    </body>
</html>
```

This page includes a tag called `details`, which then has a child element called `summary`. In addition, the `details` tag itself contains additional information: an unordered list in this case. If you open this in Chrome, it will display as you see in Figure 10-1.

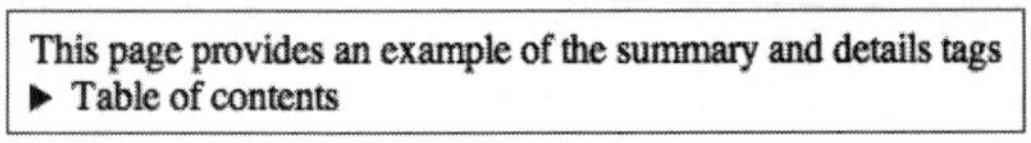

This page provides an example of the summary and details tags
▶ Table of contents

FIGURE 10-1

By default, this shows only the contents of the `summary` tag. If you then click on the arrow to the left of the `summary`, it displays the full details (see Figure 10-2).

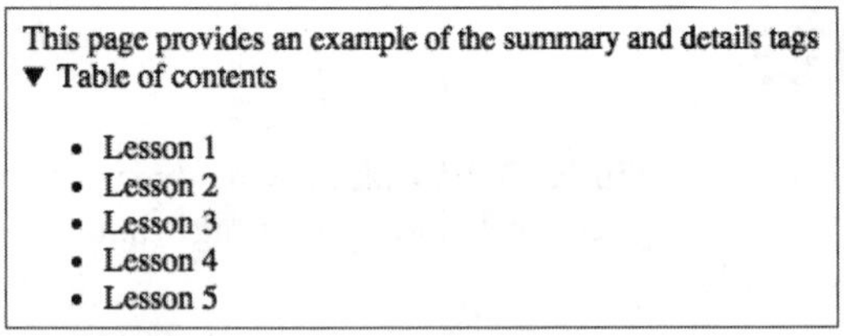

This page provides an example of the summary and details tags
▼ Table of contents

- Lesson 1
- Lesson 2
- Lesson 3
- Lesson 4
- Lesson 5

FIGURE 10-2

Notice that the arrow automatically points down to indicate that the details are being displayed. Naturally, it is possible to style these elements with CSS; you have a lot of flexibility regarding how this arrow will look to users.

Although these tags are a great addition to HTML, unfortunately browser support is currently minimal. The functionality works fine in Chrome, but if you open this same page in IE or Firefox, you will be disappointed.

If you want to know whether features are supported in various browsers, the best website available is www.caniuse.com. This details support levels for all HTML5 and CSS3 features across a wide variety of browsers. If you view the web page, www.caniuse.com/details, you can see the support level for this specific tag.

PROGRESS BAR AND METER

HTML5 also provides a native progress bar and a related element called a `meter`.

You will begin by looking at the `meter` element because this is slightly simpler. This element can be used to show a value within a range. For instance, if you wanted to show a value that was 60 percent of a target, you could add the following element to a web page:

```
<meter value="6" min="0" max="10">6 our of 10</meter>
```

If you add this to a simple template web page, it should display as you see in Figure 10-3:

FIGURE 10-3

Notice that, in this case, you have specified a minimum and a maximum value of 0 and 10 respectively, and then set the value of the element to 6. Because `min` and `max` default to 0 and 1 respectively, this could also have been expressed as follows:

```
<meter value="0.6" >60%</meter>
```

The value between the tags is not needed; I have just added that for clarity.

The color used for the meter can take on meaning when you use additional attributes supported by the element. For instance, the following meter contains an expected range along with a possible range:

```
<meter value="1" high="8" low="3" min="0" max="10">6 our of 10</meter>
```

In this case, you have stated that the value is expected to be between 3 and 8. Because the value is lower than the expected range, the color of the bar changes from green to orange.

Alternatively, the following example, which is above the maximum range, displays in red:

```
<meter low="60" high="80" max="100" value="95"></meter>
```

Naturally it is possible to change these colors using CSS.

A progress bar is similar to a meter, except it is expected to change its value as an event occurs. Typically, you will use JavaScript to update the progress bar as you perform other processing.

It is possible to add a progress bar to a web page as follows:

```
<progress value="20" max="100" min="0" ></progress>
```

Figure 10-4 shows a static progress bar, one-fifth complete.

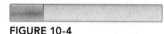

FIGURE 10-4

Naturally a static progress bar is not much use; therefore, the following is an example of a progress bar that updates 1 percent every 200 milliseconds seconds. Don't worry about the JavaScript for now; this will be explained over the next few lessons:

```
<!DOCTYPE html>
<html lang="en">
    <head>
        <meta charset="utf-8">
        <script>
        setInterval(updateProgessBar, 200);

        function updateProgessBar() {
        var progressBar = document.getElementById("progressBar");
progressBar.value += 1;
        }
        </script>
    </head>
    <body>
        <progress id="progressBar" value="0" max="100"></progress>
    </body>
</html>
```

One of the hardest things about progress bars is that it is often not possible to determine how far through an operation you are. If you would like to indicate to the user that you do not know how much time is remaining, you can simply remove the value and the progress bar will look like Figure 10-5.

FIGURE 10-5

This is referred to as a progress bar with an indeterminate value.

RANGE ELEMENT

The `progress` and `meter` elements you have looked at are a mechanism for displaying a value to the user. The `range` element is similar, except it is designed to allow the user to choose a value within a range.

The `range` element is therefore a form input type, except the possible values that the user can select are controlled by the minimum and maximum values for the range.

As an example, consider a case where you want the user to indicate how complete a task is as a percentage. You might add the following to a form:

```
0%<input type="range" name="percentComplete" min="0" max="100"
    step="5" value="50">100%
```

Notice that this is a simple `input` element, but the `type` is set to `range`.

This example specifies a minimum possible value of 0, a maximum possible value of 100, and a default value of 50. It also states that any movement of the range will step by 5. Thus, it is not possible to choose a value of 23—the user would need to choose 20 or 25. Figure 10-6 shows an example of a `range` element.

FIGURE 10-6

Notice that the labels for the minimum and maximum value have been added manually: These are not part of the element.

My biggest criticism of the `range` element is that browser implementations typically do not provide an easy mechanism to show the user the value that they have chosen; it is therefore necessary to do this manually with JavaScript. For instance, in the preceding example, it would be difficult for the user to know whether they had chosen a value of 20 or 25.

POLYFILLS

The features outlined in this lesson pose a quandary to programmers. Although these elements provide interesting functionality, all browsers do not support them. For instance, IE, prior to IE 10, does not support the `meter` and `progress` elements.

Thus, if you elect to use these features, some users may receive a lower-quality experience. For instance, when the range element is not supported, it simply displays as an input field. This is becoming less of an issue as browsers move to use auto-updating release models because most users have up-to-date browsers; many users in corporate environments, however, are still restricted to older versions of browsers.

This section will look at an approach that provides a workaround to browser support issues. It allows you to use native HTML5 functionality where it is available but provide custom implementations where it is not: This is a technique referred to as "polyfills."

In order to support polyfills, your web page needs to perform two distinct tasks:

➤ Determine whether the browser supports the features you wish to use

➤ Provide a JavaScript-based implementation if support is missing

Modernizr is a popular JavaScript library for performing these tasks. It is available from `http://modernizr.com/`.

The example that follows uses a version of Moderinzr from the Lesson 10 resources, or you can download your own version. The basic usage of Modernizer typically looks like this:

```
<!DOCTYPE html>
<html lang="en">
    <head>
        <meta charset="utf-8">
        <script src="modernizr.js"></script>

        <script>
        if (!Modernizr.inputtypes.range) {
        // provide JavaScript implementation
        }
        </script>
    </head>
    <body>
        0%<input type="range" name="percentComplete" min="0"
            max="100" step="5" value="50">100%
    </body>
</html>
```

In the `head` section, the Modernizr script is imported. Once this has been imported, it is possible to test whether features are available. In this example, you will notice the code:

```
if (!Modernizr.inputtypes.range) {
```

This states that if the `range` element is not available, the JavaScript block following the statement should be executed. Modernizr allows you to test for a wide range of features using similar statements that return `true` or `false`, depending on whether the feature is supported.

Within this block, it is necessary to provide a polyfill. The Modernizr website has links to many JavaScript polyfills, each with their own instructions on how they should be used.

TRY IT

This Try It will allow you to experiment with the elements introduced in this lesson. It will not contribute anything to the Contacts web application so you do not need to follow the instructions exactly if you choose. Instead, it is an opportunity to experiment.

The website for this book contains a file called `tryit.html` with a complete example, or you can watch the screencast online if you need extra help.

Lesson Requirements

You will also need a text editor and a web browser.

Step-by-Step

1. Start by creating a simple HTML5 web page that you can use to add the elements outlined in this lesson.

2. Imagine you wish to provide information on a patient's heart rate for a medical website. Start by creating a meter tag with a maximum possible value of 200 and a minimum possible value of 0.

3. Indicate the likely range for a healthy individual: Set the low value to 60 and the high range to 100.

4. Experiment with various different values for the meter—for instance, 20, 70, or 120—and observe what happens to the color of the bar.

5. Now imagine that instead of presenting the heart rate to the user, you want to allow a doctor to input a patient's heart rate.

6. Add a `range` element to the web page and set the minimum and maximum possible values to 0 and 200 respectively. In addition, set the step to be 3 because you do not need the input to be so precise.

7. Add a summary and detail section to the bottom of the page. Within this, the summary section should state "List of patients with high heart rates."

When the user clicks to view details, show a table with patient names and heart rates.

Your completed version should look like the screenshot in Figure 10-7.

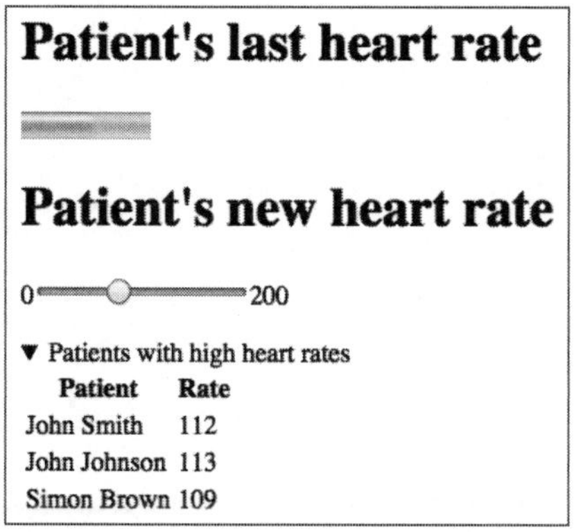

FIGURE 10-7

REFERENCE *Please select the video for Lesson 10 online at* www.wrox.com/go/ html5jsjquery24hr. *You will also be able to download the code and resources for this lesson from the website.*

PART II
Dynamic HTML5 Web Applications with JavaScript and jQuery

11

JavaScript

JavaScript has been around almost as long as web browsers themselves. It first appeared in 1995 with Netscape Navigator 2.0 and is the only programming language supported by all the most popular browsers. As a result, if you want to build dynamic websites, you need to know JavaScript.

For a long time, JavaScript was dismissed as a second-rate language, only appropriate for implementing basic functionality such as field validation. In the last five years, JavaScript's reputation has improved dramatically. This happened partly as a result of the massive performance increases that have occurred with JavaScript engines, beginning in Chrome and rippling out to all the other major browsers. More important, however, programmers began to re-evaluate the language itself and learned to harness its power.

Although JavaScript contains more than its fair share of idiosyncrasies, and although the designers of the language made some unusual decisions, JavaScript turns out to be a powerful and flexible language when it is used correctly. The goal of the next few lessons is to not only introduce the language, but also to offer some advice on how you should use the language if you want to write large and complex web applications.

This lesson will provide a quick introduction to the data types and syntax of JavaScript. These aspects of the language are reasonably conventional and are easy to pick up for anyone with a background in other programming languages.

JAVASCRIPT CONSOLE

In this lesson, you will write JavaScript directly in the Chrome JavaScript console. In order to use this, open the `contacts.html` web page from Lesson 8, and open the development tools using:

➤ Command+Option+i on OS X

➤ F12 or Ctrl+Shift+I on Windows

Once the development tools are open, click the Console tab. This provides a command prompt for writing JavaScript and allows you to directly manipulate the current web page. In order to see this, type the equation `1 + 1` at the command prompt. This should display the result immediately, as shown in Figure 11-1.

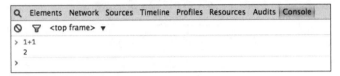

FIGURE 11-1

Pressing Enter always executes the statement in the console; therefore, if you need to write code that spans more than one line, hold down the Shift key when you press Enter.

In the sections that follow I will insert a > to show I am writing code into the console. You should omit this when you write the same code. Additionally, I will show the response on the next line if appropriate. For instance:

```
> 1 + 1
2
```

DATA TYPES

You will start your look at JavaScript by examining the different types it uses to represent data.

Strings

Character strings in JavaScript can be surrounded by either single or double quotes. To see an example, type the following into the console:

```
> "Welcome to JavaScript"
```

This is referred to as a string literal because the statement evaluates to the string itself. It is of course possible to assign a string to a variable. For instance:

```
> s1 = "Welcome to JavaScript";
```

> **NOTE** *A semicolon should terminate statements in JavaScript. The semicolon is technically optional, but if it is omitted, JavaScript will insert a semicolon for you, and there are some circumstances where it is inserted in unexpected locations, causing hard-to-understand bugs.*

The variable `s1` now refers to this string, and if you type `s1` at the console, the string will be printed. Additionally, you can ask JavaScript what data type the variable has:

```
> typeof s1;
"string"
```

It is also possible to perform operations on a string. Technically these are called methods, as you will see when you look at objects in Lesson 14. In order to see the available methods, simply type s1. in the console; the autocomplete feature will then show the available methods (see Figure 11-2).

This book is not a reference book so I will not you walk through the entire API, but the following methods are the most commonly used methods on strings:

FIGURE 11-2

➤ toUpperCase: Convert text to uppercase.

➤ toLowerCase: Convert text to lowercase.

➤ substr: Extract a portion of the string using a starting and (optional) ending index. For instance, s1.substr(0, 7) returns Welcome. Counting always starts at 0.

➤ indexOf: Returns the first index of a provided string inside the string; for instance, s1.indexOf('e') returns 1. Counting in JavaScript always starts at 0, so the second character is at position 1.

➤ length: This is a property of the string rather than a method; therefore, you do not use brackets when invoking it. For instance, s1.length returns 21.

➤ replace: This method replaces the first occurrence of one string for the new one provided. For instance, s1.replace('e', 'E') returns "WElcome to JavaScript".

It is also possible to append text to an existing string using the + operator. If you execute the following, a new string will be returned that concatenates the two strings:

```
> s1 + " - Let's get started";
```

If, however, you look at the value of s1 after executing this, you will see it has retained its old value:

```
> s1;
"Welcome to JavaScript"
```

Once a string has been assigned a value, it can never be modified (it is immutable). Any time an operation appears to modify a string, a new string is actually created. Therefore, to update the value of s1 you need to assign the result of the expression to it:

```
> s1 = s1 + " - Let's get started";
```

Finally, if you need to use special characters inside a string, you can prepend a backslash to it. For instance, the next example contains a ' character inside a quoted string so I use a backslash before it:

```
s2 = 'This is Dane\'s code';
```

Of course, in this case I could have simply wrapped the string inside double quotes because the quote character would have no special meaning in such a string:

```
s2 = "This is Dane's code";
```

Numbers

JavaScript uses a single numeric type for all numbers, including decimals: All numbers are technically 64-bit floating-point numbers.

Variables can be assigned numeric values as follows:

```
> n1 = 200;
> n2 = 2.432432432;
```

The `typeof` operator will confirm these are numbers:

```
> typeof n1
"number"
```

JavaScript then supports all the common mathematical operators for manipulating numbers. For example:

```
> n1 / 2
100
> n1 * (200 + n2);
40486.486486400005
```

For more advanced operations, JavaScript also provides a library called `Math` that is modeled on the same library in Java. For instance:

```
> Math.pow(3,2)
9
> Math.round(n2)
2
```

JavaScript also supports three special numeric values. These are numbers, but they cannot be represented as conventional numbers:

➤ `Number.POSITIVE_INFINITY`: This value is created when a positive number is divided by 0. Although you may have been taught that numbers cannot be divided by 0, because all numbers are floating-point in JavaScript, the language assumes that the number 0 could be a tiny, but still non-zero, number that cannot be represented in 64 bits of memory. If you divide a number by such a tiny number, the result will approach infinity.

➤ `Number.NEGATIVE_INFINITY`: This is returned when a negative number is divided by 0.

➤ `NaN`: This stands for not-a-number, but confusingly, it is still a number. This value is created when operations on numbers return values that cannot be represented as numbers. For instance: `1 / "hello"` or `Math.sqrt(-1)`. It is possible to check for this value using a special JavaScript function: `isNaN(Math.sqrt(-1))`.

Booleans

Booleans are used to capture the values `true` and `false`. For instance:

```
> b1 = true;
> b2 = false;
```

Boolean values are commonly returned by logical operations. For instance:

```
> 10 > 5
true
```

Null

Before looking at what `null` is, it is worth looking at variables in slightly more detail. When you execute a statement such as this:

```
> n1 = 200;
```

the variable n1 takes on the data type of number. The variable n1 is not intrinsically linked to numbers, however; you can change its type by assigning it a new value:

```
> n1 = "Testing";
```

Another way of looking at this is that the variable n1 starts out by referring to the number 200, and then it is changed to refer to the string "Testing". You can therefore also change n1 so that it refers to nothing at all:

```
> n1 = null;
```

null therefore means the absence of a value. JavaScript has a small quirk with null values:

```
> typeof n1
"object"
```

This is a historic bug in the language itself: Despite this, null is a distinct data type in JavaScript.

Undefined

The value of undefined is returned if you access a variable, or a property on an object, that does not exist. For instance, if you type the following at the command line, the value of undefined will be returned:

```
> typeof n3
"undefined"
```

Arrays

Arrays are not technically a distinct data type; they are a type of object, but it is still worth introducing them in this section.

An array contains zero or more elements of any data type. You can declare an array as follows:

```
a1 = [];
```

The initial elements in the array can also be provided as a comma separated list inside the square brackets:

```
a1 = [1,2,3,4];
```

You do not need to declare the size of the array; you can simply start inserting elements, and it will expand to support them:

```
a1[2] = 20;
a1[1] = "hello"
```

Because arrays are objects, they also support methods; for instance, this will add a new element at the end of the array.

```
a1.push(200);
```

while this will sort the array:

```
a1.sort()
```

You can access elements in the array by specifying their position inside the square brackets:

```
> a1[1]
"hello"
```

The lessons ahead will make extensive use of arrays, and many additional features will be introduced.

Objects

All other values in JavaScript are objects. You will spend a lot of time looking at these over the next few lessons so I will not discuss them here.

Functions

Functions are the basic building blocks of many JavaScript applications. A function in JavaScript accepts zero or more parameters, executes a series of statements, and then optionally returns a value.

You can create a function as follows (remember to hold down the Shift key when entering a new line into the console; you may also decide to copy and paste the code from a text editor):

```
function doubleTheNumber(num) {
    var result = num * 2;
    return result;
}
```

In this example, you are creating a function called `doubleTheNumber` and have stated that it accepts a single parameter called `num`.

In the body of the function you then multiply `num` by 2 and store the result in a local variable called `result`. Finally, on the last line of the function you return this variable. The curly brackets denote the code block relating to the function.

You can then execute this function as follows:

```
> doubleTheNumber(9);
18
```

Notice that the variable `result` is declared with the `var` keyword. This means that the variable is local to the function, and is automatically destroyed when the function ends. The `var` keyword can be omitted, and the function will still work. To prove this, change the function as follows:

```
function doubleTheNumber(num) {
    result = num * 2;
    return result;
}
```

If you execute this, it will continue to work as expected:

```
> doubleTheNumber(10);
20
```

The overall outcome is not the same, however. The variable `result` has been created as a global variable, and will exist even after the function has finished executing. You can see this by executing the following:

```
> result;
20
```

Using global variables is dangerous and should be kept to a minimum because there is always the possibly that two independent blocks of code will accidentally use the same variable name.

You will return to look at functions in substantially more detail in Lesson 13.

CONTROL STRUCTURES

JavaScript includes a standard set of control structures for looping and branching. These will be familiar to anyone with a programming background because they use the same basic syntax as those in Java, C#, and Python (among others).

It is possible to perform looping with either a for loop or a while loop. The following example uses a for loop to add the contents of an array together:

```
> a1 = [3,6,4,1,4,9]
> var result = 0;
> for (var i = 0; i < a1.length; i++) {
      result = result + a1[i];
  }
> result
27
```

The for loop consists of three distinct portions:

➤ A variable called i is declared to act as the counter; this is initially set to the value 0.

➤ You declare that looping should continue while the value of i is less than the length of the array (6).

➤ You declare that the variable i should have its value increased by 1 (i++) each time the loop completes a cycle.

The loop also uses curly brackets to denote its scope so each time the loop executes, the following statement will be executed:

```
result = result + a1[i];
```

Because the first index of an array is 0, the first iteration will therefore set the result variable to 3, and so on, until all the elements in the array have been evaluated.

If you would like to see more details as the loop executes, you can add console.log statements to print logging information to the console. For instance:

```
for (var i = 0; i < a1.length; i++) {
    console.log('The value of i is ' + i);
    console.log('The value in the array is ' + a1[i]);
    result = result + a1[i];
}
```

The second main loop variant is the while loop. While loops evaluate an expression with each iteration. While this is true, they keep iterating through the loop; if it is ever false the loop ceases. For instance:

```
var result = 0;
var counter = 0;
```

```
    while (counter < a1.length) {
        result = result + a1[counter];
        counter++;
    }
    result;
```

You will notice that this still initializes a counter variable to 0 and increments its value with each iteration, but these are done before the loop starts and inside the loop respectively, not in the loop declaration.

JavaScript supports break and continue statements to control loop execution. I will introduce these along with the next subject: control structures. The following function accepts two parameters: an array of positive numbers, and a number. It then adds together all the even numbers in the array and returns true if this sums to more than the number passed as an argument to the second parameter:

```
function checkCountEven(a1, n1) {
    var result = false;
    var count = 0;
    for (var i = 0; i < a1.length; i++) {
        var number = a1[i];
        if (number % 2 != 0) {
            continue;
        }
        count = count + number;
        if (count > n1) {
            result = true;
            break;
        }
    }
    return result;
}
```

You can call this as follows:

```
> a1 = [3, 6, 4, 1, 4, 9]
> checkCountEven(a1, 20)
false
```

This function starts by declaring two local variables and then starts looping through the array using a for loop.

Inside the for loop, you start by extracting the number from the array for the position you are at. You then check whether this is an odd number using the expression number % 2 != 0. This expression literally states "return true if the remainder of dividing the number by 2 is not 0". If this is true, the if block executes.

If the statement returns true, you do not want to count the number so you use the continue keyword to skip immediately to the next loop iteration.

If the number is even, you add it to the result and then check to see whether the running total is greater than the number passed in using another if statement. If this evaluates to true, you know that the overall result must be true, and therefore you do not need to check any more numbers in the loop. You therefore use the break keyword to jump out of the loop immediately, and the function simply returns its result.

Conditional expressions can also support if else and else statements. For instance:

```
function describeNumber(num) {
    if (num >= 0 && num % 2 == 0) {
        console.log(num + ' is a positive even number');
    } else if (num >= 0 && num % 2 == 1) {
        console.log(num + ' is a positive odd number');
    } else if (num < 0 && num % 2 == 0) {
        console.log(num + ' is a negative even number');
    } else {
        console.log(num + ' is a negative odd number');
    }
}
```

Notice in this example that you combine multiple Boolean expressions with the and (&&) operator. When this is used, the entire expression returns true only if both sub-expressions are true.

> **NOTE** *This example has used* == *to determine if two values are equal. You should generally avoid this because it still returns* true *if the data types are different. For instance, the string "1" is equal to the number 1. In general, you should use the* === *operator to determine if values are equal and the* !== *operator to determine if values are not equal, since this also checks the data-types are the same.*

JavaScript also supports a switch statement and a ternary operator for performing conditional logic. Although these will not be introduced, they work in a manner familiar to anyone who has used them in other languages.

TRUTHY AND FALSY VALUES

One unique aspect of JavaScript is that every value and every expression evaluates to either true or false. To see this in action, create the following function:

```
function whatAmI(v1) {
    if (v1) {
        console.log('I am true');
    } else {
        console.log('I am false');
    }
}
```

Notice that because values evaluate to true or false, you can simply state if (v1) to determine if the argument passed in is true. You can now call this with a variety of values:

```
> whatAmI("hello")
I am true
> whatAmI("")
I am false
```

```
> whatAmI(22)
I am true
> whatAmI(null)
I am false
> whatAmI(8 + 9)
I am true
```

There are some surprising results here. The following are not true:

➤ `false`

➤ `0` (zero)

➤ `""` (empty string)

➤ `null`

➤ `undefined`

➤ `NaN` (this value is neither true or false, which is why the `isNaN` function is needed to detect it)

All other values evaluate to `true`.

You can actually simplify this function down to a single line as follows:

```
function whatAmI(v1) {
    console.log('I am '+ !!v1);
}
```

`!` is the not operator so if it is applied to any variable, it returns the opposite of its Boolean value. You can then negate this with an additional `!` operator to return its actual truthy value.

JavaScript code makes extensive use of the fact that values are either true or false in `if` statements. For instance, if you only want to print the string held in s1 if it has a value, you can use the following:

```
if (s1) {
    console.log(s1);
}
```

DYNAMIC TYPING

JavaScript is a dynamically typed language. This means that the types of variables are only determined at runtime. Although dynamically typed languages are very flexible in many ways, they are also prone to bugs when types are not as expected. Consider a function such as this:

```
function add(n1, n2) {
    return n1+n2;
}
```

This function operates as expected when called with two numbers, but what happens if you invoke this as follows?

```
> add(1, '0')
```

In this case, the result is the string value `10`. This may or may not be what you were expecting.

In a statically typed language, you would declare that n1 and n2 were numbers and refuse to allow it to be invoked with strings. This is not possible in JavaScript.

This is made slightly worse due to the fact that JavaScript is very forgiving. Consider the following examples:

```
> add(1, [])
"1"
> add(1, true)
2
```

JavaScript does have its own internal logic to explain these results, but they are seldom intuitive or expected. In order to circumvent issues such as this, it is common to write functions so that they generate errors if they are passed unexpected data types. For instance:

```
function add(v1, v2) {
    if (typeof v1 === "number"
&& typeof v2 === "number") {
        return v1+v2;
    } else {
        throw "both arguments must be numbers";
    }
}
```

Notice the `throw` statement in this example: This will generate an error to the caller, as shown in Figure 11-3.

This is still not as explicit as a compile time error, but at least it ensures that, if the program fails, it is obvious why it has failed.

```
> add(1, true)
⊗ "both arguments must be numbers"
```

FIGURE 11-3

TRY IT

In this Try It, you will use the techniques you have learned in this lesson to write two utility functions. If you get stuck on either of these examples, you may want to watch the screencast, which will walk through both examples. Completed versions of both functions are available on the book's website.

Lesson Requirements

You will use the Chrome console for these examples. It is, however, recommended that you write the code in a text editor and copy the completed versions into the Chrome console.

Step-by-Step

The first utility function you will create will accept a single parameter, which should be a string, and will return the reverse of the string: If it is passed "Hello," it will return "olleH."

1. Start by creating a function called `reverse` and declare that it accepts a single parameter.

2. Check that the argument passed in is a string: If it is not, then throw an error for the caller.

3. You will construct an empty string variable to hold the result of the operation.

4. You can now iterate through the string one character at a time using a `for` loop. You will need to initialize a counter variable with an initial value of 0, and loop while this is less than the length of the string.

5.   With each iteration, you want to extract the character at the position "length of the string – current count - 1". This will ensure that you extract the last character of the string on the first iteration, the second to last on the second iteration, and so on. For instance, if the string has seven characters, you will extract the character at position 6 on the first iteration (remember that the count starts at 0 so the last position in a string with seven characters is 6). You can use the `charAt` method to extract a character at a given position.

6.   Once the character has been extracted, you need to append it to the result variable using the + operator.

7.   Once the loop completes, you need to return the result.

Once the function is complete, you should be able to call it as follows:

```
> reverse("Hello");
"olleH"
```

The second utility function will accept an array of numbers, and return `true` if the sum of all the positive numbers is greater than the sum of the absolute value of all the negative numbers.

1.   Start by creating a function called `calculateSums`, and declare that it accepts a single parameter, which in this case will be an array.

2.   Create two variables to hold the result of the positive and negative numbers respectively. These should be initialized to 0.

3.   You will use a `while` loop in this example so you also need to create a counter variable and initialize it to 0.

4.   Create a `while` loop, and add curly brackets for its code block. The `while` loop should test that the counter is less than the length of the array.

5.   Inside the code block, you need to add an if-else block to determine if the number is greater than 0.

6.   If the number is greater than or equal to 0, simply add it to the sum of positive numbers. If it is less than 0, you need to calculate its absolute value using `Math.abs()` and add the result to the sum of negative numbers.

7.   You also need to remember to increase the counter variable by 1 inside the loop. If you omit this, the `while` loop will run forever: This is called an infinite loop.

8.   After the loop finishes, you can simply return whether the sum of positive numbers is greater than or equal to the sum of negative numbers.

It should be possible to call the function as follows:

```
> calculateSums([-1,2])
true
> calculateSums([-1,2,-3])
false
```

> **REFERENCE** *Please go to the book's website at* www.wrox.com/go/html5jsj-query24hr *to view the video for Lesson 11, as well as download the code and resources for this lesson.*

12

Debugging

Now that you have some working code, it is worth taking a step back to look at the development tools provided by Chrome to help analyze JavaScript-based web applications.

Probably the most important tool for development purposes is a debugger. Debuggers allow you to examine an application while it is running and therefore diagnose the cause of any problems or bugs.

All major browser vendors have introduced development tools such as debuggers into their browsers. For instance, Firefox supports similar tools to the ones you will look at here with the Firebug plugin.

This lesson is very much a practical lesson. It will consist of two Try It sections, and you are encouraged to follow along with the examples.

Both Try It sections will use the same web page to demonstrate the various features in the debugger. This is available from the book's website in the Lesson 12 folder under the name `tryit.html`, but you can also choose to write it yourself:

```
<!DOCTYPE html>
<html lang="en">
<head>
    <meta charset="utf-8">
    <script>

    function calculateAbsoluteSumOfArray(a) {
        var result = 0;
        for (var i = 0; i < a.length; i++) {
            var num = a[i];
            result = result + Math.absolute(num);
        }
        return result;
    }
```

```
function calculateSumOfArray(a) {
    var result = 0;
    for (var i = 0; i < a.length; i++) {
        var num = a[i];
        result = result + num;
    }
    return result;
}

function findHighestSum(arrays) {
    var result = Number.NEGATIVE_INFINITY;
    for (var i = 0; i < arrays.length; i++) {
        var a = arrays[i];
        var sum = calculateSumOfArray(a);
        if (sum > result) {
            result = sum;
        }
    }
    console.log('The largest sum is '+ result);
}

var arrays = [[1,2,3,4,5],[6,4,2],[1.9]];

</script>
</head>
<body>
This page is for trying out the debugger
<p>
<button onclick="findHighestSum(arrays)">Click me to sum arrays</button>
<p>
<button onclick="calculateAbsoluteSumOfArray(arrays[0])">Click me cause an
error</button>
</body>
</html>
```

TRY IT

In the first Try It, you will debug two functions that are responsible for processing a two-dimensional array that has been defined as follows:

```
var arrays = [[1,2,3,4,5],[6,4,2],[1.9]];
```

> **NOTE** *A two-dimensional array is simply a conventional array where each element is itself an array.*
>
> *The first function, called* findHighestSum, *will iterate through all the inner arrays in the array provided, and pass each array in turn to another function called* calculateSumOfArray *that will sum the numbers in the array. The job of* findHighestSum *is to determine which of the inner arrays sums to the highest value.*

Lesson Requirements

In order to complete this lesson, you will need the Chrome web browser and the `tryit.html` web page mentioned previously.

Step-by-Step

1. In order to start the debugger, first open the `tryit.html` page in Chrome. Then use one of the following approaches to open the development tools:

   ➤ Command+Option+i on OSX

   ➤ F12 or Ctrl+Shift+I on Windows

2. Once the development tools are open, click the Sources tab. Once in this tab, you will notice that the `tryit.html` page appears in the left-hand panel: Double-click on this to open it in the middle panel (see Figure 12-1).

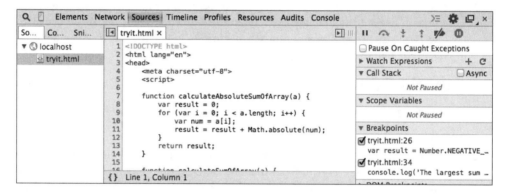

FIGURE 12-1

3. The first step in debugging code is defining a breakpoint. A breakpoint is the point in the processing when you want the program to pause so you can examine it line by line. Find the first line of the `findHighestSum` function and click once in the margin where its line number is shown—for me this was line 26. A blue marker should appear in the margin, as shown in Figure 12-2.

```
24
25      function findHighestSum(arrays) {
26          var result = Number.NEGATIVE_INFINITY;
27          for (var i = 0; i < arrays.length; i++) {
28              var a = arrays[i];
29              var sum = calculateSumOfArray(a);
```

FIGURE 12-2

4. Click the button Click Me to Sum Arrays. As soon as you click this, the program should display a message stating "Paused in debugger," and the various panels of the debugger will populate. In addition, the line that the program is currently paused on will be shaded blue, as shown in Figure 12-3.

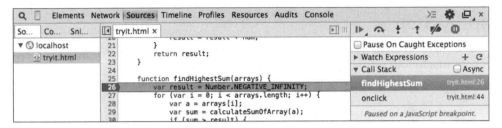

FIGURE 12-3

5. Now that the program is paused, you can begin interacting with it. One of the most common uses of the debugger is to step through the execution of the program line by line. You can achieve this with a set of buttons in the top right of the debugger, as shown in Figure 12-4.

FIGURE 12-4

6. If you hover over these buttons, their tooltips will tell you their purpose. You will start by using the second button from the left, which should have the tooltip "Step over next function call." If you press this button, the execution will jump to the next line in the function. Press this two more times so that the blue line is shading line 29, as shown in Figure 12-3.

7. As the function executes code, a number of local variables have been assigned values. For instance, the `arrays` variable contains the two-dimensional array, the `a` variable contains the array you are about to sum up, and the `i` variable contains the current counter value of the `for` loop. You can see the values for these variables in the right-hand side of the console, as shown in Figure 12-5. To see the values in any of the arrays, simply click the arrow next to them.

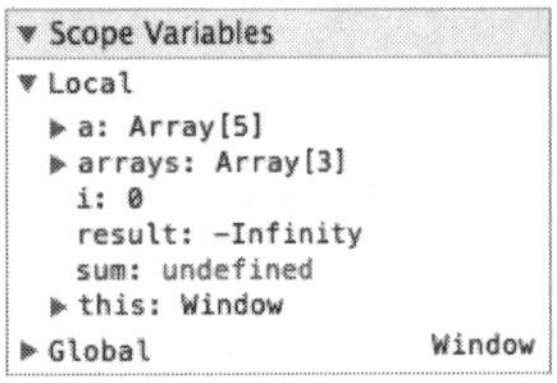

```
▼ Scope Variables
▼ Local
  ▶ a: Array[5]
  ▶ arrays: Array[3]
    i: 0
    result: -Infinity
    sum: undefined
  ▶ this: Window
▶ Global          Window
```

FIGURE 12-5

8.   It is also possible to interact with the program as it executes. For instance, if you swap to the Console tab, you can write code that uses the variables currently in scope, and you can even modify their values (see Figure 12-6).

```
Q   Elements  Network  Sources  Timeline  Profiles  Resources  Audits  Console
    ⊘  ▽  <top frame> ▼
>  a
   [1, 2, 3, 4, 5]
>  a[2] = 7
   7
>  a
   [1, 2, 7, 4, 5]
>
```

FIGURE 12-6

This is a great way to try out code before adding it to the web page because you receive immediate feedback from the Console.

There is also a mini-console at the bottom of the Sources tab that can be used for the same purpose, and means you do not need to swap back and forward between tabs.

9.   Switch back to the Source tab. You will now step into a function call rather than step over it so click the button with the tooltip Step into next function call. When you do this, execution should jump into the `calculateSumOfArray` function, and you can now step through this function. Step through this function until it finishes, and watch the local variables update as it executes.

10. When `calculateSumOfArray` finishes executing, the debugger will immediately return to the `findHighestSum` function where it left off. Rather than stepping through the rest of the execution, you may decide you want to jump immediately to the line that prints information to the console. In order to do this, add a breakpoint to this line by clicking in the margin, and then press the Resume Script Execution button. When you do this, the debugger should pause on the appropriate line, and the local variables will have been updated to reflect the processing that has occurred.

11. In order to finish the debugging session, simply press Resume Script Execution one more time.

Finding Errors

Debuggers are an excellent way to understand the behavior of a program as it executes, but they are most commonly used to diagnose problems. Programming bugs can be difficult to find in JavaScript code because if a problem occurs the JavaScript simply ceases to execute.

The user of the web page will not even necessarily be aware that an error has occurred; she will simply notice that a piece of functionality does not work as she expects.

This section will therefore walk you through an example of a program with a bug in it, and look at how you can identify and remedy the problem.

Try It

In this Try It, we will press a button that invokes a faulty JavaScript function. This uses the same web page as the previous Try It, so ensure that you have opened this in Chrome.

Lesson Requirements

In order to complete this lesson, you will need the Chrome web browser and the `tryit.html` example mentioned previously.

Step-by-Step

1. In order to start the debugger, first open the `tryit.html` page in Chrome. Then use one of the following approaches to open the development tools:

    ➤ Command+Option+i on OSX

    ➤ F12 or Ctrl+Shift+I on Windows

2. Identify the toolbar shown in Figure 12-7, and press the pause button (on the right-hand side of the toolbar with the tooltip Pause on Exceptions). When you click this, it should turn blue, and an additional checkbox should appear. For this example, it will not matter if you select this checkbox.

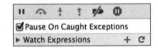

FIGURE 12-7

3. In order to run the faulty code, click the button with the label Click Me to Cause an Error. As soon as you click this, the debugger should pause on the line that has the error, despite the fact that you did not add a breakpoint to this line. This is shown in Figure 12-8.

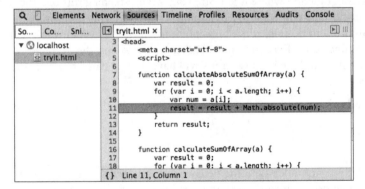

FIGURE 12-8

4. In order to determine why this line is faulty, copy it from the editor using your keyboard shortcut. Then open the Console tab, paste it in, and press Enter. The cause of the error will be displayed, as shown in Figure 12-9:

```
Q  Elements  Network  Sources  Timeline  Profiles  Resources  Audits  Console
⊘  ▽  <top frame> ▼
> result = result + Math.absolute(num);
⊗ ▶ TypeError: undefined is not a function
> |
```

FIGURE 12-9

5. This shows that you are calling a function that does not exist. The function name has been specified as absolute rather than abs; you can confirm this by executing this alternate version of the code with the function name corrected, as shown in Figure 12-10.

```
Q  Elements  Network  Sources  Timeline  Profiles  Resources  Audits  Console
⊘  ▽  <top frame> ▼
> result = result + Math.absolute(num);
⊗ ▶ TypeError: undefined is not a function
> result = result + Math.abs(num);
  1
> |
```

FIGURE 12-10

6. Once the problem has been identified, you can fix up your source code and try again.

> **REFERENCE** *Please go to the book's website at* www.wrox.com/go/html5jsj-query24hr *to view the video for Lesson 12, as well as download the code and resources for this lesson.*

13

Functions

Functions may seem simple in JavaScript, but beneath this simplicity lies enormous power. Gaining an understanding of this power is one of the keys to mastering the JavaScript language.

In Lesson 11, you created simple functions and invoked them from the console. For instance:

```
function isPositive(num) {
    return num >= 0;
}
```

In JavaScript, functions are objects so it is possible to assign them to variables:

```
f1 = function isPositive(num) {
    return num >= 0;
}
```

If you ask JavaScript the type of f1, it will respond as follows:

```
> typeof f1
"function"
```

This is another example of JavaScript being slightly disingenuous. Functions are not a distinct data-type; they are objects and therefore support all the features you will learn about in the next lesson, such as the ability to invoke methods on them.

Once you have assigned a function to a variable, you can invoke it via its variable name by appending brackets and parameters:

```
> f1(9)
true
```

In fact, you can use this variable wherever you can use any other variable in JavaScript; for instance, you can pass it as a parameter to another function.

Consider an example where you want to write a function that counts how many positive numbers are in an array. With the power of functions, you can do this by writing a generic algorithm as follows:

```
function countForArray(array, condition) {
    var result = 0;
    for (var i = 0; i < array.length; i++) {
        var element = array[i];
        if (condition(element)) {
            result++;
        }
    }
    return result;
}
```

This algorithm accepts an array and a function. It then loops through every element in the array and passes it to the function provided. If the function returns `true`, the count is incremented by one. You can then call this as follows:

```
> a = [1,2,-3,2,-5]
> countForArray(a, f1)
3
```

Notice that you are passing a reference to the function you defined earlier. It may not looked like you have gained much in this example; after all, the `countForArray` method could have very easily checked if the number was positive without using the function passed in.

The beauty of `countForArray`, however, is that it is a generic function that can be made to behave differently very easily. For instance, if you want to count the negative numbers you can use the following code:

```
> countForArray(a, function(num) {
    return num < 0;
})
2
```

Notice that in this case you did not even create the function in advance; you simply declared it as part of the call to `countForArray`. The function that you have created does not even have a name; it is therefore called an anonymous function. Its scope is limited to the duration of this function call.

Once you have a function such as `countForArray`, you can use it for a whole variety of tasks that you may not even have thought about when you originally wrote it.

Functions that are passed to other functions are often called callback functions because they allow another function to "call back" to them at the appropriate time.

JavaScript arrays natively support a number of functions that can be used for performing common operations. For instance, one of the most common operations performed on arrays is to filter out a set of elements that do not meet a set of criteria. For instance, you might want to filter all the negative numbers out of an array, leaving only the positive numbers.

JavaScript arrays provide a `filter` method for performing this operation. Just like `count` `ForArray`, this passes each element in the array in turn to a function provided, and retains those that return `true`:

```
> a.filter(f1)
[1, 2, 2]
```

Likewise, you can filter out positive numbers with the following code:

```
> a.filter(function(num) {
      return num < 0;
})
[-3, -5]
```

You may have noticed that the `filter` function is not actually modifying the underlying array; instead, it is returning a new array with the relevant elements filtered out.

Another common operation performed on arrays is to transform each element in some way. With this particular array, you might want to transform the elements so that all the numbers are positive; this can be achieved with the `map` function.

The `map` function works in exactly the same way: You pass it a function, and the `map` function invokes it with each element in the array. The function you provide is responsible for modifying the element in some way and returning the modified version as a result.

The following returns an array of elements where each number has been converted to a positive value:

```
> a.map(function(num) {
      return Math.abs(num);
})
[1, 2, 3, 2, 5]
```

Because functions such as `map` and `filter` both operate on arrays and return arrays, it is possible to chain together a whole set of function calls. Imagine that you want to return the absolute value of all even numbers in an array. This can be achieved as follows:

```
> a1 = [-2,1-3,5,6]
> a.filter(function(num) {
      return num%2==0;
}).map(function(num) {
      return Math.abs(num);
});
[2, 2, 6]
```

This example is a bit harder to follow, so start by breaking out its component parts. It starts out by performing a `filter` operation:

```
> a1.filter(function(num) {
      return num%2==0;
})
[-2, -2, 6]
```

It then performs a map operation on the result: you can simulate this as follows:

```
> [-2, -2, 6].map(function(num) {
    return Math.abs(num);
})
[2, 2, 6]
```

When writing JavaScript code it is often a good idea to think in terms of simple functions that perform a single task, and do not store or modify any global state. These functions can then be combined together to create more advanced functionality. Building software in this way tends to be simpler because it is very easy to understand, develop, and test each function in isolation.

CLOSURES

Closures can be a difficult concept to explain, so I will explain them through examples.

Imagine a case where you want to write a function that can produce unique, incrementing numbers that can be used by other code in your web application. The only condition of this functionality is that if the last call to the function returned 10, the next call must return 11.

It is possible to write this functionality with a global variable:

```
> count = 0;
> function getNextCount() {
    return count++;
}
> getNextCount()
0
> getNextCount()
1
```

As has already been mentioned, however, global variables should be avoided because any other code can modify them. For instance, any other code could reset the count variable:

```
count = -1;
```

or set it to a nonsense value:

```
count = 'hello';
```

These may look like contrived examples, but as web applications grow in size, global variables such as this become the source of difficult to find bugs. Closures provide an alternative.

Before looking at the solution, consider what happens to local variables inside a function when it finishes executing. The function that follows declares a local variable called myCount.

```
function counter() {
    var myCount = 0;
    return myCount++;
}
```

If you execute this and then attempt to access the myCount variable, you will find it does not exist:

```
> counter()
0
> myCount;
ReferenceError: myCount is not defined
```

The variable is created inside the function each time it is invoked, and it is automatically destroyed when the function completes. This is why the counter function always returns 0:

```
> counter()
0
> counter()
0
```

Now, consider this slight variation on the preceding function:

```
function getCounter() {
    var myCount = 0;
    return function() {
        return myCount++;
    }
}
```

Rather than returning a number, this function returns another function. The function that it returns has the following body:

```
function() {
    return myCount++;
}
```

You can now assign a variable to refer to this function:

```
counter = getCounter();
```

There is something strange about this function though: It is referring to the local variable myCount that was defined inside the getCounter function. Based on my previous explanation, this should have been destroyed when the call to getCounter finished. Therefore you might expect that if you invoke the function returned by getCounter, it will fail.

Not only does it not fail, it gives you exactly the behavior you want:

```
> counter();
0
> counter();
1
```

The anonymous function created inside getCounter is referred to as a closure. When it is created, it "closes" over all the variables in scope at the time, and obtains a reference to them. When the call to getCounter finished, therefore, JavaScript recognized that the anonymous function still might need to use the myCount variable and did not destroy it.

Although the anonymous function can continue to use the `myCount` variable, it is completely hidden from all other code. This means that it is not possible for any other code to interfere with the value of this variable:

```
> myCount = 10;
10
> counter()
2
```

The preceding code created a global variable called `myCount`, but this does not have any impact on your counter, which continues to use the local variable of the same name.

In addition, if you were to create a second counter, it will have its own local `myCount` variable that will not impact your original counter. Instead, the new counter will also start counting from 0.

The beauty of this solution is that you have created private data. The function performing the counting is using a variable that only it has access to. This is an important technique in JavaScript because it does not support many of the mechanisms found in other languages for creating private data.

HOISTING AND BLOCK SCOPE

One interesting feature in JavaScript is the scope of variables inside functions. In most programming languages it is possible to declare variables within a sub-block (a loop for instance) and limit their scope to this block. Consider the following example:

```
function iterate(array) {
    var count = 0;
    for (var i = 0; i < array.length; i++) {
        var count = 10;
    }
    return count;
}
```

If you were to invoke this function with an array, it would always return 10 because the `count` variable declared inside the `for` loop overwrites the `count` variable declared before the loop.

Part of the reason JavaScript operates in this manner is a concept called *hoisting*. Although it is possible to declare variables anywhere in a function, when JavaScript executes a function, it first searches for all the local variables in it and moves their declaration to the top of the function. They are, however, left undefined until they are explicitly given a value in the body of the function. In order to demonstrate this, create the following function:

```
function testHoisting() {
    var num = num1 + num2;
    var num1 = 10;
    var num2 = 10;
    return num;
}
```

If you call this function, you will notice it does not fail, even though it is using local variables before they are defined:

```
> testHoisting()
NaN
```

If you tried the same thing with global variables, however, the code will fail because global variables are not hoisted:

```
> function testHoisting() {
      var num = num1 + num2;
      num1 = 10;
      num2 = 10;
      return num;
  }

> testHoisting()
ReferenceError: num1 is not defined
```

ARGUMENTS

As discussed many times, JavaScript functions can accept parameters. When you invoke a function, however, the number of arguments you pass does not need to be constrained by the number of parameters defined.

For instance, you can pass a single argument to a function accepting two parameters. In this case the second parameter will have a value of undefined.

Likewise, you can pass three arguments to a function accepting two parameters. This may not sound useful, but in fact JavaScript makes these arguments available in a special array called arguments.

Consider a case where you want to write a function to add together an arbitrary set of numbers. Obviously, you could pass an array to the function, but you can also write it as follows:

```
function add() {
    var result = 0;
    for (var i = 0; i < arguments.length; i++) {
        result = result + arguments[i];
    }
    return result;
}
```

Notice that this function declares no parameters: Instead, it uses the arguments array to extract the arguments passed to it. It is now possible to call this function with an arbitrary number of arguments:

```
> add(3,7,8,10)
28
```

BIND

Since JavaScript functions are actually objects, it is possible to invoke methods on them. This section looks at a widely used method called `bind`.

You have already seen how functions "close" over all variables in scope when they are created. This set of variables can be thought of as the environment in which the function executes.

JavaScript is even more powerful than this: It is possible to provide the environment to the function in the form of an object, therefore allowing the function to use an entirely different set of variables.

Imagine that you want to create a counter that is capable of starting from any number, not just 0. One way to achieve this is to create the function as follows:

```
function getCount() {
    return this.myCount++;
}
```

Notice in this case that you have not provided a starting value for `myCount`, and you are accessing the variable with `this invoke getCount().myCount` rather than just `myCount`. You will look at the meaning of `this` in the next lesson.

If you were to create a counter function, it would not work because it does not have a value for `myCount`.

You can instead bind this function to a new environment by providing a set of name/value pairs for the variables in the environment:

```
> var counter2 = getCount.bind({myCount:100});
undefined
> counter2()
100
> counter2()
101
```

> **NOTE** *The set of name/value pairs inside curly brackets is actually an object: You will look at how objects can be constructed in a lot more detail in the next lesson.*

As you can see, the `bind` function returns a new version of the function, permanently bound to the new environment. You can then invoke this function and obtain the appropriate results for the environment it is bound to.

TRY IT

In this Try It, you will start by writing a function that takes advantage of the techniques you have learned in this lesson. This function will implement a stand-alone version of the `map` method.

Next, you will look at another of the methods provided by arrays called `reduce`. This can be used to aggregate the values in an array—for instance, to sum them.

Lesson Requirements

In order to complete this lesson, you will need the Chrome web browser. You may, however, want to complete these exercises in a text editor and copy the results to the console.

Step-by-Step

1. Open the Chrome development tools and selecting the Console tab.

2. Define a function called `map` that accepts two parameters: an array and a function for performing the map operation.

3. In the body of the function, you first need to construct an empty array to hold the result of the function.

4. Use a `for` loop to iterate through all the elements in the array. Remember to use a counter variable and declare that the loop should continue while this counter is less than the length of the array.

5. Within the body of the `for` loop, extract the element that is at the position of the counter. Store this in a local variable.

6. Pass the element to the function provided in the second parameter, and store the result in another variable.

7. Add the mapped variable to the result array using the `push` method—for example, `result .push(value)`.

8. In order to execute this function, start by creating an array that contains a mixture of odd and even numbers.

9. Create a function that accepts a single parameter. If this parameter is even (remember, you can use the modulus operator: %), it should simply be returned; if it is odd, add 1 to the number and return it. This function therefore converts all numbers into even numbers.

10. Assign the function to a variable.

11. Call the `map` function you created earlier with the array, and the variable referring to the function to convert numbers to even. The result should be an array of even numbers.

In the second section of this Try It, you will look at the `reduce` function. This is similar to `map` and `filter`, but slightly more complex. This function is used to aggregate the data in an array to a single value such as a sum or an average (the single value can also be an object or an array if required). This function is more complex because it needs to keep track of a running total as it executes.

1. Create an array of numbers that can be summed together.

2. Create a function that can be used for summing the numbers together. This should be called `addToTotal` and will accept two parameters, a current total and a new value to add to this total.

3. In the body of the function, return the sum of the two numbers.

4. Add logging to the addToTotal so you can see what is happening: print both parameters to the console.

5. You now want to call the reduce method on the array. This accepts two arguments, a function and an initial value for the aggregation: therefore pass in addToTotal and 0.

   Remember that you are passing the function itself rather than calling it. Thus, when you pass addToTotal, you should only include its name; you should not call it with a set of parameters.

   When I run this, it produces the following output:

   ```
   [6, 2, 3].reduce( addToTotal, 0);
   Current total:
   Value: 6
   -----------------
   Current total:
   Value: 2
   -----------------
   Current total:
   Value: 3
   -----------------
   11
   ```

REFERENCE *Please go to the book's website at* www.wrox.com/go/html5jsj-query24hr *to view the video for Lesson 13, as well as download the code and resources for this lesson.*

Objects

Most of the JavaScript data types you have looked at so far have held simple atomic values such as strings or numbers. This lesson looks at objects: Objects encapsulate multiple data properties, along with a set of methods capable of operating on these properties.

Objects are potentially the most difficult aspect of JavaScript for programmers migrating from other languages because objects in JavaScript work in a fundamentally different way than most other languages. As you will see, this is not a bad thing, but if you don't understand these fundamental differences, you will struggle to write complex web applications.

OBJECT LITERALS

Objects can be created in JavaScript by enclosing a set of properties and methods within a pair of curly brackets. The following is an example of an object with two properties and one method:

```
> o = {
    firstName:'Dane',
    lastName:'Cameron',
    getFullName: function() {
        return this.firstName + ' ' + this.lastName;
    }
}
```

In this case, the two properties are `firstName` and `lastName`. These properties are both strings, but they could be any data type: numbers, Booleans, arrays, or other objects.

Notice that the property names are separated from their values with colons, and the properties are separated from one another with commas.

It is possible to access these properties in two different ways:

```
> o.firstName
"Dane"
> o['firstName']
"Dane"
```

These two mechanisms are not exactly equivalent. The second mechanism (with the square brackets) will always work, whereas the first mechanism will only work if property names follow specific rules:

➤ They start with a letter, the underscore character, or the dollar sign.

➤ They only contain these characters or numbers.

For instance, it is possible to create an object as follows:

```
> o = {
    'first name':'Dane',
    'last name':'Cameron'
}
```

Because the property names contain spaces, however, they must be declared between quotes, and the only way to access these properties is with the square bracket notation:

```
o['first name']
"Dane"
```

The method on this object is `getFullName`. You will notice that this accesses the properties on the object with the keyword `this`. Inside a method, `this` refers to the object itself so `this.firstName` means that you want to access the `firstName` property of the object, not the variable called `firstName` (which would be `undefined`). It is possible to invoke the method as follows:

```
> o.getFullName()
"Dane Cameron"
```

Methods can therefore be thought of as functions that use the special value `this` differently.

After an object has been constructed, it is still possible to add additional properties or methods to it, or redefine any existing properties or methods. For instance:

```
> o.profession = "Software Developer";
> o.getFullName = function() {
    return this.firstName + " " + this.lastName + " (" + this.profession + ")";
}
> o.getFullName();
"Dane Cameron (Software Developer)"
```

Notice that the call to `getFullName` picks up the redefined implementation, even though the object was created when the redefinition occurred.

It is possible for two variables to refer to the same object, but in this case, any changes to the objects are reflected to both variables. For instance, I can create a new variable called o2 and set it to o; calling `getFullName` will return the same value as calling the method on o:

```
> o2 = o;
> o2.getFullName();
"Dane Cameron (Software Developer)"
```

because o and o2 are referring to exactly the same object.

PROTOTYPES

One of the main reasons programming languages use the concept of objects is to allow code reuse. It is common to have many objects that share the same properties and methods but with different property values.

For instance, the example in the previous section may represent a staff member in an employee management system; you may therefore create many similar objects, all with the same property names and methods, but each with distinct data in their properties. As a result, all these objects can share the same methods. Obviously, you could just add the relevant methods to each object you create, but this would become tedious.

If you have used languages such as Java or C#, you probably think of classes as the mechanism for acquiring this reuse. Classes are templates for objects, and many languages insist that you construct classes first, and then create objects from those classes. The classes therefore contain the methods and property names that will appear in the objects, but each object has its own values for the properties.

As you will see shortly, JavaScript does support syntax for creating objects in this manner, but it is not the core mechanism for code reuse in JavaScript. Instead, JavaScript is designed around the concept of prototypes.

As it turns out, every object in JavaScript has a prototype on which it is based, and it derives properties and methods from this prototype. In order to convince yourself of this, enter the following into the console:

```
> o = {};
> o.toString()
"[object Object]"
```

In this example, you create an empty object, with no properties or methods, and then invoke a method on it called toString. The toString method comes from the new object's prototype, which happens to be called Object.

A prototype is just a regular object in its own right. When a property or method is accessed on an object, JavaScript first tries to access it on the object itself. If it is not available there, it attempts to access it on the object's prototype. In fact, as you will see shortly, the object's prototype may have a prototype of its own; therefore, there can be a whole chain of prototypes. If the property or method still cannot be found after searching the prototypes, the value of undefined is returned.

Because many objects share the same prototype, adding functionality to prototypes provides a mechanism for code reuse.

Consider the case of an array in JavaScript. Every array that is constructed in JavaScript has a prototype object called Array: This is where the methods such as pop, map, and reduce are defined. Array itself has a prototype of Object, and this provides additional methods.

Because a prototype is just a regular object, you can add additional methods to it. These methods will then automatically be available to all arrays, even arrays created before you added the method.

For instance, you might decide you would like arrays to support a method called `contains`. This would accept an argument and return `true` if this existed as an element in the array. You can define this as follows:

```
> Array.prototype.contains = function (val) {
    for (var i = 0; i < this.length; i++) {
        if (this[i] === val) {
            return true;
        }
    }
    return false;
}
```

`Array`, in this case, is a constructor function (you will look at these shortly), whereas `Array.prototype` allows you to access the object that acts as the prototype to all arrays. Notice that within the method you add, you can use `this` to refer to an array itself.

You can then write code as follows:

```
> a1 = [1,5,3,8,10]
[1, 5, 3, 8, 10]
> a1.contains(8)
true
> a1.contains(9)
false
```

Prototypes can also solve the code reuse problem discussed earlier with the staff member objects. You can construct a single object that will act as the prototype of all staff member objects, and then set this as the prototype of any staff member object you construct.

You will start by defining an object with methods on it to act as the prototype:

```
staffPrototype = {

    increasePay : function(percentage) {
        this.salary = this.salary + ((this.salary * percentage) / 100);
    },

    getFullName : function() {
        return this.firstName + " " + this.lastName + " (" + this.profession + ")";
    }
}
```

Notice that this accesses four properties: `firstName`, `lastName`, `salary`, and `profession`. None of these properties has been defined on the object itself; therefore it is not possible to call these functions and have meaningful results returned. Despite this, the object definition is still considered valid by JavaScript.

You now need a mechanism to set this object as the prototype for other objects. The best way to do this is with the following function:

```
> function extend(obj) {
    function T(){};
    T.prototype = obj;
    return new T();
}
```

You will use this function first and then come and look at how it works. Start by creating a new object with the following call:

```
> s1 = extend(staffPrototype);
```

Now add the relevant properties to s1:

```
> s1.firstName = 'Morgan';
> s1.lastName = 'Thomas';
> s1.salary = 50000;
> s1.profession = 'Graphic Designer';
```

Now, you should be able to use the methods added to the prototype and have these methods use the properties in your newly constructed object:

```
> s1.getFullName()
"Morgan Thomas (Graphic Designer)"
> s1.increasePay(10)
> s1.salary
55000
```

You can construct as many objects as you like from this same prototype:

```
> s2 = extend(staffPrototype);
> s2.firstName = 'Sam';
> s2.lastName = 'Donaldson';
> s2.salary = 60000;
> s2.profession = 'HR Manager';
```

All of these objects will use the methods you defined on the prototype but will have their own distinct values in each of the properties.

Although this clearly works, the extend function is rather mysterious. The first line of this function defines another function called T. Although this is a normal function, as you will see, it will be used as a constructor function, just as Array was.

Constructor functions are normal functions, but they are intended to be invoked with the new keyword. You will look at these in-depth in the next section. When they are invoked with the new keyword (as you can see on the third line), they implicitly return a new object.

The second line of the function is where all the magic happens however: On this line, the object passed into the function (staffPrototype in this case) is set as the prototype of the constructor function. This means that any objects constructed from this function will have this object set as their prototype.

Finally, it's important to understand that prototypes are read-only. For instance, the following code might be executed on one of the objects to redefine the getFullName method:

```
> s1.getFullName = function() {
    return this.lastName + ", "+ this.firstName + " (" + this.profession + ")";
}
```

This code does succeed, but it only has the effect of providing a new definition of the method for the s1 instance of the object. The underlying prototype is not affected, and any other objects based on this prototype will also be unaffected.

CONSTRUCTOR FUNCTIONS

The previous section briefly touched on the subject of constructor functions. These are the closest JavaScript has to classes because they provide a mechanism to construct new objects, and initialize their properties, all in a single step.

For instance, the following is a constructor function for initializing objects with the four properties used in the previous section:

```
function Staff(firstName, lastName, salary, profession) {
    this.firstName = firstName;
    this.lastName = lastName;
    this.salary = salary;
    this.profession = profession;
}
```

There is really nothing special about this function other than the following:

➤ It starts with a capital letter, when all the other functions and methods you have written start with lowercase letters. This is a convention to remind you that this function is a constructor function: You will see why this convention is important shortly.

➤ The body of the constructor function uses this to refer to a number of properties. As you will see, constructor functions implicitly return a new object, and properties can be set on the new object using this.

It is now possible to construct an object using this constructor function as follows:

```
s3 = new Staff('Brian', 'Downing', 40000, 'Software Tester');
```

This will create a new object and set its properties according to the arguments passed to the function.

This only constructs and initializes an object because it is invoked with the new keyword. If this were omitted, the function would still succeed, except it would not construct a new object:

```
> s4 = Staff('Brian', 'Downing', 40000, 'Software Tester');
undefined
```

As you can see, the function now returns the value of undefined. You may be wondering what happened to the calls inside the function such as this.salary. If a function is invoked without the new keyword, this refers to the JavaScript global namespace, which is the window object. The values passed to the function have therefore been created as global variables, overwriting any other global variables with the same name in the process:

```
> firstName
"Brian"
> salary
40000
```

This is why it is important to name constructor functions with leading capital letters: to remind yourself that they are constructor functions, and ensure that you precede them with the `new` keyword.

MODULES

Most programming languages that support objects support a mechanism for controlling how data is accessed. For instance, consider the `salary` property from the objects in the previous section. Any code that has access to an object can set it to any value it wants, as you can see here:

```
s1.salary = 100000000;
```

In a real-world application, you may want to control the values that `salary` can be set to. For example:

```
> s1.updateSalary = function(newSalary) {
    if (newSalary > 0 && newSalary < 200000) {
        this.salary = newSalary;
    } else {
        throw 'The salary must be between 0 and 200000';
    }
}
```

Although it is possible to expose methods such as this, this does not stop code from accessing the object's properties directly.

This may not sound like an important issue because you have full control over the code base, and you can therefore check that no one updates the `salary` property directly. This becomes increasingly difficult as the code base grows, however, and you introduce more and more rules about how properties should be accessed and updated.

Fortunately, there is a solution to this problem, and it relies on closures. The following is an example:

```
function createStaffMember(initialSalary, firstName, lastName) {
    var  salary = null;
    o = {
        setSalary : function() {
            if (initialSalary > 0 && initialSalary < 200000) {
                salary = initialSalary;
            } else {
                throw 'The salary must be between 0 and 200000';
            }
        },
        getSalary : function() {
            return salary;
        },
        firstName : firstName,
        lastName : lastName
    };
    o.setSalary(initialSalary);
    return o;
}
```

Notice that this function declares a local variable called `salary` and then constructs an object that uses this local variable. When the object is returned at the end of the function, it retains a reference to the `salary` variable so it is not destroyed. Despite this, there is no way any other code can set this variable without using the method `setSalary`, and this ensures the value is always within the acceptable range.

An object can be constructed from this function as follows:

```
> s5 = createStaffMember(50000, 'Tom', 'Braithwaite');
```

It may appear the `salary` property can be set as follows:

```
> s5.salary = 1000000000;
```

However, if you invoke the `getSalary` method, you will discover that the actual salary has not been modified:

```
> s5.getSalary();
50000
```

You will also notice that the object's methods do not access the `salary` variable with the `this` keyword. This is because `salary` is not a property of the object; it is a local variable the object has a reference to. Also notice that you need to provide a method (getSalary) for returning the current value of salary because there is no other way code outside the object could access this value.

The approach outlined in this section is a *design pattern*, which is a reusable solution to a well-known problem. This design pattern is referred to as the *module design pattern* and is used extensively in JavaScript programming.

TRY IT

In this Try It, you will use the module design pattern within the CRM web application. Although it will not do much at this point, it will provide a well-structured base on which to add additional functionality over the next few lessons.

Lesson Requirements

In order to complete this lesson, you will need the CRM web application as it stood at the end of Lesson 8. This can be downloaded from the book's website if you have not completed Lesson 8. You will also need a text editor and the Chrome browser.

Step-by-Step

1. Start by creating a standalone JavaScript file called contacts.js. This should be placed in the same folder as the contacts.html file.

2. Within this, start by creating a function called contactsScreen. This should accept a single parameter called mainID, and should return an empty object.

3. Define a local variable within the function (not within the object returned), called appScreen, and set this to the parameter passed into the function. You are going to pass the main element of the contacts.html page to this function when you eventually invoke it,

4. Create another local variable called initialized and set this to false.

5. Create a method inside the object returned called init. Add this method, and declare an empty code block for it. This is where you will place any logic that needs to execute when the web page first loads.

6. You want to make sure you only initialize the screen once. Therefore, at the top of the init method, check if initialized is true: If so, simply invoke return.

7. Copy the JavaScript code from contacts.js (minus the script tags: leave these in place), and add them to the body of the init method. In addition, set initialized to true at the end of the init method.

    My completed version of the JavaScript file is available on the book's website.

8. You now need to link the JavaScript file to the HTML page to ensure it loads when the web page loads. In order to do this, add the following to the body of the head element:

```
<script src="contacts.js"></script>
```

> **NOTE** *If you have used earlier versions of HTML, you may be expecting to add a* type *attribute to the* script *tag to specify the script is JavaScript. This is no longer required because JavaScript is the assumed default.*

9. Now, pass the main element to the contactsScreen function and store the resulting object in a local variable called appScreen. This needs to occur inside the script block at the bottom of contacts.html.

10. Invoke the init method on the appScreen object. Your code block now looks as follows:

```
<script>
    var mainElement = document.getElementById('contactScreen');
    var appScreen = contactsScreen(mainElement);
    appScreen.init();
</script>
```

11. If you now load the screen, you can add a breakpoint to the first line of the init method by selecting the contacts.js file from the Sources tab.

12. You can now reload the page and step through the init function to ensure it loads correctly.

> **REFERENCE** *Please go to the book's website at* www.wrox.com/go/html5jsj-query24hr *to view the video for Lesson 14, as well as download the code and resources for this lesson.*

15

JSON

JSON (commonly pronounced Jason) stands for JavaScript Object Notation. It is a data format for representing the properties of a JavaScript object as a string.

In computing, there are often instances where you need to convert data from one format to another. For instance, if you consider a JavaScript object, you may want to convert it into a String so that:

➤ You can send it across a network to another computer.

➤ You can store it in a file.

➤ You can use it with other JavaScript APIs that only support strings.

Conversely, you may eventually want to convert this string back into an object so that you can use it in your JavaScript application.

The process of converting an object into a string is referred to as *serialization*, while the process of converting it back is referred to as *de-serialization*.

In order to convert an object into a string, you need a data-format that specifies how the object should be mapped to a character string—for instance, how do you denote the properties and values of an object, and how do you encode the various data types such as numbers and arrays?

Historically most data formats have been binary: This meant that it was not possible for a human to read the formatted data and gain an understanding of its underlying structure or meaning. Typically, data was converted to and from the binary format using a proprietary algorithm.

In recent years, there has been a move toward plain-text data formats. The most notable example is XML, which uses a similar structure and syntax to HTML in order to differentiate properties from their values.

There is nothing inherently wrong with using XML to serialize JavaScript objects, and many web applications do use XML. For instance, this is a possible representation of a contact in XML:

```xml
<?xml version="1.0" encoding="UTF-8"?>
<contact>
    <contactName>William Jones</contactName>
```

```
            <phoneNumber>555-2941</phoneNumber>
            <emailAddress>william@testing.com</emailAddress>
            <company>
                <code>123</code>
                <name>ABC Incorporated</name>
            </company>
            <notes></notes>
            <lastContacted>2014-09-25</lastContacted>
        </contact>
```

There are three main drawbacks with XML:

> ➤   The ratio of tags to content in XML is reasonably high: In the previous example, far more than half the message consists of tags.

> ➤   A JavaScript library is required to convert between the JavaScript object and XML because JavaScript does not natively support XML.

> ➤   Although XML is simple in principle, numerous technologies have grown up around it, such as namespaces and schemas, and they can complicate XML considerably.

JSON alleviates all of these issues. The main beauty of JSON is that it maps directly to JavaScript. If you were to write out the structure of a JavaScript object on paper using the same syntax JavaScript uses for declaring objects, it would probably look identical to JSON.

JSON is also natively supported in the latest versions of JavaScript; therefore you do not need any libraries to work with JSON.

Finally, JSON is incredibly simple. It is described in a few hundred words on the following website: http://www.json.org.

The JSON representation of a contact may look like this:

```
{
    "contactName":"William Jones",
    "phoneNumber":"555-2941",
    "emailAddress":"william@testing.com",
    "company":{
        "code":123,
        "name":"ABC Incorporated"
    },
    "notes":null,
    "lastContacted":"2014-06-30T05:50:46.659Z"
}
```

Notice how similar this looks to the literal notation for declaring a JavaScript object?

It is possible to convert a JavaScript object into a string using the utility function JSON.stringify. In order to demonstrate this, start by creating a contact object using the object literal notation:

```
> c1 = {
    contactName: "William Jones",
    phoneNumber:"555-2941",
    emailAddress:"william@testing.com",
    company:{
```

```
        code:123,
        name:"ABC Incorporated"
    },
    notes:null
    lastContacted: new Date()
}
```

Next, execute the following to store this as a string in the variable `contactString`:

```
> contactString = JSON.stringify(c1)
"{"contactName":"William Jones","phoneNumber":"555-2941","emailAddress":"william@
testing.com","company":{"code":123,"name":"ABC Incorporated"},"notes":null,"lastCon
tacted":"2014-06-30T06:06:56.306Z"}"
```

Notice that the properties and values are all retained, but property names are all automatically embedded in double quotes.

JSON allows all the JavaScript data types to be represented in the serialized version. This ensures that when the string is eventually converted back into an object, the various properties retain their original data types.

➤ Strings always appear inside double quotes. Multiple examples can be seen in this example—for instance `"William Jones"`.

➤ Numbers appear literally, and do not need to be quoted; for instance, the `code` property has a value of `123`.

➤ Although not shown in this example, Boolean values are represented with the unquoted keywords `true` and `false`.

➤ The unquoted keyword `null` is used to represent a null value, as you can see with the `notes` property.

➤ Objects can encapsulate child objects, as the `company` property demonstrates. This nesting can go to as many levels as you require.

➤ Arrays can be used as the value for any property. These use the familiar square brackets to indicate the start and end of the array, while elements are separated with commas.

You can convert the string back into an object using the `JSON.parse` function. The example in Figure 15-1 shows this and demonstrates that you can access the properties of the de-serialized object:

```
> contact = JSON.parse(contactString);
▶ Object {contactName: "William Jones", phoneNumber: "555-2941", emailAddress: "william@testing.com", company: Object,
  notes: null…}
> typeof contact
  "object"
> contact.contactName
  "William Jones"
```

FIGURE 15-1

Although the JSON format is great for serializing properties, it cannot be used for serializing methods: Any methods present on the object are simply ignored when `JSON.stringify` is invoked.

REPLACING AND REVIVING

Although JavaScript is great for working with most JavaScript data types, it does come with certain limitations. One of the most difficult data types to handle is the `Date` object.

There are many different ways to serialize dates. For instance, you could use their time in milliseconds:

```
new Date().getTime()
1404088573560
```

The time in milliseconds is a number that represents the number of milliseconds that have passed since midnight on January 1, 1970. This is not an ideal way to represent a date; among other reasons, it does not contain time-zone information.

You could also use the `toString` method on the `Date` object:

```
new Date().toString()
"Mon Jun 30 2014 12:36:01 GMT+1200 (New Zealand Standard Time)"
```

This is better because it does contain time-zone information. However, it also contains unnecessary information: The day of the week is implied by the date.

Ultimately, it does not really matter what format you choose, as long as it stores all the information you require. The most important thing is that everyone agrees on the same format, thereby allowing any serialized objects to be de-serialized by your web application.

For this reason, the JavaScript `Date` object now supports a method called `toJSON`, as you can see in the following example:

```
new Date().toJSON();
"2014-06-30T00:37:09.348Z"
```

This produces a date in the UTC time zone (essentially the same as Greenwich Mean Time), regardless of the time zone of the computer itself. The timezone is denoted by the trailing Z on the date format. The entire date/time string is formatted according to an ISO standard, which is widely used in computing.

If you look at the JSON example earlier in this lesson, you will see that the date was converted into a string conforming to this standard.

You may have noticed a problem in our example, however. When `JSON.parse` was used to transform the string back into an object, the `lastContacted` property was left as a string, rather than converted back into a `Date` object.

This is not the desired behavior: You always want the serialization process to be completely reversible by the de-serialization process. Fortunately, there is a way around this problem.

The `JSON.parse` function supports an optional second parameter referred to as a "reviver." This can be used to convert values as they are transformed back onto the object. This parameter expects to be passed a function, which in turn will be passed every property as it is parsed. Where appropriate, the reviver can decide to modify the value of the property before it is set on the object.

In order to parse dates with a reviver function, you need to perform two tasks:

➤ Identify that a value is a date. The most common way to do this is with regular expressions.

➤ Convert it from a string to a `Date` object. The `Date` object has a constructor that supports the ISO format; therefore, this is a simple process.

You saw regular expressions earlier in the book when you validated form fields. JavaScript supports a literal notation for defining regular expressions: Any unquoted character string that starts with a forward slash is assumed to be a regular expression.

The regular expression that follows is reasonably complex, so it is not important that you understand it, but you should understand the approach:

```
dateReviver = function(name, value) {
    var regExp = /^(\d{4})-(\d{2})-(\d{2})T(\d{2}):(\d{2}):(\d{2}(?:\.\d*)?)Z$/
    if (value && typeof value === 'string' && value.match(regExp)) {
        return new Date(value);
    } else {
        return value;
    }
}
```

This code starts by defining a regular expression that describes the pattern of characters you expect to find in a date field.

Next, the `if` statement checks that you have been passed a value and that the value has a data type of `string`. Finally, the `if` statement checks whether the value matches the regular expression: If it does, then the `match` method will return a non-null value.

If the value is determined to be a serialized version of a date, it is simply passed to the constructor of `Date`, and the resulting object is returned. If it is not a date, you simply return the value untouched.

You can now use this function to de-serialize the contact into a new variable:

```
contact2 = JSON.parse(contactString, dateReviver);
```

If you now examine the `lastContacted` property, you can confirm it is a `Date`:

```
> typeof contact2.lastContacted
"object"
> contact2.lastContacted.toString()
"Mon Jun 30 2014 18:06:56 GMT+1200 (NZST)"
```

Notice that even though the serialized version used the UTC time zone, the de-serialized version has been converted back into my local time zone.

Just as the `JSON.parse` function supports a reviver, the `JSON.stringify` function supports an optional replacer function. This is identical to the reviver, except it allows you to convert values as they are serialized.

TRY IT

In this Try It, we will experiment with the JSON data format. As you have already seen, JSON is an extremely simple data format so you will use it for a slightly different purpose: cloning objects. To clone an object is to make a copy of it: We will look at how this can be achieved with JSON.

Lesson Requirements

In order to complete this lesson, you will need the Chrome web browser. You may, however, want to complete these exercises in a text editor and copy the results to the console.

Step-by-Step

1. Start by creating a sample object that you can clone. Make sure that this contains child objects and arrays. My object looked like this:

    ```
    o = {
        studentName: 'William Jones',
        school: 'Middletown High School',
        grades: [
            {subject: 'English',
             grade: 'A'},
            {subject: 'Algebra',
             grade: 'B+'},
            {subject: 'Geometry',
             grade: 'C'},
        ]
    }
    ```

2. Create a clone function; this should declare a single parameter, which is the object to clone.

3. Within the function, call JSON.stringify on the object passed in, and store the result in a new variable.

4. Parse the string stored in Step 3 using JSON.parse, and store the result in a new variable.

5. Return the newly created object from the function.

6. Confirm that you can change the value of properties in the newly created object and that these are not reflected in the original object.

> **REFERENCE** *Please go to the book's website at* www.wrox.com/go/html5jsj-query24hr *to view the video for Lesson 15, as well as download the code and resources for this lesson.*

16

Document Object Model

The Document Object Model (DOM) and the DOM API have been mentioned several times already in this book, but now it's time to step back and look at them in depth.

As you will see over the next few lessons, you can largely avoid an in-depth understanding of the DOM API if you use jQuery. jQuery is essentially a wrapper around the DOM; it provides all the same basic functionality but with a more intuitive API.

It is, however, wise to have at least a basic understanding of how the underlying DOM technology works before starting with jQuery because this places it in a wider context, and helps you understand what jQuery is trying to achieve.

NODES AND OBJECTS

The Document Object Model is the in-memory browser representation of a web page. When the browser loads a web page, it parses all the HTML tags and their content, and generates a model for display in the browser.

As you have already seen, the DOM model may differ from the literal HTML in several ways. For example:

➤ It will close any unclosed tags, such as self-closing tags.

➤ It will convert attribute names to lowercase.

➤ It will rearrange tags closed in the wrong order, per the rules in the HTML5 specification.

➤ It will add certain tags that may be missing such as the body tag.

You have also seen how the DOM is represented as a tree-like structure via the Elements tab in the Chrome developer tools.

The DOM is actually more complex than the Elements tab implies. In order to understand the DOM, you need to think in terms of nodes rather than elements: The DOM is a hierarchy of nodes.

In this section you will gain an understanding of the DOM constructed for the following web page:

```
<!DOCTYPE html>
<html lang="en">
<head>
    <meta charset="utf-8">
</head>
<body>
    <h1>This is the header</h1>
</body>
</html>
```

The DOM for this HTML will be modeled as you see in Figure 16-1. Each square box in this diagram is called a node in the DOM tree. As you can see, there are many nodes that are not simple elements in the document.

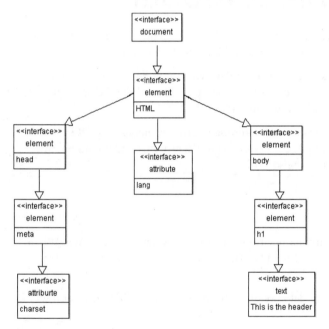

FIGURE 16-1

Figure 16-1 also lists the interface or object type of each node. The DOM represents each node as an object (a JavaScript object in this case), and this object exposes an interface consisting of a set of properties and methods.

You can see that the top-level node is called the document, and the html element is its child. Along with the element nodes, you can also see examples of text and attr nodes in the tree because the DOM models these as independent objects.

The following are the most common types of object:

➤ document: A document object represents the entire document. This can be accessed within the browser using the global variable document. When you start using the DOM API shortly, you will always do so from the context of the document.

➤ element: This object is used to represent the elements, or tags, in the document. Every tag—such as td, head, or h1—is represented by an instance of this object, but their content and attributes are modeled as independent objects.

➤ attr: The attr object type represents attributes. Each element can have zero to many attr objects as its children.

➤ text: When the body of an element contains text, this is represented by a separate object called the text object. In some cases an element can have multiple text nodes. For instance, with the following HTML fragment <p>Left sideinnerright side</p>, the p tag has two text nodes, one for the text on either side of the em tag, while the em tag also has a text node.

You may be wondering why you need all these different object types. The primary reason is that you want to do different things to different nodes in the document. For instance, the API exposed by the document may contain functionality to determine the doctype, whereas the API exposed by the attr object may contain functionality to change the attribute value. Alternatively, the element object allows you to navigate, add, remove, and change its child nodes, whereas this is not possible with text nodes.

The API used for interacting with, and manipulating all these types of node is called the DOM API. Browsers implement the DOM API in JavaScript, but the DOM API can be written in any language and can exist outside a web browser.

The purpose of the DOM API is mainly to allow the DOM to be manipulated after the web page has loaded. This allows you to implement dynamic functionality within web pages without resorting to page refreshes. There are four essential aspects to the DOM API that allow this manipulation:

➤ Selecting nodes from the DOM—for example, finding all the nodes with a particular class

➤ Traversing from a selected node to another set of nodes—for example, finding the children for a particular node

➤ Manipulating the nodes in the DOM—for example, adding, replacing or deleting nodes

➤ Responding to events generated by nodes—for example, responding to the user clicking an element

Each of these will be briefly discussed in the text that follows. Before starting, it is worth mentioning that the DOM API is very large, and I will only scratch the surface of what is possible. The idea is to be introduced to broad themes rather than understand every aspect of the API.

The examples that follow will use the following web page:

```
<!DOCTYPE html>
<html lang="en">
<head>
    <meta charset="utf-8">
</head>
```

```
<body>
    <h1 class="mainHeader">This is the title</h1>
    <ol id="daysOfWeek">
        <li>Monday
        <li>Tuesday
        <li>Wednesday
        <li>Thursday
        <li>Friday
    </ol>
</body>
</html>
```

You can either download this from the book's website (it is called `domexample.html`), or you can write it yourself.

This web page contains a heading and a list of days in an ordered list. You will interact with this web page from the Chrome console, but the code could also be added to a script block in the page itself.

Selecting Elements

You select elements from the DOM using the same basic criteria as CSS: Specifically, you select elements by their type, their classes, or their IDs.

To select an element by ID, you can use the following method on the `document` object:

```
> document.getElementById('daysOfWeek');
```

This returns a single object, which is why it is very important you never duplicate IDs on a web page.

Whenever you select an object from the DOM, you can determine its type by using the `nodeType` property. For example:

```
> document.getElementById('daysOfWeek').nodeType;
1
```

The DOM API uses numbers to represent the various types of node: 1 represents an element node, 2 represents an attribute node, 3 represents a text node, and so on.

Alternatively, you can determine the name of the element:

```
> document.getElementById('daysOfWeek').nodeName;
"OL"
```

It is also possible to select nodes by class name:

```
> document.getElementsByClassName('mainHeader');
```

or tag name:

```
> document.getElementsByTagName('li')
```

Both of these methods return an array of objects rather than a single object. Therefore, if you know only a single object will be returned, you still need to access it from the first index in the array before using it:

```
> document.getElementsByTagName('ol')[0].nodeName
"OL"
```

Traversing the DOM

Once nodes have been selected, it is common to navigate from these nodes to other nodes. The examples that follow demonstrate how it is possible to navigate from nodes to their children, and from child nodes to parents:

```
// obtain a reference to the daysOfWeek node
o = document.getElementById('daysOfWeek');
// find all the children for this node (i.e., the li elements)
o.childNodes
// find the parent of this node, i.e., the body element
o.parentNode
// find the first child of this node
o.firstElementChild
```

The DOM API also supports a number of shortcuts for traversing from one node to another. For instance, you can traverse from the document node to the body node as follows:

```
> document.body
```

Manipulating the DOM

Selection and traversal operations are used to select a set of nodes; these can then be manipulated to dynamically change the appearance of the web page after it has loaded in the browser.

For example, you may want to add a new li element with the value Saturday. This is a two-part process: First, you need to construct the nodes that represent the new li element, and then you need to insert it into the DOM at the appropriate location.

To start, you will create the li node, and assign this to the variable newLi. The node created will not be part of the DOM at this stage; it will be a standalone DOM object, commonly referred to as a document fragment.

```
> newLi = document.createElement('li');
```

Next, you will create a new text node, also using a method on the document itself. Like the li node, this will not be part of the DOM:

```
> saturday = document.createTextNode("Saturday");
```

Next, you will set the text node to be the first child of the new li node:

```
> newLi.appendChild(saturday);
```

Finally, you can add the li node into the DOM at the appropriate location. Many methods are available for controlling where nodes are inserted in relation to other nodes, but you will use the appendChild method; this simply adds the node as the last child of an existing node:

```
> document.getElementById('daysOfWeek').appendChild(newLi);
```

As soon as you invoke this final line, a new li element will appear in the web page. In addition, if you look at the Elements tab in the developer tool, you can see that the DOM has been updated (see Figure 16-2).

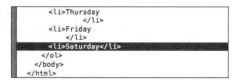

FIGURE 16-2

As you can see, working with the DOM API is somewhat convoluted: This code will be significantly simplified once you introduce jQuery.

Responding to Events

The final aspect of the DOM API you need to understand is events. In fact, you have already seen these when you wrote the drag-and-drop–based web page in Lesson 9.

Each type of DOM object supports a wide variety of events. These are primarily categorized as:

➤ Keyboard events, such as keyup and keydown

➤ Mouse events, such as onclick and onmousedown

➤ Document events, such as onload and onresize

➤ Form events, such as onchange and onselect

In this section, you will take advantage of two mouse events. You will add functionality so that if the user hovers over the header (a mouseenter event), the list will be displayed (its display property will be set to block). When the mouse moves away from the header (a mouseleave event), the list will be hidden again.

You will change the web page so that the list of days is initially hidden by adding the following to the head element:

```
<style>
ol {
    display:none;
}
</style>
```

Next you will add the appropriate event listeners in the script block before the closing body tag.

```
<script>
document.getElementsByClassName('mainHeader')[0]
    .addEventListener("mouseenter", function(event) {
        document.getElementById('daysOfWeek').style.display = 'block';
});

document.getElementsByClassName('mainHeader')[0]
    .addEventListener("mouseleave", function(event) {
        document.getElementById('daysOfWeek').style.display = 'none';
});
</script>
```

In this example, you add two event listeners to the h1 element. One is fired when the mouse enters the box of the header element; the other fires when the mouse leaves the box.

Within each event listener you simply locate the ol node, and either hide it or show it as appropriate. This is achieved by updating its display style to either block or none.

TRY IT

In this Try It, you will take the CRM web application from Lesson 14 and add two dynamic features to it:

➤ You will change the contact details form so that it is initially hidden and only displayed if the user clicks a link to add a new contact.

➤ You will create a hover effect for displaying notes: If the user hovers over the last contacted time, you will display the notes to the user in a popup box.

Lesson Requirements

In order to complete this lesson, you will need the Chrome web browser and the CRM project files from Lesson 14.

Step-by-Step

This step-by-step will be broken into two distinct sections. Work through each in turn, ensuring that the functionality works as expected before moving on.

Displaying Form Dynamically

1. To start, you need to hide the section with the id contactDetails in the HTML. This can be accomplished via an inline style on the element itself, which will set its display property to none.

2. Add a hyperlink to the bottom of the contactList section (after the closing table tag) that the user can click to add a new contact. The href for this should simply be # because you will not use browser-based navigation (you will respond to the user click in JavaScript). You need to also ensure the hyperlink has an id so you can select it from the DOM. You can choose how this looks, but I added the following:

```
<div class="controls">
    <a href="#" id="addContact">Add a new contact</a>
</div>
```

I also added the following to contacts.css to improve its appearance:

```
.controls {
    padding:15px;
}
```

3. Within the init method of contacts.js, select the hyperlink by id using document.getElementById, and add an event listener to the object returned using addEventListsner. The first parameter to addEventListener is the type of event you are listening for, which in this case is click. The second parameter is a function that accepts a single parameter called event. Create this as an anonymous function.

4. Within the function, you first need to disable the default behavior of clicking a hyperlink to request a new page from the server. This can be achieved by calling the method preventDefault() on the event itself.

5. Select the element `contactDetails` by `id`, and set its `style.display` property to `block`.

6. If you reload the page and click the hyperlink, the contact details section should immediately appear.

Showing Notes

You will now change the time field so that when the user hovers above it, the notes are displayed, as shown in Figure 16-3.

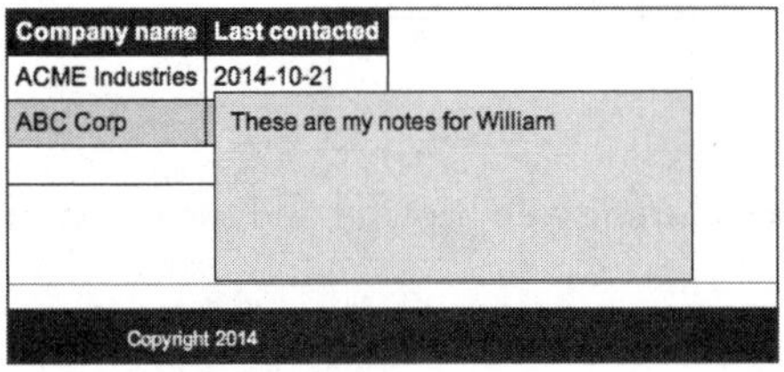

Company name	Last contacted
ACME Industries	2014-10-21
ABC Corp	These are my notes for William
Copyright 2014	

FIGURE 16-3

1. In order to display notes, you first need to ensure that they are present, but hidden, in the DOM when the page loads. Identify any table cells that contain `time` elements, and modify them so that they contain an additional element with notes information. For example:

```
<td>
    <time datetime="2014-09-12">2014-09-12</time>
    <div class="overlay">These are my notes for William</div>
</td>
```

Notice that I have also added a class called `overlay` to the `div`.

2. You now need to add a CSS rule for the overlay class. Try to add this yourself based on the following specification:

➤ Set the `height` of the `div` to 100px.

➤ Set the `width` of the `div` to 300px.

➤ Add a 1px solid `border` to the `div` with a color of `#333333`.

➤ Set the background color to `#eeeeee`.

➤ Add 10px of padding between the content and the border.

➤ Set the initial `display` to `none`.

➤ Use the `position` element to remove the element from the flow of the page, and ensure that, when it is displayed, it does not impact the position of any other elements in the DOM. Think about which `position` value most closely meets these needs.

➤ Set the `z-index` so that when the `div` is displayed, it appears over the top of the table.

My CSS looked like this:

```
.overlay {
    position: fixed;
    height: 100px;
    width: 300px;
    border: 1px solid #333333;
    background: #eeeeee;
    display: none;
    z-index:1;
    padding:10px;
}
```

3. You need to add event listeners to each of the time elements. Select all the time elements using document.getElementsByTagName. Once these have been found and stored in a local variable, iterate through them in a for loop.

4. Within the for loop, you need to add two different event listeners, one for mouseenter and one for mouseleave. Create skeleton implementations for each of these and make sure the anonymous function passed as their second parameter accepts the parameter event.

5. Within the function passed to each event listener, you need to find the notes div that is closest to the time element that the mouse is hovering over. You can first find the time element they are hovering over using event.target. You can then find the next sibling of this element using nextElementSibling and set the display property to either block or none, depending on whether you are hiding or showing the div.

The next sibling element allows you to find the next element in the DOM with the same parent as the specified element. In the case of the time element, that will be the div element containing the notes.

6. If you reload the page and hover the mouse over the time elements, the notes should display and then immediately disappear if you hover away.

> **REFERENCE** *Please go to the book's website at* www.wrox.com/go/html5jsj-query24hr *to view the video for Lesson 16, as well as download the code and resources for this lesson.*

17

jQuery Selection

In this lesson, you will start gaining an understanding of jQuery and the way in which it can simplify interaction with the DOM.

jQuery is an open-source library written entirely in JavaScript. Although it is intended to simplify interaction with the DOM, it does not do anything that could not be achieved with the DOM API. In fact, it uses the DOM API to perform its operations.

The following are the main reasons why jQuery is used in so many web applications:

➤ It provides an intuitive and easy-to-learn API for performing the most common tasks in website development. For instance, the selection API you will use in this lesson is based on CSS selectors.

➤ It provides genuine cross-browser support and hides some of the quirks that exist in the DOM API implementations of certain browsers (most notably, older versions of IE).

➤ It is very easy to write plugins to enhance the capabilities of jQuery, and there are extensive libraries of freely available plugins on the Internet.

➤ The jQuery website contains extremely good documentation, and there is a wide variety of help available on the Internet if you encounter problems.

jQuery is not the only library designed to assist with DOM interaction, but it has become the *de facto* standard, and has a higher market share than all its competitors combined. Therefore, if you are going to learn one JavaScript library, it makes sense for it to be jQuery.

LOADING JQUERY

Before using jQuery, you need to import it into your web pages. There are two ways you can do this:

➤ You can download the relevant version of jQuery, store it on your server, and link to it via a relative URL in a source tag. This is generally the best approach while developing a web application.

➤ Link to a version hosted by an external party. Many Content Distribution Networks (CDNs), such as Google, provide hosted versions of popular JavaScript libraries, including jQuery. This is generally the best option for production websites because CDN delivery tends to be faster.

In this section, you look at how you can use both approaches.

The jQuery library used in this book is available from the book's website, but these instructions show you how to download your own version of the library. In order to download a version of jQuery, first navigate to `www.jquery.com`. Find the Download link on the homepage and click it.

In this book, you will use the 2.*x* release of jQuery. This does not support some older browsers, such as IE8. Therefore, if you are developing a website that must support older browsers, you can use the 1.*x* release of jQuery, which provides most of the same functionality.

Click to download the development version of the latest 2.*x* release of jQuery. The version used in this book is 2.1.1, but the latest 2.*x* release can be used. jQuery offers both a production and a development version. The only difference between these is that the production version is "minimized," which essentially means the code has been compressed. The code in both versions is, however, functionally equivalent; it is just very hard to debug the minimized version.

Once it is downloaded, store it in the CRM directory along with `contacts.html`.

Now, simply import it into the web page using a `source` tag in the `head` of the document:

```
<script src="jquery-2.1.1.js"></script>
```

If you now load the page, you can test if jQuery is installed. In order to confirm this, type **jQuery** in the console. It should produce the output shown in Figure 17-1.

```
Q  Elements  Network  Sources  Timeline  Profiles  Resources  Audits | Console |
⊘  ▽  <top frame> ▼
> jQuery
  function ( selector, context ) {
        // The jQuery object is actually just the init constructor 'enhanced'
        // Need init if jQuery is called (just allow error to be thrown if not included)
        return new jQuery.fn.init( selector, context );
  }
>
```

FIGURE 17-1

If you choose to load jQuery via a CDN, you do not need to download jQuery; you can simply add the following `source` tag to the `head` section of the web page:

```
<script src=http://ajax.googleapis.com/ajax/libs/jquery/2.1.1/jquery.min.js >
</script>
```

If you now load the page, you can test if jQuery is installed. In order to confirm this, type **jQuery** in the console. It should produce the output shown in Figure 17-2 (notice that this is a minimized version of the library so the output is different):

```
Q   Elements  Network  Sources  Timeline  Profiles  Resources  Audits | Console |
⊘   ▽   <top frame> ▼
> jQuery
    function (a,b){return new n.fn.init(a,b)}
>
```

FIGURE 17-2

SELECTING ELEMENTS

You are now ready to start selecting elements with jQuery. Selecting elements has no inherent value; it is simply the first step in a sequence of operations. Typically, once you have selected a set of elements, you will manipulate them in some way, but that is the subject of future lessons.

In this lesson, you will select elements from the contacts.html web page using the Chrome console.

If you remember back to the lesson on the DOM API, elements were selected using methods on the document object. With jQuery, you select elements by placing a selection string inside the following structure:

```
$('selection string')
```

The dollar sign is an alias to the jQuery function and is intended to save on typing. It is also possible to use the following construct:

```
jQuery('selection string')
```

The great thing about selection strings in jQuery is that they mostly use the same syntax as CSS. Therefore, to select all the td elements from the document, simply type the following:

```
> $('td');
```

This is an element selector, and like all jQuery selections, will return a jQuery object that provides access to the underlying elements selected.

It is also possible to select elements using their ID, as you can see in this example:

```
> $('#contactList');
```

and by class name, as you can see in the following example:

```
> $('.controls');
```

Notice that in all these cases, the selection syntax is identical to the syntax used with CSS.

My discussion of CSS selectors skipped over one additional type of selection: selecting elements based on their attributes. In order to select all elements with a particular attribute, simply add the attribute name between square brackets:

```
> $('[datetime]');
```

It is also possible to state the element that the attribute is relevant to by prepending it to the selection; this is useful when several different element types share the same attribute:

```
> $('time[datetime]');
```

And it is possible to specify that the attribute should have a specific value:

```
$('time[datetime="2014-10-21"]');
```

or not equal a certain value:

```
$('time[datetime!="2014-10-21"]');
```

Notice that in both of these cases, the value is provided in double quotes. Because you are providing a string inside a string, you mix and match double and single quoted strings. You could have also used the following syntax:

```
$("time[datetime!='2014-10-21']");
```

PSEUDO-SELECTORS

You can also use pseudo-selectors to select elements, just as with CSS pseudo-classes. This particular example will select all the even numbered `tr` elements in the `tbody` element:

```
> $('tbody tr:even');
```

Pseudo-selectors are always prepended with a colon.

Notice also that the space between `tbody` and `tr` implies that the `tr` elements must be children of a `tbody` element, just as it did in CSS.

The following are some of the most useful pseudo-selectors:

- ➤ `:even` finds all even numbered elements in a selection.
- ➤ `:odd` finds all odd numbered elements in a selection.
- ➤ `:not(selection)` finds all elements that do not match the selection.
- ➤ `:gt(selection)` finds all elements with an index greater than the supplied number.
- ➤ `:checked` finds radio buttons or check boxes that are checked.
- ➤ `:selected` finds options in select boxes that are selected.
- ➤ `:contains(text)` finds elements that contain a given piece of text.
- ➤ `:empty` finds all elements that have no children.
- ➤ `:focus` finds the element that currently has focus.
- ➤ `:first` finds the first element in a set.
- ➤ `:last` finds the last element in a set.

For instance, the following finds the first `section` in the web page:

```
> $('section:first');
```

while this finds all the `tr` elements, except the first one, in the page:

```
> $('tr:gt(0)');
```

The pseudo-selectors are not identical to the pseudo-classes in CSS, and in many cases they are used to provide shorthand for a selection that could still be performed with conventional selectors. For instance, this selection returns all the form input fields, including fields that do not use the `input` element such as `select` and `textarea`:

```
> $(':input');
```

This same selection could have been performed as follows:

```
> $('input,select,textarea');
```

The other great thing about jQuery pseudo-selectors is that it is possible to write your own. For instance, you may find that you are constantly writing the following selector to find input fields:

```
> $('input[type="email"]');
```

You can therefore add the following code to your web page (making sure jQuery has been loaded before this is executed) to add your own special pseudo-selector called `email`.

```
> $.expr[':'].email = function(elem) {
    return $(elem).is("input") && $(elem).attr("type") === "email";
}
```

Don't worry too much about the first line of this example; it is simply the mechanism used for adding a new pseudo-selector to jQuery. Once this has been loaded, it can be used as follows:

```
> $(':email');
```

and it can be combined with other selectors:

```
> $('form :email');
```

jQuery will automatically pass the pseudo-selector every element in the web page (unless filtered out by one of the other selectors in the selection string), and the pseudo-selector will check:

➤ Is the element a type of input field? `$(elem).is("input")`

➤ Does it have an attribute with the name email? `$(elem).attr("type") === "email";`

If it meets these criteria, the selector returns `true`.

SELECTION WITHIN A CONTEXT

You have already seen how it is possible to select elements that are children of other elements. For instance, the following finds all the `tr` elements that are children of `tbody` elements:

```
> $('tbody tr:even');
```

Selecting elements within the context of a specific sub-tree of the DOM is very common. For instance, in your CRM web application you may want to always select elements in the context of the `main` tag for the page. This will ensure that even if your contacts web page is embedded in a larger web application, it will only select elements that are relevant to it.

> **NOTE** *It is very common to write single page web applications. In a single web page application, the entire web application is loaded as a single page, even though it contains many logical pages. When the user navigates around the application, they appear to be loading new pages from the server, but instead the DOM is being manipulated in real time to hide and show the relevant portions of the DOM. Single page web applications tend to provide a much faster experience to the user because traditional navigation requires a whole set of resources to be retrieved from the server whenever a navigation event occurs.*

Because selecting elements in the context of other elements is so common, jQuery provides two additional mechanisms for achieving it. The first mechanism uses the `find` method:

```
> $('#contactScreen').find('tr');
```

This will first find the element with the ID `contactsScreen` and then will look inside the result for any `tr` elements.

The other way of achieving exactly the same result is to use the optional second parameter to jQuery after the selection string:

```
> $('tr', '#contactScreen')
```

The second parameter provides the context within which the selection should occur.

WRAPPED OBJECTS

If you consider the following line of jQuery again:

```
> $('#contactScreen').find('tr');
```

you will see that jQuery is not simply returning a DOM object because DOM objects do not support a `find` method.

In this particular case, jQuery has returned its own type of object wrapped over the DOM objects, and it is the jQuery object that `find` is executed against.

As it happens, every jQuery selection returns a jQuery-specific object, not the underlying DOM objects. The object returned is capable of masquerading as an array, however, and accessing specific indexes returns the native DOM objects.

The following code assigns a native DOM object to the `domObject` variable:

```
> var domObject = $('td')[0];
```

It is always possible to convert a native DOM object into a jQuery object by embedding it in the selection structure:

```
> $(domObject);
```

This then gives you access to all the additional features provided by jQuery. For instance, the following returns the text of the element:

```
> $(domObject).text()
```

while this call queries whether the text of the element contains the word "contacts":

```
> $(domObject).is(':contains("contacts")');
```

You will typically work with jQuery objects rather than native DOM objects in the remainder of this book, but you can always use this technique if you need to convert native DOM objects to jQuery objects.

TRY IT

In this Try It, you will try out a number of the selection techniques discussed in the lesson. If you want, you can follow along with these examples in the screencast.

Lesson Requirements

You will need the CRM web application, and you will need to have loaded the jQuery library using one of the techniques outlined earlier in this lesson. Once the web page is loaded, you can perform jQuery selections against the web page using the Chrome Console.

Step-by-Step

1. Select all the elements from the web page that have the class `overlay`.

2. Select all the `input` elements that have a `name` attribute on them. This will involve first selecting the `input` elements using an element selector, and limiting this with an attribute selector.

3. Find the element in the `form` that has a `name` attribute with the value `companyName`. Assign the result to a variable called `companySelector`.

4. Invoke the `find` method on `companySelector` and have it return all the `option` elements within it, except for the first one. You can achieve this with the `gt` pseudo-selector discussed earlier in this lesson.

5. Find the `label` for the `phoneNumber` field (using an attribute selector with a value), and print out its text.

6. Find the odd numbered `tr` elements in either the `tbody` or the `tfoot` elements (but not the `thead`).

> **REFERENCE** *Please go to the book's website at* www.wrox.com/go/html5js-jquery24hr *to view the video for Lesson 17, as well as download the code and resources for this lesson.*

18

jQuery Traversal and Manipulation

In the previous lesson, you learned how to select elements from the DOM with jQuery. This lesson will build on that knowledge and teach you how to:

> ➤ Traverse from those elements to another set of related elements.

> ➤ Manipulate the nodes in the DOM—this includes adding new nodes, modifying existing nodes, and removing nodes from the DOM.

TRAVERSAL

When you execute a jQuery selection, the result is a jQuery object encapsulating a set of elements. The traversal operations allow you to traverse from the initially selected elements to a new set of elements. The result of a traversal is therefore also a jQuery object encapsulating a set of elements.

You have already seen one instance of a traversal operation: the `find` method in the previous lesson was a traversal operation because it began by finding an element (or set of elements), and then finding other elements that are children of these elements.

It is also possible to traverse from elements to their parents. For instance, the following starts by finding all the `time` elements, and then finds their parents, which are `td` elements:

```
> $('time').parent();
```

This will return two `td` elements.

The `parent` function returns immediate parents; if you want to find elements that are indirect parents, you can use the `parents` function. This returns any element that is an ancestor of the selected elements, but it is possible to provide a selection to this function as a parameter. For instance, you might want to return the `form` that is the parent of all the input fields. This can be achieved as follows:

```
> $(':input').parents('form');
```

This only returns unique results; therefore a single `form` element is returned from this selection.

It is also possible to create a result set that contains the original elements along with the newly selected elements. For example, the following selects all the input fields and the `form` element in a single selection list using the `andSelf` function:

```
> $(':input').parents('form').andSelf();
```

Another common traversal is to select elements that are siblings of other elements (elements are siblings if they have the same parent). For instance, you may want to select all the labels that are siblings of input fields, but only if they contain the `required` attribute. In the "Manipulation" section later in this lesson, you will modify the way these labels are displayed:

```
> $(':input[required]').siblings('label');
```

With most traversal functions, you can choose to add a selection filter (`'label'` in this case), or omit the parameter to receive all siblings.

There are a number of other traversal functions that find specific siblings:

➤ `last`: Find the last sibling that (optionally) meets specific criteria.

➤ `first`: Find the first sibling that (optionally) meets specific criteria.

➤ `next`: Find the next sibling that (optionally) meets specific criteria.

➤ `prev`: Find the previous sibling that (optionally) meets specific criteria.

There are a couple more important traversal functions you need to know before moving on:

➤ `add`: This provides a mechanism to join together two different selections. For instance, the following can be used to create a selection list of all the input fields and all the labels.

```
> $(':input').add('label')
```

➤ `closest`: The `closest` function finds the closest ancestor of an element, meeting specific criteria, but, unlike the `parents` selector, considers the original element. Imagine if you want to select the closest `td` element to any element that contains the text "Bob". You can use the following:

```
> $(':contains("Bob")').closest('td')
```

If the element containing the text is a `td` element, it is added to the result set. Otherwise, jQuery ascends up through the parents of the element, searching for the first `td` element.

➤ `eq`: The equals operator can be used to return the element at a specific index—for example, the following returns the second section in the document:

```
> $('section').eq(1)
```

CHAINING

Traversal functions also highlight another great strength of jQuery:

➤ The traversal functions are executed on a selection of jQuery elements.

➤ The traversal functions return a selection of jQuery elements.

To put it another way, the input for traversal functions is the same data type as their output. This means that it is possible to chain together a whole set of traversal functions in a single statement. Consider the following call:

```
> $('time').siblings('.overlay').parents('tr').last();
```

This code performs the following:

➤ Selects all `time` elements

➤ Selects any sibling of these elements that has the overlay class

➤ Selects the `tr` element that is a parent of these elements

➤ Selects the last element returned from the list

Effectively, this code selects the last row that has a `time` element with an overlay. This chaining can continue almost indefinitely.

MANIPULATION

Now that you have written code to find elements, you can get to the interesting part of jQuery: manipulating the DOM to provide dynamic behavior to the user.

Consider the selection earlier that found all the labels of input fields that had the `required` attribute:

```
> $(':input[required]').siblings('label');
```

You may decide that you want to change the text of labels such as this to display in red. This can be achieved as follows:

```
> $(':input[required]').siblings('label').css('color', 'red');
```

Running this single line of code is sufficient to color all the labels red.

Red labels are potentially overpowering so you will instead add a red asterisk next to each label. Your goal is to create the following structure:

```
<label for="contactName" style="color: red;">
    Contact name<span class="requiredMarker">*</span>
</label>
```

You will start by adding a class to `contacts.css` to match the `requiredMarker` class:

```
.requiredMarker {
    color: red;
    padding-left:7px;
}
```

The first task is to create a new element to add to each of the labels:

```
$('<span>').text('*').addClass('requiredMarker');
```

This performs the following:

➤ Creates a new span node that can be added to the DOM

➤ Adds an * as its text

➤ Adds the class redMarker to the span

➤ Returns the new span element as a result

Next, you select all the labels that you want to add the span to, and you use the append function to insert this single span into all the labels:

```
$(':input[required]').siblings('label').append($('<span>').text('*').
addClass('requiredMarker'));
```

Notice how this complex operation can be expressed in a single statement. If you run this and select to create a contact, the relevant labels will appear as you see in Figure 18-1.

FIGURE 18-1

Once this line of code has been tested in the Console, you can add it to the init method in contacts.js to ensure it always runs when the page loads.

Naturally, you could have added the asterisks to the labels manually, but the advantage of this approach is that you are deriving this content directly from the data: If you mark a new field as required, you do not need to remember to add an asterisk to the label. It is functionality such as this that helps maintain consistency as the web application grows in size.

When adding new elements in relation to an existing element, there are four positions for which you may want to insert new nodes. For instance, consider the h2 element selected in Figure 18-2:

```
▼<main id="contactScreen">
  ▼<section id="contactDetails" style="display:none">
      <h2>Contact details</h2>
    ▶<form method="post">…</form>
    </section>
  ▶<section id="contactList">…</section>
  </main>
```

FIGURE 18-2

➤ You may want to insert a new element as a sibling of the h2 element, but before it in the DOM. This can be achieved with the before function. For example:

```
$('h2').before('<span>before</span>')
```

➤ As a sibling of the h2 element, but after it in the DOM. This can be achieved with the after function.

➤ As the first child of the h2 element. This can be achieved with the prepend function.

➤ As the last child of the h2 element. As already shown, this can be achieved with the append function.

Any of these functions can either be passed a string of HTML markup or a DOM object.

Figure 18-3 shows where a span element would be inserted using each of these functions.

```
▼<section id="contactDetails" style="display: block;">
    <span>before</span>
  ▼<h2>
      <span>prepend</span>
      "Contact details"
      <span>append</span>
    </h2>
    <span>after</span>
```

FIGURE 18-3

Along with adding new nodes to the DOM, it is simple to remove nodes from the DOM with the `remove` function. This can be seen in the following example:

```
> $('.requiredMarker').remove();
```

This function returns all the elements that have been removed.

CHANGING ELEMENTS

The manipulation techniques you have looked at so far are designed to add or remove nodes from the DOM. jQuery also provides the capability to modify existing elements.

For instance, you can directly manipulate the `text` of an element as follows:

```
> $('#contactDetails h2').text('CONTACT DETAILS');
```

or you can modify its HTML as follows:

```
> $('#contactDetails h2').html('<span>Contact Details</span>');
```

This line of code positions the text inside a span element. jQuery is a very flexible library, so there are typically many different ways to accomplish the same task. For example, the following code also adds a span element around the text of the h2 element:

```
> $('#contactDetails h2').wrapInner('<span>');
```

It is also possible to set the value of form inputs using the `val` function. For example:

```
> $('[name="contactName"]').val('testing 123');
```

Any of these functions can be used without an argument to access the current value. The following displays the current value of the `contactName` field:

```
> $('[name="contactName"]').val();
```

When used in this mode, only a single value will be returned so if you invoke these functions on a set of elements, only the value of the first element will be returned. Additionally, because these functions do not return jQuery objects, it is not possible to chain other jQuery functions onto their results.

Earlier in this lesson, you saw how individual CSS properties can be set using the `css` function, and how classes can be added to an element with `addClass`. It is also possible to remove classes with `removeClass`. For example, this will remove the class you added to all the span elements containing asterisks:

```
> $('label span').removeClass('requiredMarker');
```

One additional useful function is `toggleClass`. This adds a class to an element if it does not already have it, and removes it if it does. You will come back to this function when you look at jQuery events.

Finally, it is possible to access and modify the attributes of an element. For instance, the following returns the `maxlength` of the `textarea` in the form:

```
> $('textarea').attr('maxlength');
```

while the following modifies the value of the attribute (or adds the attribute if it does not already exist):

```
> $('textarea').attr('maxlength', 200);
```

Alternatively, an attribute can be removed as follows:

```
> $('textarea').removeAttr('maxlength');
```

ITERATION

A common requirement once a set of elements has been selected is to iterate through each element and perform an operation on it. Because the result of a jQuery selection mimics an array, it is possible to use a `for` loop to iterate through it.

An easier approach to iteration is to use a jQuery helper function called `each`. jQuery contains a number of helper functions that can be invoked directly rather than on a jQuery selection.

In this section you will write a function that iterates through all the input fields in the form, extracts their name and value, and constructs an object of these name/value pairs. Essentially this function is serializing the form to an object: You will then be able to use this object in your web application.

Start by creating a new method on the object returned from the `contactsScreen` function. This should come immediately after the `init` function and be separated from it by a comma:

```
function contactsScreen(mainID) {
    var screen = mainID;
    var initialized = false;
    return {
        init: function() {
            // body omitted
        },
        serializeForm: function() {

        }
    };
}
```

The first thing the function should do is obtain a reference to the input fields on the `form`. You also want to create an empty object that can be returned as a result of the function:

```
var inputFields = $(screen).find('form :input');
var result = {};
```

Remember that you always want to select elements in the context of the `screen` element (which was set to the `main` element).

Next, you want to iterate through all the input fields using each. The each function accepts two arguments: a jQuery selection, and a function that should be passed the index and value of each element in the selection:

```
$.each(inputFields, function(index, value) {

});
```

Notice that the call to each is prepended with $. rather than just $: This indicates that each is a helper function rather than a jQuery selection.

You now need to write the implementation of the function itself. This should first check whether the input field has a name attribute. (This lets you omit input fields such as the submit button.) If it does, it should write a property to the object using the name attribute as the property name and the value of the input field as the value. The final version will look like this:

```
serializeForm: function() {
        var inputFields = $(screen).find('form :input');
        var result = {};
        $.each(inputFields, function(index, value) {
            if ($(value).attr('name')) {
                result[$(value).attr('name')] = $(value).val();
            }
        });
        return result;
}
```

Notice that each time the value is accessed, it is converted into a jQuery object using the following syntax: $(value). This allows you to invoke methods, such as val and attr.

You can now invoke this from the console:

```
> appScreen.serializeForm();
```

Figure 18-4 shows the results of invoking this method with a given set of values in the input fields.

```
> appScreen.serializeForm();
<- ▼ Object {contactName: "Dane Cameron", phoneNumber: "555 433 3331",
    companyName: "1"
    contactName: "Dane Cameron"
    emailAddress: "dane@cisdal.com"
    lastContacted: "2014-11-06"
    notes: "Notes"
    phoneNumber: "555 433 3331"
    ▶ __proto__: Object
> |
```

FIGURE 18-4

You will make more use of this method in the lessons ahead.

TRY IT

In this Try It, you will try out a number of the traversal and manipulation techniques discussed in the lesson. If you want, you can follow along with these examples in the screencast.

Lesson Requirements

You will need the CRM web application, and you will need to have loaded the jQuery library using one of the techniques outlined earlier in this lesson. Once the web page is loaded, you can perform jQuery selections against the web page using the Chrome Console.

Step-by-Step

1. Write a jQuery selection that starts by finding any `time` elements in the `contacts.html` web page and then traverses from these to find each element's parent `tr` element. Essentially, you are finding all the rows in the table that contain a `time` element.

2. Find the input field in the document with the attribute `autofocus`. Traverse from this to its parent element, ensuring that this is a `div` with the class `formRow`. Now, find the next sibling of this node (which should also be a `div` with the class `formRow`), and find an input field within this `div`. You should be able to achieve this entire operation in a single line of jQuery.

3. Imagine that you want to add `placeholder` text to every input field that has the required attribute specifying, "This field is required." Write a selection that finds all input fields that match this selection and add a `placeholder` attribute with the appropriate text.

4. Write a line of jQuery to set the value of the `companyName` select box to 2.

5. Use the `each` function to iterate through all the input fields that have `pattern` attributes. Inside the loop, append a sibling to each input field to display this pattern. The result should display as you see in Figure 18-5.

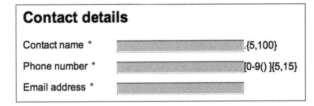

Contact details

Contact name *		.{5,100}
Phone number *		[0-9()]{5,15}
Email address *		

FIGURE 18-5

REFERENCE *Please go to the book's website at* www.wrox.com/go/html5jsj-query24hr *to view the video for Lesson 18, as well as download the code and resources for this lesson.*

19

jQuery Events

Although you have come a long way in your understanding of jQuery, it is not possible to unlock the full power of jQuery until you are introduced to jQuery events.

jQuery is typically used to manipulate the DOM after the page has loaded, but an event needs to trigger this. This event might be:

➤ A mouse event, such as the user clicking on an element

➤ A keyboard event, such as the user typing into an input field

➤ A form event, such as the value of a select element changing

➤ A screen event, such as the window being resized

Just as it is possible to listen for events such as these using the native DOM API, it is possible to listen for these events with jQuery. In fact, jQuery is actually providing a wrapper around DOM events so all the events discussed in this lesson are ultimately based on the underlying DOM events.

Although this lesson is technically an introduction to jQuery events, I will use it as an opportunity to bring together everything you have learned about jQuery so far.

REGISTERING EVENT LISTENERS

Registering event listeners begins with selecting the element that will generate the event. Once selected, the appropriate method is invoked to register an event listener, and it is passed a callback function that should be invoked when the event occurs. For instance, this code can be added to the `init` function in `contacts.js` to add a mouse click listener to the submit button:

```
$(screen).find('form input[type="submit"]').click(
    function(evt) {
        evt.preventDefault();
    }
);
```

This code first finds the submit button inside the form, and then calls the `click` method on it. As you can see, the callback function accepts an event object that contains important contextual information about the event that has occurred. In this example, you are invoking a method on the event object to prevent the default behavior of the submit button, which would be to post the form data to the server.

You can now enhance the event listener to perform a number of other tasks:

➤ Check whether the form is valid according to the rules you added in Lesson 8.

➤ If the form is valid, extract a serialized version of the form using the function you wrote in the previous lesson.

➤ Create a new `tr` element based on the data in the serialized object.

➤ Add the new `tr` element to the table body.

The event listener for this will be one of the most complex blocks of code you have seen so far, so take a look at it first: I will then walk you through it line by line:

```
$(screen).find('form input[type="submit"]').click(
    function(evt) {
        evt.preventDefault();
        if ($(evt.target).parents('form')[0].checkValidity()) {
            var contact = this.serializeForm();
            var html = '<tr><td>'+contact.contactName+'</td>'+
                '<td>'+contact.phoneNumber+'</td>'+
                '<td>'+contact.emailAddress+'</td>'+
                '<td>'+contact.companyName+'</td>'+
                '<td><time datetime="'+contact.lastContacted+'">'+
                contact.lastContacted+'</time>'+
                '<div class="overlay">'+contact.notes+'</div></td></tr>';
            $(screen).find('table tbody').append(html);
        }
    }.bind(this)
);
```

You have already looked at the purpose of the first line of the function. The second line of the function tests whether or not the form is valid. First, this line finds the jQuery element that has generated the event `$(evt.target)`; from this you can use the `parents` function to find the `form` that the event occurred within.

Once the `form` has been found, you can use the native DOM method `checkValidity` to determine if the form is valid. Because this is a native DOM method, you convert the jQuery selection to a native DOM object by accessing the first (and only) element in the selection using `[0]`. It is also possible to use `.get(0)` to achieve the same result.

You only want to execute the rest of the functionality in this event listener if the form is valid so the remainder of the function is inside an `if` statement.

Once you have confirmed that the form is valid, you next use the `serializeForm` method to create an object from the data in the form. Because this method resides on the same object, you would expect to invoke this method by prefixing it with `this`:

```
var contact = this.serializeForm();
```

There is, however, more to this line of code than meets the eye. The event listener itself is a function inside a method. When a function is placed inside a method, the object it uses as its environment is not the object itself, as you can see in the following simple example:

```
var obj = {
    methodA : function() {
        console.log('Outer this is '+this);
        function inner() {
            console.log('Inner this is '+this);
        }
        inner();
    }
}
obj.methodA();
```

This block of code creates an object with a single method called methodA. Inside this method, a function is created called inner, which is then invoked. At the end, methodA is invoked: This will cause both the method and the inner function to write to the console the identity of their this reference. Somewhat surprisingly, it prints the following:

```
Outer this is [object Object]
Inner this is [object Window]
```

Because the inner function uses the window as its this object, it cannot invoke methods or properties on the object it is actually executing within.

There are two common solutions to this problem. The first is to declare a local variable with a reference to this, and use that inside the function. Traditionally, the local variable is named that.

```
var obj = {
    methodA : function() {
        console.log('Outer this is '+this);
        var that = this;
        function inner() {
            console.log('Inner this is '+that);
        }
        inner();
    }
}
obj.methodA();
```

Executing this now produces the expected results:

```
Outer this is [object Object]
Inner this is [object Object]
```

The other way to solve this problem is to use the bind method I introduced earlier in the book. As you remember from Lesson 12, the bind method allows you to provide an object that will act as the this reference for a function, and it returns a new function permanently bound to it. You can therefore rewrite this functionality as follows:

```
var obj = {
    methodA : function() {
        console.log('Outer this is '+this);
        inner   = function() {
```

```
                    console.log('Inner this is '+this);
                }.bind(this);
                inner();
        }
    }
    obj.methodA();
```

Notice that you are now saying that `inner` is a function bound to the `methodA`'s `this` reference (which is the object); thus, both the method and the function have the same reference to `this`, and the function produces the expected results:

```
    Outer this is [object Object]
    Inner this is [object Object]
```

This can be a difficult concept to grasp, so you may want to work through the preceding examples to assure yourself exactly how it works.

As you can see, this is exactly the approach you have used with the click event listener, and therefore `this.serializeForm()` works inside the event listener, just as it would outside the event listener.

If you need further evidence of the problem being solved here, remove `.bind(this)` once you have the code working: Without this code, `this.serializeForm()` will attempt to access a function called `serializeForm` on the `window` object, which will be `undefined`.

Once the object has been extracted from the form, you use simple string concatenation to create a `tr` element populated with data. String concatenation such as this is somewhat error prone, so you will find a better solution to this functionality in the next lesson.

Once the HTML has been constructed, it is simply added as the last child of `tbody` using the `append` function.

Once you have a working example, you will add two additional lines to the end of the event listener to:

➤ Clear the form of all values (thereby leaving it ready to add a new contact).

➤ Hide the input section of the page.

This can be achieved with the following two lines:

```
    $(screen).find('form :input[name]').val('');
    $(screen).find('#contactDetails').hide();
```

Notice that the second line simply uses the helper method `hide`, rather than setting the display property to `none`: This achieves the same result, but is more concise.

DELEGATED EVENT LISTENERS

You may have noticed a couple of problems with the save functionality. For a start, the company name does not display properly (I will address this later in the book). Second, if you add notes and hover over the last contacted field, the popup does not display because the event listeners you added for the `time` elements were added when the DOM loaded, and this new `time` element did not exist at that point.

One solution to this is to add relevant event listeners after you add new elements to the DOM. This is an error-prone approach, however. A better solution is to use delegated events.

With a delegated event, you select an element you know is in the DOM when the page loads (such as the tbody element), and bind an event listener to any of its descendants (such as time elements). The great thing about delegated events is that the descendants do not need to exist when the event listener is registered; any newly added descendants will automatically be bound to the relevant event listener.

You can therefore rewrite this block of code from earlier in the book using jQuery delegated events:

```
var timeElements = document.getElementsByTagName('time');
for (var i = 0; i < timeElements.length; i++) {
    timeElements[i].addEventListener("mouseenter", function(event) {
        event.target.nextElementSibling.style.display = 'block';
    });
    timeElements[i].addEventListener("mouseleave", function(event) {
        event.target.nextElementSibling.style.display = 'none';
    });
}
```

You can use the jQuery on method to add a delegated event listener to a particular sub-tree of the DOM. The on method accepts the following parameters:

➤ A space-separated list of events to listen for

➤ A selector to find the descendants that will generate the events

➤ The function to execute when the event occurs

Replace the preceding code with the following:

```
$(screen).find('tbody').on("mouseenter mouseleave", "td > time",
    function(evt) {
        if (evt.type === "mouseenter") {
            $(evt.target).siblings('.overlay').show();
        } else {
            $(evt.target).siblings('.overlay').hide();
        }
    }
);
```

Notice in this case that you register a single event listener and then determine from the event object which type of event has occurred. You then use the show and hide methods to dictate whether the popup is displayed or hidden.

If you now reload the page, first ensure that the popup functionality works for existing rows. If you now add a new contact, and save it along with a date and notes, the popup will display when the user hovers over it, just like it did for rows in the table when the page loaded.

The events you have looked at in the last two sections have dealt with mouse-based events. The other most common mouse-based events that can be listened for are:

➤ dblclick: Similar to click, but fires only if the same element is clicked twice in quick succession

➤ mousedown: Fires when the user presses the mouse button down

➤   `mouseup`: Fires when the user releases the mouse button

➤   `mousemove`: Fires any time the mouse moves. Naturally, this event is fired often so it is important not to perform intensive processing every time this event fires.

FORM EVENTS

The previous sections have focused on mouse events. The other main categories of event are form events and keyboard events. These two categories are inherently linked because the focus for keyboard events will be form elements. Thus, you will group these two categories of event together.

In this section, you will create an event listener that displays how many characters the user has typed into a `textarea`. To begin, you will add a new `span` element next to the `textarea` in the form:

```
<div class="formRow">
    <label for="notes">Notes</label>
    <textarea cols="40" rows="6" name="notes" class="validated" maxlength="1000">
</textarea>
    <span class="textCount"></span>
</div>
```

The span will be updated to include a character count every time the user types a character into the `textarea`.

Once this is in place, the following can be added to the `init` method in `contacts.js`:

```
$(screen).find('textarea').keyup(function(evt) {
    if ($(evt.target).siblings('.textCount')) {
        var characters = $(evt.target).val().length;
        $(evt.target).siblings('.textCount').text(characters + ' characters');
    }
});
```

This code starts by finding any `textareas` in the form, and then uses the `keyup` method to add an event listener whenever the user releases a keyboard key while typing in the `textarea`. When this occurs, you will determine if the `textarea` has a sibling `span` element for recording text counts. If it does, you will determine the number of characters currently typed into the field and update the text on the `span` accordingly.

If you now reload the web page and start typing into the `textarea`, you should see a text count updating in real time, as shown in Figure 19-1.

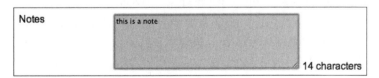

Notes this is a note

14 characters

FIGURE 19-1

The great thing about this solution is that it is generic. You can enable this functionality for any future `textareas` by adding the relevant `span` as its sibling.

The other most useful form and keyboard events are as follows:

➤ `change`: This event is called whenever the value in a form field changes. This can be applied to any form input field, but in the case of text-based input fields, the event only fires once the user leaves the field. This is the reason you could not use `change` in the example earlier in this section.

➤ `focus`: This event is invoked when an input field receives focus.

➤ `keydown`: This is essentially the same as `keyup`, but is fired as soon as the key is pressed.

➤ `keypress`: This event is not covered by official documentation so it can vary from browser to browser. As a general rule, this is equivalent to `keydown`, but only fires if the key pressed would produce a visual character; for example, it would not be fired if the Shift key were pressed.

SCREEN EVENTS

The final major category of event is screen events. The most useful screen event is `ready`. The JavaScript examples so far have placed JavaScript at the end of the web page to make sure the DOM has loaded before element selection begins.

The `ready` event provides a safer way to ensure that the DOM has fully loaded before you attempt to manipulate it. It is possible to register a `ready` event listener by enclosing the browser's `document` object in a jQuery selector and invoking the `ready` method on it. For instance, you could change the code in `contacts.html` as follows:

```
$(document).ready(function(evt) {
    var mainElement = document.getElementById('contactScreen');
    var screen = contactsScreen(mainElement);
    screen.init();
});
```

A companion function for `ready` is `load`. This is similar, but only executes when all the resources (such as JavaScript source files, images, and CSS files) have finished loading.

> **NOTE** *Notice that I have also renamed the variable* `screen` *rather than* `appScreen`. *You cannot name a global variable* `screen` *because JavaScript already contains a global variable with this name, but it is possible in this case because the scope of the variable is the function passed to* `ready`.

The other main browser-based event is the `resize` event. This fires whenever the user resizes the window. This event should be bound to the browser's `window` object:

```
$(window).resize(function(evt) {
```

ANIMATION

Earlier in this lesson, you looked at how the `hide` and `show` functions could be used instead of changing the display type of an element. As it happens, jQuery supports many other helpers for displaying and hiding elements, complete with animated effects. These are a great way to make the web page feel more alive to users.

In order to see how simple this can be, change the event listener for hiding and showing the `notes` popup as follows:

```
if (evt.type === "mouseenter") {
    $(evt.target).siblings('.overlay').slideDown();
} else {
    $(evt.target).siblings('.overlay').slideUp();
}
```

If you reload the web page and hover over a `time` element, you will notice that the popup is displayed as though it is being dragged down like a projector screen. Likewise, when it is hidden, it is as though the projector screen has been released again.

It is possible to control how long the entire effect takes by providing a time in milliseconds as the first parameter to these functions: The default is 400 milliseconds (0.4 of a second). It is also possible to control many other aspects of the animation process. These features will not be discussed in this book, but you can easily learn more from the jQuery website.

jQuery also supports other effects. For instance the `fadeIn` and `fadeOut` functions can be used to animate the opacity of an element as it is displayed or hidden. This has a similar effect to approaching an object through a thick fog: It starts out pale and blurry and eventually becomes fully opaque.

TRY IT

In this Try It, you will use event listeners to add new functionality to the table. When the user hovers over any row, you will change it so that the background color becomes blue and the foreground color becomes white. This will help users read across the row if they are phoning or emailing the contact. The finished result will look like Figure 19-2 when the user hovers over a row in the table.

Sales leads				
Contact name	Phone number	Email address	Company name	Last contacted
William Smith	555-642-7371	william@testing.com	ACME Industries	2014-10-21
Bob Morris	555-999-2991	bob@testing.com	ABC Corp	2014-09-12
				2 contacts displayed

FIGURE 19-2

Lesson Requirements

You will need the CRM web application, and you will need to have loaded the jQuery library using one of the techniques outlined earlier in this section of the book.

In order to work through this example, you might want to start with a simple event listener and place a breakpoint to allow you to debug code when the event is fired. This will allow you to try out code in the context of an event. Once you have working code, you can copy it into the JavaScript file.

Step-by-Step

1. As with all the event listeners, you will add code to the init method in contacts.js.

2. Because new rows can be added to the table after the DOM has loaded, the event listener will need to be a delegated event listener. Therefore, start by selecting the tbody element, and use the on method to register an event listener.

3. The two events that you should listen for are mouseenter and mouseleave. Add these as the first parameter to on.

4. The second parameter to on is the element that will generate the event. Because you want to be able to hover over any element in the row, add tr as the selector.

5. Add a function as the third parameter to on, and have this accept a single parameter called evt.

6. Within the event listener function, use the event object passed as the parameter to determine the event that has occurred. This can be extracted from the type property of the event.

7. If the event is a mouseenter event, you need to change two styles on the target of the event. This can be achieved using the css method on the target of the event, as you saw earlier in this lesson:

   ➤ Change the color property to white.

   ➤ Change the background property to #3056A0.

8. If the event is a mouseleave event, you want to clear the inline styles added. This can be achieved by using the removeAttr method to remove the style attribute.

9. If you reload the web page now and try this out, you will notice a problem. Only a single cell will be shaded when the user hovers over it, not the entire row.

10. In order to determine the cause of this problem, set a breakpoint on the first line of the event listener.

    With the breakpoint in place, hover over a cell. Once the breakpoint is hit, move to the Console tab and type evt.target. This will confirm that the target of the event is actually a td element rather than the tr element that the event listener was registered with. This is because the td element is the specific element the user was hovering over when the event occurred.

11. In order to circumvent this problem, you can use the closest traversal operation to find the closest tr element to the element that fired the event, and modify the style of this element.

    There is one remaining problem with this solution. Because of CSS inheritance, the color of the text in the overlay is also white now, meaning it cannot clearly be read. This is a perfect opportunity to use the `!important` attribute in CSS so add the following to the `.overlay` rule in `contacts.css`:

```
color: #333333 !important;
```

Your finished version of the code should look like this:

```
$(screen).find('tbody').on("mouseenter mouseleave", "tr", function(evt) {
    if (evt.type === "mouseenter") {
        $(evt.target).closest('tr').css('color', 'white');
        $(evt.target).closest('tr').css('background', '#3056A0');
    } else {
        $(evt.target).closest('tr').removeAttr('style');
    }
});
```

> **REFERENCE** *Please go to the book's website at* www.wrox.com/go/html5jsj-query24hr *to view the video for Lesson 19, as well as download the code and resources for this lesson.*

20

Data Attributes and Templates

In this lesson, you will look at two additional HTML5 features:

➤ **Data attributes:** These allow you to define your own attributes on any element and thus bind data directly to the element. This has a number of useful purposes, as you will see shortly.

➤ Templates: Templates are a relatively new HTML5 feature. They allow a document fragment to be created independently of the DOM itself. The document fragment can then be programmatically filled with data and added to the DOM. This will provide an alternative approach to the complex string concatenation used in the previous lesson.

Although this lesson introduces these two technologies together, there is no fundamental connection between them.

TEMPLATE TAG

In the previous lesson, you used string concatenation to create a new row in the contacts table. As mentioned at the time, this is a problematic approach because it is very easy to make a mistake with the String concatenation.

A preferable approach to string concatenation is to define the structure of the HTML using regular tags but leave placeholders for the actual data. When you need to create a row, you could simply add data to this structure, and add it to the DOM. The `template` tag has been added to HTML5 to support this exact approach.

> **NOTE** *The template tag is not currently supported in Internet Explorer; thus, it is best to confirm support across relevant browsers before using it. There are, however, many other templating libraries available for JavaScript, and many have more advanced features than the* `template` *tag introduced in this lesson.*

In order to start using the `template` tag, you simply add it anywhere in the HTML and include the relevant HTML structure inside it. You also typically provide an `id` for the template so you can locate it. Therefore, start by adding the following immediately before the closing `main` tag:

```
<template id="contactRow">
    <td></td>
    <td></td>
    <td></td>
    <td></td>
    <td><time></time>
    <div class="overlay"></div></td>
</template>
```

If you reload the web page, you will notice that this HTML does not display within the browser. In addition, although it is possible to select the template element using DOM and jQuery selectors, it is not possible to select its children. For instance:

```
$('#contactRow td')
[]
```

When you use the template, you need to populate it with the appropriate data. Clearly, you could simply set the contact name in the first child, the phone number in the second child, and so on.

Where possible, it is best to find generic solutions to common problems. Therefore, you will write an algorithm that can take any template and any object, and will populate the template with the data in the object based on a set of conventions.

In order to achieve this, you will use another technology called *data attributes*.

DATA ATTRIBUTES

In order to create the generic algorithm mentioned in the previous section, you need some way of marking tags in the template with the property names from the object that should be used to populate them.

There are several ways you could do this. For instance, if a `td` element should be populated with the data in the `contactName` property, you could specify the `td` as follows:

```
<td id="contactName"></td>
```

The obvious problem with this approach is that IDs must be unique within the document, and therefore you would need to make sure that the property names in your objects never conflicted with the IDs of elements in the document.

An alternative approach is to specify the property name as a class:

```
<td class="contactName"></td>
```

There is nothing inherently wrong with using class names for non-CSS purposes; an obvious problem with this solution, however, is that your CSS may contain a class that matches one of the properties.

Another approach that has been used historically is to use attributes that are supported by the specification but are not used by the browser. The most common attribute used for this purpose is `rel`:

```
<td rel="contactName"></td>
```

The problem with this approach is that, although browsers do not use this attribute, the `rel` attribute does have meaning, and is used by search engines when used on a tags.

As you can see, historically, there has not been a good way of linking program-specific data to an element. HTML5 offers a much better way to solve this problem. It is possible to specify your own attributes on any element, provided they are prefixed with `data-`. You can see this in the following example:

```
<template id="contactRow">
    <td data-property-name="contactName"></td>
    <td data-property-name="phoneNumber"></td>
    <td data-property-name="emailAddress"></td>
    <td data-property-name="companyName"></td>
    <td><time data-property-name="lastContacted"></time>
    <div data-property-name="notes" class="overlay"></div></td>
</template>
```

Data attributes should follow the naming conventions shown here, specifically:

➤ They must start with `data-`.

➤ They should contain only lowercase characters.

➤ They should use hyphens to separate logical words.

You will look at why these conventions are important shortly.

Just like any attribute, data attributes can be assigned values. In this case, the value has been defined as the property name from the object that should be used to populate the text of the element.

Once elements have been logically associated with property names, you can write a function that binds the property values in the object to a document fragment. Add the following as a global function within `contacts.js`:

```
function bind(template, obj) {
    $.each(template.find('[data-property-name]'), function(indx, val) {
        var field = $(val).data().propertyName;
        if (obj[field]) {
            $(val).text(obj[field]);
        }
    });
    return template;
}
```

This may look complex, but if you walk through it line-by-line it is reasonably straightforward. You start by iterating through every element that has a `data-property-name` attribute using the jQuery each helper.

As shown in earlier lessons, you provide a callback function to `each`. Because this passes the index and value of each element to the function provided, the parameter `val` will represent an element with the `data-property-name` attribute.

On the next line, you extract the value of the `data-property-name` attribute. You may expect that this line would read:

```
var field = $(val).attr('data-property-name');
```

This would be valid, but as you can see, calling the `data` method on an element provides access to all the data attributes as properties on an object. This also automatically converts the names from the conventions used on attributes to the convention used for property names, so:

```
data-property-name
```

becomes:

```
propertyName
```

On the next line, you check to see whether the object you were passed has a property with this name:

```
if (obj[field]) {
```

Notice that you use the square bracket notation here for accessing the property. If the property does exist, you simply set its value as the text of the element; if not, you do nothing.

The advantage of this code is that it does not need to know anything about the document fragment or the object it has been passed; it only needs to know the convention you are using. Property names in the object match data attributes on elements. This is known as "programming by convention," and is a very efficient mechanism for writing generic, reusable code.

USING THE TEMPLATE

Now that you have a template, and a function for binding data to a template, you need to put it all together. Start by adding a new method called `save` to the object returned in `contacts.js`. Place it between the `init` and `serializeForm` methods:

```
save: function(evt) {
    if ($(evt.target).parents('form')[0].checkValidity()) {
        var fragment = $(screen).find('#contactRow')[0].content.cloneNode(true);
        var row = $('<tr>').append(fragment);
        var contact = this.serializeForm();
        row = bind(row, contact);
        $(screen).find('table tbody').append(row);
        $(screen).find('form :input').val('')
        $(screen).find('#contactDetails').hide();
    }
},
```

This method will replace the functionality in the submit button click listener; therefore, you start by checking the validity of the form. Next, you find the `template` element with the ID `contactRow`. Once you find this, you convert it to a native DOM object by accessing it as the first element in the array returned.

If you access the `content` of a template directly in the DOM, you will notice that the value returned is a document-fragment, as you can see in Figure 20-1.

```
> document.getElementById('contactRow').content
  ▼#document-fragment
     <td data-property-name="contactName"></td>
     <td data-property-name="phoneNumber"></td>
     <td data-property-name="emailAddress"></td>
     <td data-property-name="companyName"></td>
   ▶ <td>…</td>
> |
```

FIGURE 20-1

Unlike other nodes in the DOM, a document fragment does not have a parent, and therefore it is not part of the DOM.

Your goal is to create a DOM node that contains the elements represented by the template; therefore, you access the content of the template using its content property and clone (create a copy of it) using the cloneNode method. The true value passed to the cloneNode method indicates you also want to clone any children elements.

Once you have a copy of the document fragment, you append it to a tr element. Ideally, you would have worked directly with the document-fragment, but unless you add it to another node, the content of the document fragment cannot be queried by jQuery.

> **NOTE** *When you write code such as $('<tr>'), you are creating jQuery-specific document fragments (it does not have a parent, and is not part of the DOM). Therefore, think of the preceding approach as adding an HTML5 document fragment to a jQuery document fragment.*

Once the object and the template are obtained, you simply call the bind function to populate the template:

```
row = bind(row, contact);
```

You can now change the submit button click event listener as follows:

```
$(screen).find('form input[type="submit"]').click(
    function(evt) {
        evt.preventDefault();
        this.save(evt);
    }.bind(this)
);
```

Notice how you have broken the functionality in the save operation down to a number of distinct components, each with its own generic, and reusable, implementation:

➤ Serializing the object from the data in the form

➤ Providing a template for a new row in the table

➤ Binding an object to a template

One of the keys to writing a large, maintainable web application is to write self-contained functions or methods that each perform a specific task, but do so in a generic manner.

Once you have self-contained functions, you can enhance them over time. For instance, the current implementation of bind does not add the datatime attribute to time elements; you can easily rectify this as follows:

```
function bind(template, obj) {
    $.each(template.find('[data-property-name]'), function(indx, val) {
        var field = $(val).data().propertyName;
        if (obj[field]) {
            $(val).text(obj[field]);
            if ($(val).is('time')) {
                $(val).attr('datetime', obj[field]);
            }
        }
    });
    return template;
}
```

TRY IT

In this Try It, you will look at how you can modify the template created in this lesson to allow you to delete rows from the table. Each row in the table will have a delete button, and clicking this will remove the row from the table.

Lesson Requirements

You will need the CRM web application from Lesson 19. This lesson can then be completed in a text editor and tested in Chrome.

Step-by-Step

1. Start by removing the tr elements from the tbody in contacts.html. From now on, you will not have any rows when the screen initially loads. Later in the book, you will save contacts, but for now you will need to create contacts each time the screen loads.

2. Add an additional th column to the thead element with the text "Actions," and set the td element in tfoot to span six columns. The table should now look like this:

```
<table>
    <thead>
        <th>Contact name</th>
        <th>Phone number</th>
        <th>Email address</th>
        <th>Company name</th>
        <th>Last contacted</th>
        <th>Actions</th>
    </thead>
    <tfoot>
        <tr>
            <td colspan="6">2 contacts displayed</td>
        </tr>
    </tfoot>
    <tbody>
    </tbody>
    <caption>Sales leads</caption>
</table>
```

3.   Change the `template` to include a new `td` element at the end. The `td` element will contain a hyperlink for deleting rows from the table. This hyperlink will in turn contain a data attribute describing its role:

```
<td><a href="#" data-delete-button>Delete</a></td>
```

4.   Add an event listener within the `init` method that fires when the user clicks an element with the attribute `data-delete-button`. Because these elements will not be in the DOM when the screen loads, you will need to use the `on` method, as described in the previous lesson. My version can be found at the end of this section.

5.   Within the event listener, start by preventing the default behavior of a hyperlink (to load a new page). The event listener should call a method called `delete` (which you will write in the next step) on the object, and pass it the event.

6.   Add a new method to the main object in `contacts.js` called `delete`. This should accept a parameter called `evt`, which will be the event object.

7.   Use the target of the event, and find its closest parent that is a `tr` element. Once this is located, use the `remove` method to remove it from the DOM.

8.   Add a new method to the object called `updateTableCount`. This method should check how many rows are in the table and then update the `tfoot` cell to display a count, for instance "3 contacts displayed." Once this is written, it should be called after the `save` or `remove` method completes.

My event listener looked like this:

```
$(screen).on("click", "[data-delete-button]",
    function(evt) {
        evt.preventDefault();
        this.delete(evt);
    }.bind(this)
);
```

And my delete method looked like this:

```
delete: function(evt) {
    $(evt.target).parents('tr').remove();
},
```

My version of `updateTableCount` looked like this:

```
updateTableCount: function(evt) {
    var rows = $(screen).find('table tbody tr');
    $(screen).find('table tfoot td').text(rows.length + ' contacts
displayed');
},
```

> **REFERENCE** *Please go to the book's website at* www.wrox.com/go/html5jsj-query24hr *to view the video for Lesson 20, as well as download the code and resources for this lesson.*

21

jQuery Plugins

In the lessons covered so far in this section, you have learned most of what you need to know to start writing dynamic web applications. This lesson will cover one final subject that can enhance dynamic web applications: jQuery plugins.

One of the reasons jQuery is so popular is that it is very easy to extend with plugins. As a result, a huge number of jQuery plugins are freely available, and these can often be used as an alternative to writing your own code.

In this lesson, you will briefly look at one of the most popular jQuery plugins, called jQuery UI. This plugin provides a set of user interface components, such as date pickers and dialog boxes, and is used extensively, including on some of the Internet's most popular websites.

It is also possible to write your own jQuery plugins. A typical jQuery plugin uses a jQuery selector to identify a set of elements, and then performs an operation on these elements, returning the modified elements as a result.

Although it is obviously possible to modify elements without encapsulating the code in a jQuery plugin, writing plugins provides a convenient mechanism for packaging code.

JQUERY UI

jQuery UI is probably the most widely used jQuery plugin. This plugin provides a variety of user interface components, all of which work seamlessly across all the most common browsers. jQuery UI can therefore be used to provide polyfills for native HTML5 components, such as date pickers and progress bars.

jQuery UI can be downloaded from `http://jqueryui.com`. This website also contains a set of live demos for all the components included in the plugin, along with comprehensive documentation on all components.

Many of the UI components provided by jQueryUI mirror equivalents in HTML5, including the following:

➤ A **date-picker component**

➤ A **progress bar:** Implements the same basic functionality as the HTML5 progress bar, but works in all modern browsers.

➤ A **slider:** Implements the same basic functionality as the HTML5 `range` input field, although again, in a cross-browser manner, and with additional configuration options.

➤ A **spinner component:** Implements the same functionality seen on `number` input fields in Chrome.

➤ **Drag and drop components:** These include more advanced features not supported by HTML5, such as the ability to resize components, and the ability to reposition elements onscreen without specifically dropping them on other elements.

jQuery UI also contains more advanced widgets not currently found in HTML5, including the following:

➤ A **tab component:** Allows an interface to provide a set of tabs to the user.

➤ A **dialog widget:** Provides an implementation of all common varieties of dialog box, such as confirmation, warning, and error dialogs.

➤ An **accordion component:** Allows panels to be expanded and collapsed. This has some similarity to the summary/detail tags seen earlier in the book, but allows for many summary/detail blocks to work together, and assumes one detail block will always be expanded. This component is named after its passing resemblance to an accordion musical instrument.

A version of jQuery UI is included with the Lesson 21 resources on the book's website. Because jQuery UI is a large library, it is possible to tailor the download to the specific components needed, and it is also possible to customize the themes of the components (such as colors and fonts) when downloading the library. The version provided contains all components, and the default theme.

The jQuery UI resources comprise the following:

➤ `jquery-ui.js`: Contains all the JavaScript code implementing the various components.

➤ `jquery-ui.css`: Contains the CSS used for styling the components.

➤ An `images` folder: Contains all the images needed by the components. For instance, the date-picker uses arrows for moving between months: These are represented by images.

Copy all these resources to the folder containing `contacts.html`.

In this section, you will change the `date` input field in `contacts.html` to use the jQuery UI implementation, rather than the native HTML5 implementation.

To begin, the jQuery UI JavaScript file and CSS file must be imported into the `head` of the web page. It is essential that the JavaScript file is imported after the main jQuery file because jQuery UI extends the capabilities of jQuery:

```
<link rel="stylesheet" type="text/css" href="jquery-ui.css">
<script src="jquery-ui.js"></script>
```

Next, change the `lastContacted` input field from a date-based field to a text-based field:

```
<input name="lastContacted" type="text" class="validated"/>
```

Once this is done, all that is required to enable the jQuery UI date-picker on the field is to execute the following code:

```
$('[name="lastContacted"]').datepicker();
```

Notice that this begins by selecting an element with a regular jQuery selector, and then calls a `datepicker` method on the result. The `datepicker` method was provided by the jQuery UI library, but notice that it is available on a regular jQuery selection.

Add this code to the `script` block at the bottom of `contacts.html`.

If you now open the web page and click in the `lastContacted` field, a date-picker will be displayed, as you can see in Figure 21-1.

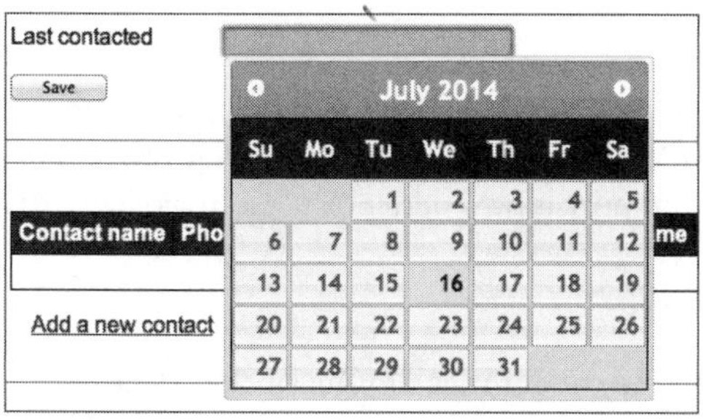

FIGURE 21-1

All jQuery UI components follow this same model: An element (or set of elements) is selected from the DOM and converted into a dynamic component using a method provided by jQuery UI.

jQuery UI components accept a variety of configuration parameters, and in many ways are more flexible than their HTML5 counterparts. Because of the large number of potential parameters (the date-picker itself supports more than 50 different configuration parameters), and the fact that all of these parameters are optional, any parameters required are provided within an object with properties representing the required options.

For instance, the following sets the maximum date the date-picker will accept to today (0 means zero days from today), and the minimum date to 6 months ago (-6m):

```
$('[name="lastContacted"]').datepicker({
    minDate: "-6m",
    maxDate: 0
});
```

With these parameters set, any dates outside this range will be disabled.

The jQuery UI website contains excellent documentation on all the options available for this component, and all the other components supported by jQuery UI.

WRITING A PLUGIN

You will now switch from using plugins developed by other programmers, to writing your own plugins. The basic premise of a jQuery plugin is that it is passed a selection of elements; it then performs an operation on these elements and (usually) returns the modified elements.

In this section, you will write a plugin that accepts time elements with a datetime attribute, and changes the content of the element to contain a more readable representation of the date. Once this is implemented, you will be able to select time elements and transform them to display the date as you see in Figure 21-2.

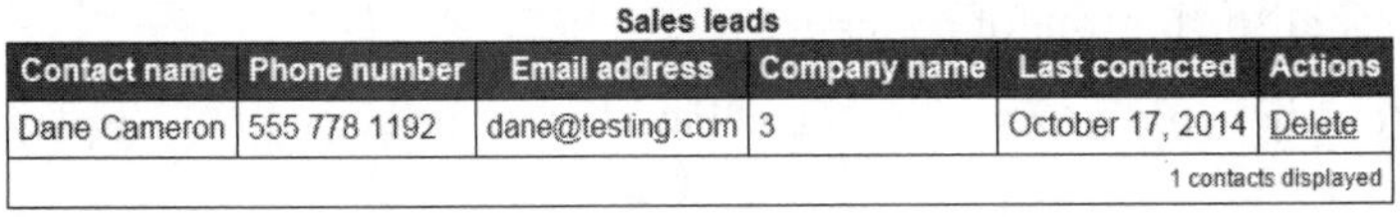

Contact name	Phone number	Email address	Company name	Last contacted	Actions
Dane Cameron	555 778 1192	dane@testing.com	3	October 17, 2014	Delete

Sales leads

1 contacts displayed

FIGURE 21-2

Because plugins should be reusable across websites, I recommend that you add them to a new JavaScript file. Start by creating an empty JavaScript file called jquery-time.js. Place this in the same directory as the other project resources, and import it into contacts.js (make sure the import occurs after the main jQuery library).

```
<script src="jquery-time.js"></script>
```

In order to add a plugin to jQuery, you need to extend the capabilities of jQuery. Specifically, you need to extend an object that can be accessed via jQuery.fn, and add a new method to it. The boilerplate code for adding a plugin to jQuery therefore looks like this:

```
(function($) {
    $.fn.extend({
        setTime: function() {
            return this;
        },
    });
})(jQuery);
```

This code uses a technique you have not seen previously: It declares an anonymous function that accepts a single parameter (represented by $). The code then immediately calls this function (on the last line) and passes it the jQuery function (which is the same function you have been accessing through its $ alias).

This is a great technique when you only want a function to be executed a single time when the web page loads: Because this is an anonymous function, and is not referred to by any variables, it can never be executed again.

Once you have a reference to fn, you call a method on it called extend, and pass this an object. This object will contain definitions of the methods you wish to add to jQuery: In this case, a single method will be added called setTime.

If you reload the web page, you can use this plugin immediately. Figure 21-3 demonstrates an example where you select a time element from the web page and then call setTime on the selection:

```
Q  Elements  Network  Sources  Timeline  Profiles  Resources  Audits  Console
⃠  ▽   <top frame> ▼
> $('time').setTime()
  [<time data-property-name="lastContacted" datetime="07/17/2014">07/17/2014</time>]
> |
```

FIGURE 21-3

As you can see, the `setTime` method returns the selection it is passed. This is due to the fact that the method returned `this`. The `this` variable can be used inside a plugin to extract the elements selected, but can also be returned at the end to allow chaining. For example, it is possible to write code such as the following:

```
> $('time').setTime().parent()
```

With the plugin skeleton in place, you can start writing the functionality of the plugin. JavaScript does not contain a library for formatting dates, although there are numerous open-source libraries available. You will therefore write your own rudimentary code for date formatting:

```
(function($) {
    $.fn.extend({
        setTime: function() {
            months = ['January','February', 'March', 'April', 'May', 'June',
                'July','August','September','October','November', 'December'];
            $.each(this, function(indx, val) {
                if ($(val).attr('datetime')) {
                    var date = new Date($(val).attr('datetime'));
                    var display = months[date.getMonth()] + ' ';
                    display += date.getDate() + ', ';
                    display += date.getFullYear();
                    $(val).text(display);
                }
            });
            return this;
        },
    });
})(jQuery);
```

JavaScript represents the months of the year with the numbers 0–11, so you begin by creating an array that allows you to place a textual representation of each month in an array at its relevant index.

Next, you use the jQuery `each` method to iterate through the selected elements. The method then checks to see whether the element has a `datetime` attribute: This plugin will be compatible with elements containing the `datetime` attribute, and therefore will not do anything if this attribute is missing.

Because the `datetime` attribute contains an ISO-compliant representation of a date, it can be converted into a JavaScript `Date` object using its constructor. Once a `Date` object is created, its component parts (month, day, year) can be accessed through its methods.

The rest of this method uses simple string concatenation to create a textual representation of a date, using the `months` array to find the textual representation of the month, and extracting the other important date components with the relevant methods. Once a textual representation of a date is created, it is set on the element using the `text` method.

If you load the screen, and ensure the table contains a row with a date in it, you can convert this into a more readable representation with the following call:

```
> $('time').setTime();
```

It is also possible to pass parameters to the plugin. As with jQuery UI, it is customary to pass an object with relevant parameters and provide defaults for all parameters. For instance, you may want the user to specify either a short or long form of the date: A short form will only print the first three characters of the month and the last two numbers in the year.

In the following example, the `params` object can contain a `style` property: If this has a value of `short`, the month and year will be truncated.

```
(function($) {
    $.fn.extend({
        setTime: function(params) {
            months = ['January','February', 'March', 'April', 'May', 'June',
                'July','August','September','October','November', 'December'];
            $.each(this, function(indx, val) {
                if ($(val).attr('datetime')) {
                    var date = new Date($(val).attr('datetime'));
                    var m = months[date.getMonth()];
                    if (params && params.style === 'short') {
                        m = m.substr(0, 3);
                        var display = m + ' ';
                        display += date.getDate() + ', ';
                        display += (date.getFullYear() % 100);
                    } else {
                        var display = m + ' ';
                        display += date.getDate() + ', ';
                        display += date.getFullYear();
                    }
                    $(val).text(display);
                }
            });
            return this;
        },
    });
}) (jQuery);
```

This can then be called as follows to use the `short` representation:

```
$('time').setTime({'style':'short'})
```

The great thing about jQuery plugins is that they are completely reusable on other web pages. Each plugin performs its own specific operation, and provided it is passed elements it is compatible with, it does not need to know anything else about the web page.

You want to ensure that this plugin is called automatically whenever a new row is added to the table so change the `save` method to invoke it as follows (the remainder of this function has been excluded for brevity):

```
row = bind(row, contact);
$(row).find('time').setTime();
$(screen).find('table tbody').append(row);
```

TRY IT

In this Try It, you will use one more feature in the jQuery UI library and write a new plugin of our own.

Lesson Requirements

You will need the CRM web application from Lesson 20, but it is also assumed you have been following this lesson, and have imported the jQuery UI resources. If not, you need to do this before continuing with the Try It. This lesson can then be completed in a text editor and tested in Chrome.

Step-by-Step

In addition to providing a set of components, jQuery UI contains a set of more advanced animation effects than are found in jQuery itself. You will therefore use one of these effects when displaying the contacts form.

1. The `init` method in `contacts.js` adds an event listener for displaying the form that uses the following code:

   ```
   document.getElementById('contactDetails').style.display = 'block';
   ```

   This uses the native DOM API: In order to use a jQuery UI effect, change this as follows:

   ```
   $(screen).find('#contactDetails').toggle( "blind" );
   ```

2. Load the web page, and click to add a contact. The form should slide down slowly from the top.

3. In order to use jQuery UI effectively, you need to be able to access its documentation. Therefore, open `http://api.jqueryui.com/` in your web browser and click the Effects category on the left-hand side. You should be able to find documentation on the `blind` effect and learn about its various options.

4. The form section is hidden with the following code in the `save` method:

   ```
   $(screen).find('#contactDetails').hide();
   ```

   This can be replaced with the exact same code used in step 1: Because the `toggle` method is being used, a visible element will be automatically hidden.

You will now change the code that populates the contact count in the table footer to operate as a jQuery plugin.

1. Start by creating a new plugin called `jquery-tables.js` and add the same boilerplate code from `jquery-time.js` to this.

2. Import the new plugin into `contacts.html`.

3. Add a method to the plugin called `updateFooter`. This should accept a single parameter called `params`.

4. This plugin will operate on tables that contain `tfoot` and `tbody` children. Therefore, use the `each` method to iterate through the selection provided to the plugin, and check that each element has these child elements before processing the element further.

5. Within the `if` statement, start by counting how many `tr` elements are in the `tbody`. Remember that the `length` property can be used for ascertaining this. Store the number in a local variable.

6. Update the `td` element in the `tfoot` to contain the text "X rows in table," where X is the count retrieved in Step 5.

    You should now be able to update the footer by invoking the plugin on the table, as shown in Figure 21-4.

```
Q  Elements  Network  Sources  Timeline  Profiles  Resources  Audits │ Console │
⊘  ▽  <top frame> ▼
>  $('table').updateFooter()
   [▶<table>…</table>,  ▶<table class="ui-datepicker-calendar">…</table>]
> |
```

FIGURE 21-4

7. The message displayed in the table should be configurable. Therefore, if the `params` object contains a property called `message`, use its value instead of "rows in the table." When writing the code to use this, remember that both the `params` object and the `message` property may be undefined.

8. You can now change the `updateTableCount` method to use this plugin. I have used the following code:

```
$(screen).find('table').updateFooter({'message':' contacts displayed'});
```

    The full version of my plugin looks like this:

```
(function($) {
    $.fn.extend({
        updateFooter : function(params) {
            $.each(this, function(indx, val) {
                if ($(val).find('tbody') && $(val).find('tfoot')) {
                    var count = $(val).find('tbody tr').length;
                    if (params && params.message) {
                        $(val).find('tfoot td').text(count + ' ' + params.
message);
                    } else {
                        $(val).find('tfoot td').text(count + ' rows in the
table');
                    }
                }
            });
            return this;
        },
    });
})(jQuery)
```

> **REFERENCE** *Please go to the book's website at* www.wrox.com/go/html5jsj-query24hr *to view the video for Lesson 21, as well as download the code and resources for this lesson.*

PART III
HTML5 Multimedia

22

HTML5 Audio

The third section of the book will cover many of the multimedia enhancements added in HTML5, beginning with HTML5's audio capabilities.

Audio has been part of the web almost since browsers first appeared but, unlike images that are natively supported by the browser, audio support has always been provided by third-party plugins such as QuickTime. Browser plugins are supported by the HTML `object` tag, and are used to support a wide selection of media types such as audio, video, PDF files, and animations.

There are a number of problems with plugins, however:

➤ They often rely on the user installing a plugin manually, and this can be an inconvenience for users. Additionally, users are typically required to update plugins independently of the browser's update cycle, which can lead to further frustration.

➤ Plugins can effectively do anything they want on the computer running the browser (or at least, anything that the browser could do). This presents a security loophole, and has been exploited on many occasions.

➤ Plugins can cause stability issues in browsers because a bug in a plugin can cause the browser to crash.

➤ Plugins are not standards-based for the most part, and therefore they encourage lock-in to proprietary formats.

In order to counteract these issues, HTML5 supports an `audio` tag (along with a `video` tag, as you will see in the next lesson). The `audio` tag is intended to remove the need for plugins, and has begun to find widespread adoption.

FILE FORMATS

Although HTML5 specifies an `audio` tag, it does not specify an audio format. In fact, it does not even specify a single default format that all browsers are required to support.

As you will see, this is not such a problem for audio because the two most popular formats are well supported, but it is a bigger issue for video.

There are good reasons why there are multiple audio formats. Different formats compress audio in different ways, and these in turn present trade-offs in terms of quality on the one hand, and file size on the other.

Because raw audio files are extremely large, it is almost always necessary to compress them in some manner. This compression fits into two main categories:

➤ **Lossless compression:** This means the size of the audio file is reduced, but no audio quality is lost. This is similar to zipping a text file: The file size is reduced, but the text can be fully recovered at a later date.

➤ **Lossy compression:** This means that some information is lost during the compression process, but the algorithm tries to lose information that will not be noticed by the listener. Most audio formats use lossy compression.

The other main difference between audio formats relates to patents and licensing:

➤ Some audio formats require a license or the payment of royalties to create or stream files using the audio format.

➤ Some audio formats are protected by patents but are available royalty free.

➤ Some audio formats are unencumbered by patents and royalties completely.

This can present problems to browser vendors, particularly in the open source world, and is the reason Firefox historically has not supported some of the most popular file formats.

> **NOTE** *Even in cases where an audio format is unencumbered by patents, it is possible patent holders will assert their rights in the future. The main reason HTML5 could not specify a single default audio or video format was for fear that once the format achieved critical mass, a patent holder would assert their rights over the technology.*

Before looking at the various formats, it is important to distinguish two different types of format. This will become even more important when you start looking at video:

➤ **Container formats:** A container format is used for storing the data, and dictates the file extension. A container format is like an envelope: It contains the audio data along with any other relevant information about the file.

➤ **Codec format:** The codec format specifies the way in which the audio should be encoded and decoded.

In many cases a single container format supports many different codecs. One of the responsibilities of the container format, therefore, is to describe the codec format.

The most common audio codecs are as follows:

➤ **MP3:** This format is in many ways the de-facto standard for music files and uses lossy compression. The degree of loss can be specified when an MP3 file is created by specifying the bit rate per second. Many organizations have claimed patent rights over various aspects of the MP3 format, and a license is required to stream MP3 content on a commercial site.

MP3 is technically a codec, but it does perform many of the functions of a container, and therefore does not need to be placed inside a container format.

➤ **AAC (Advanced Audio Coding):** This format is in many ways the successor to MP3, and generally achieves superior sound quality at equivalent bit rates. It is not necessary to pay royalties to stream AAC content, which makes it an attractive option over MP3.

AAC files can exist as a raw bit stream (typically with the `.aac` extension) but are usually packaged in the MPEG-4 container and given a variety of extensions such as `.mp4`, `.m4p`, and `.m4a`.

➤ **Vorbis:** This is a free audio format that performs lossy compression. This format can technically be stored in any container format but is most commonly stored inside the OGG container format. It is also often used in conjunction with the WebM container format.

➤ **Opus:** This is another free, lossy format that has been standardized by IETF. Like Vorbis, Opus is supported by both the OGG and WebM container formats. As you will see in the next lesson, this is becoming increasingly popular for encoding the audio stream of a video.

Table 22-1 outlines the support of the various formats in the most common browsers.

TABLE 22-1: Audio Support in Browsers

	MP3	ACC (MP4)	VORBIS (OGG, WEBM)	OPUS (OGG, WEBM)
CHROME	Yes	Yes	Yes	Yes
FIREFOX	Partial	Partial	Yes	Yes
INTERNET EXPLORER	Yes	Yes	No	No
OPERA	Yes	Yes	Yes	Yes
SAFARI	Yes	Yes	Supported with the OGG container format	No

The main outlier here is Firefox. Older versions of Firefox did not support the royalty encumbered audio formats, but newer versions of Firefox do support these formats, as long as the underlying operating system provides support (both OS X and Windows do).

AUDIO TAG

The following is a simple example of the `audio` tag in use:

```
<audio controls>
    <source src="test.ogg" type="audio/ogg">
Your browser does not support the audio element.
</audio>
```

The `test.ogg` audio file referred to can be downloaded from the book's website: This contains an audio version of one of the book's screencasts, so feel free to use your own audio file if you would prefer. This file uses the Vorbis codec and the OGG container format.

If you embed this in an HTML page, and open the page in Chrome, it will display as you see in Figure 22-1.

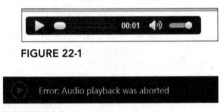

FIGURE 22-1

If, on the other hand, you open this in Internet Explorer, it will display as you see in Figure 22-2

This should not come as a surprise because the OGG format is not supported in Internet Explorer.

FIGURE 22-2

In order to circumvent this, it is possible to specify more than one audio file in a single audio tag. For example:

```
<audio controls>
    <source src="test.ogg" type="audio/ogg">
    <source src="test.mp4" type="audio/mp4">
Your browser does not support the audio element.
</audio>
```

The `test.mp4` file can also be downloaded from the book's website and contains an AAC encoded audio stream inside an MP4 container.

Where multiple formats are provided, the browser will use the first version that it supports.

You will notice that this example specifies the MIME type of each audio file. Specifically, it contains information on the type of the container because the container itself contains information on the codec. Although it is optional, it is recommended that you add the `type` attribute. If it is omitted, the browser will sample each file until it finds one that is in a compatible format, and this will likely cause a delay.

You will notice that when the file is displayed in Chrome, it contains a set of components for controlling playback. This has been provided because the `controls` attribute has been added to the tag. If this was omitted, the controls would not be shown.

It is common to omit the controls if you want the audio to play in the background when the page loads. Although this is a major annoyance to many users, setting the `autoplay` attribute supports it:

```
<audio autoplay>
```

In order to annoy users even further, the `loop` attribute can be added to make the audio track play in a loop indefinitely:

```
<audio autoplay loop>
```

The final attribute supported by the audio tag is `preload`. This can be set to the following:

➤ `auto`: A hint to the browser that it should load the audio when the page loads. This should be used if you are reasonably confident the user will play the file.

➤ `none`: A hint to the browser that it should not begin downloading the file until the user selects to play it.

➤ `metadata`: A hint to the browser that only metadata should be downloaded when the page loads.

CONTROLLING PLAYBACK

Rather than relying on the default browser controls, it is possible to add your own set of controls and interact with the audio track via JavaScript. The audio element is represented in the DOM by an object that supports an assortment of methods, properties, and events.

In this section, you will write your own set of controls to create the interface shown in Figure 22-3.

Play Pause Stop

FIGURE 22-3

This contains the following controls:

➤ A progress bar that shows how far through the track is as it plays

➤ Three hyperlinks for controlling playback

Start by creating the following page and save it as `audio.html`:

```
<!DOCTYPE html>
<html lang="en">
    <head>
        <meta charset="utf-8">
        <script src="jquery-2.1.1.js"></script>
    </head>
    <body>
        <audio id="audioTrack">
            <source src="test.ogg" type="audio/ogg">
            <source src="test.mp3" type="audio/mpeg">
                Your browser does not support the audio element.
        </audio>
        <div id="controls">
            <progress></progress>
            <div id="buttons" style="padding:5px;">
                <a href="#" id="play">Play</a>
                <a href="#" id="pause">Pause</a>
                <a href="#" id="stop">Stop</a>
            </div>
        </div>
    </body>
</html>
```

In order to simplify your interaction with the DOM, you will use jQuery so ensure that the jQuery file is in the same directory as `audio.html`.

Once you confirm that the page looks as expected, you can start adding JavaScript to the page, so create a `script` block immediately before the closing `body` tag.

You will begin by writing the code for updating the progress bar. This will be triggered via a `timeupdate` event generated by the `audio` element. As the track plays, the audio element will generate one of these events approximately every second.

In order to register an event listener for this event, you can use the following code:

```
$("audio").on('timeupdate', function(evt){
});
```

> **NOTE** *Notice that you are omitting the selector as the second element. This is optional, and therefore jQuery will bind the* `'timeupdate'` *event to the audio tag.*

By default, a progress bar starts at 0 and ends at 1 so you need to find:

➤ **How long the audio file is:** This is supported by the `duration` property on the DOM object and returns the time in seconds.

➤ **How much of the audio has been played so far:** This is supported by the `currentTime` property on the DOM object and also returns the time in seconds.

The `target` of the event will be the DOM object representing the audio tag; therefore, the properties can be accessed directly from this. Once you know the value of these two properties, you can simply divide the current position by the total duration (which will be a value between 0 and 1) and update the value of the progress bar.

```
$("audio").on('timeupdate', function(evt){
    var duration = evt.target.duration;
    var current = evt.target.currentTime;
    $('progress').val(current/duration);
});
```

You can now add jQuery click listeners to the three hyperlinks as follows:

```
$('#play').click(function(evt) {
    evt.preventDefault();
    $("audio")[0].play();
});

$('#pause').click(function(evt) {
    evt.preventDefault();
    $("audio")[0].pause();
});

$('#stop').click(function(evt) {
    evt.preventDefault();
    $("audio")[0].currentTime = 0;
    $("audio")[0].pause();
});
```

The play functionality simply invokes the `play` method on the underlying DOM object, and the pause functionality uses the `pause` method. The stop functionality is slightly more complex; in this case, you want to:

➤ Pause the audio if it is playing.

➤ Set the current position back to the start of the audio file. As you can see, the `currentTime` property is writable.

The functionality of these controls will be enhanced in the Try It section, and additional API methods will be introduced in the next lesson, but this example gives you an idea of how simple it is to interact with an audio file.

TRY IT

In this Try It, you will enhance the controls by adding a range input field. The user will be able to use this component to select the position in the audio file that they want to jump to. Figure 22-4 shows the finished version of the audio controls.

Play Pause Stop

FIGURE 22-4

Lesson Requirements

You need to have created the `audio.html` file outlined in this lesson. Alternatively, you can download `audio_pre.html` from the book's website, along with the audio files.

Step-by-Step

1. Start by adding an `input` element with a `type` attribute set to `range`. This should have a `min` attribute set to 0, and a `max` attribute set to 100.

2. You need to add an event listener for detecting changes to the input field. This can be achieved by selecting the `range` input field with jQuery and using the `change` method to specify an event listener.

3. Start by finding the value of the `range` input field using the jQuery `val` method. Store the value in a local variable.

4. Find the duration of the audio file using the `duration` property on the native DOM object. Remember that you need to access this property on the native DOM object, not the jQuery wrapper.

5. Given that the value of the range field is a number between 0 and 100, you can consider this as a percentage. Therefore, work out what position you should set the audio file to in order to represent this percentage. For instance, if the audio file was 90 seconds long, and the user chose a value of 50 with the range control, you would want to set the position to 45 seconds.

6. Once you determine the position the audio file should be set to, set the `currentTime` property to this value. Additionally, call the `play` method on the audio just in case it was not playing when the user interacted with the `range` input field.

My input field looked like this:

```
<input type="range" min="0" max="100" value="0" id="setLocation"/>
```

And my event listener looked like this:

```
$('#setLocation').change(function(evt) {
    var val = $(evt.target).val();
    var duration = $("audio")[0].duration;
    var location = duration*(parseInt(val)/100);
    $("audio")[0].currentTime = location;
    $("audio")[0].play();
});
```

> **REFERENCE** *Please go to the book's website at* www.wrox.com/go/html5jsj-query24hr *to view the video for Lesson 22, as well as download the code and resources for this lesson.*

23

HTML5 Video

Like audio, video has been widely supported in browsers for many years, but has gained increased prominence in recent years with the advent of sites such as YouTube and Netflix. Although the technical capabilities to deliver video over the Internet have been around for a long time, the increased prominence of video is largely a result of faster Internet connections because video tends to be bandwidth intensive.

As with audio, video has been supported in browsers via plugins. Adobe Flash currently dominates the video plugin market, largely due to the overwhelming success of YouTube, but many other plugins also support video, such as QuickTime and Silverlight.

HTML5 provides native support for video inside a browser. The HTML5 video capabilities are essentially the same as the audio capabilities, but obviously the format types for video are quite different from the format types for audio. As with audio, the HTML5 standard does not specify a default video format that all browsers must support.

HTML5 video has received more attention than HTML5 audio, and received an extra boost when Apple declined to support Adobe Flash on phones and tablets, suggesting instead that HTML5 should be used in its place. As you will see later in this lesson, there are still some impediments to the commercialization of HTML5 video, but it continues to gain traction. Even YouTube now supports HTML5 video for much of its content.

FILE FORMATS

Video formats are slightly more complex than audio formats because the container format is required to encapsulate an audio and a video stream. In fact, the same video container may support multiple audio streams to provide audio in multiple languages. Thus, a video file typically consists of the following formats:

➤ A container format such as OGG, WebM, or MP4

➤ A video codec such as H.264 or VP8

➤ An audio codec such as AAC or Vorbis

The following are the main video codecs and their accompanying container and audio formats:

➤ **Theora:** Theora is an open, royalty-free video format using lossy compression. There was a concerted push from some quarters to make Theora the standard HTML5 video format, but because of resistance from some browser vendors, those efforts have largely failed. Theora is typically used with the Vorbis audio format and packaged in the OGG container format.

➤ **H.264:** H.264 is an extremely common video codec, used for everything from Blu-Ray discs, to YouTube, to iTunes. H.264 supports both lossy and lossless compression, but most commonly is used in a lossy mode.

H.264 is a patent-encumbered format, and there has been a certain amount of controversy surrounding the use of H.264 in browsers. Google has suggested support may be removed from Chrome in the future, and Firefox only supports H.264 where it is natively supported by the operating system.

H.264 is typically used with the MP4 container format and the AAC audio format.

➤ **VP8:** VP8 is a competitor of H.264 and produces very similar quality to H.264 for similar sized files. Google acquired the intellectual property behind VP8, but it has released all patents pertaining to the VP8 codec.

VP8 is typically used with the WebM container format and the Vorbis audio format.

➤ **VP9:** VP9 is the successor to VP8. It is also developed by Google, and is also royalty free. Unlike VP8, VP9 is based on open standards. VP9 is likely to grow in prominence due to the resources Google has spent on the project.

VP9 is typically used with the WebM container format and the Opus audio format.

Table 23-1 demonstrates support for these formats across the most popular browsers.

TABLE 23-1: Video support in browsers

	THEORA	H.264	VP8	VP9
Chrome	Yes	Yes	Yes	Yes
Firefox	Yes	Partial	Yes	Yes
Internet Explorer	No	Yes	No	No
Opera	Yes	Yes	Yes	Yes
Safari	No	Yes	No	No

A video tag can be added to a web page as follows:

```
<video width="800" controls>
    <source src="test.m4v" type="video/mp4">
Your browser does not support the video element.
</video>
```

The video file referenced is available on the book's website, and is a 90-second section from one of the screencasts. Naturally, you can use your own video file if you wish.

You will notice that this example contains a `width` attribute for controlling the size of the video element. As with the `image` tag, it is considered acceptable to provide `height` and `width` directly on the tag, rather than through CSS, even though these attributes do affect presentation.

As with images, it is generally advisable to only provide a `height` or a `width`, and if the size is omitted, the size will be based on the size of the encoded video.

As with audio, multiple formats can be specified. In addition, the `type` attribute specifies the container format, just as with the `audio` tag, but it is also possible to specify the codecs supported by each container. For example:

```
<video width="800" controls>
    <source src="test.ogg" type='video/ogg; codecs="theora, vorbis"'>
    <source src="test.m4v" type="video/mp4">
Your browser does not support the video element.
</video>
```

Specifying the codecs can helping the browser make a quicker decision about whether it supports a particular file.

Another interesting attribute supported by the video tag is the `poster`. This allows a static image to be used in place of the video before it begins playing:

```
<video width="800" controls poster="poster.png">
    <source src="test.ogg" type='video/ogg; codecs="theora, vorbis"'>
    <source src="test.m4v" type="video/mp4">
Your browser does not support the video element.
</video>
```

The `poster.png` file is available from the book's website.

Finally, the `video` tag also supports an attribute called `muted`. This allows the video to be played with mute initially enabled, and is useful when video is set to play automatically. The user can then decide to increase the audio as required.

```
<video width="800" controls muted autoplay poster="poster.png">
```

CONTROLLING VOLUME

Just as it is possible to interact with audio files with JavaScript, it is also possible to interact with video files. All of the methods and properties you looked at in the previous lesson are also supported by video. In this lesson, you will look at a number of additional methods supported by both audio and video.

In this lesson, you will also look at an alternative approach for interacting with native DOM objects with jQuery. Up until this point, when you have needed to set properties on native DOM objects, you have accessed them through the array of elements returned by jQuery. For instance:

```
$('table')[0].nodeType
```

This allowed you to access the underlying DOM object. jQuery also supports alternative mechanisms for achieving this without accessing the native DOM object:

```
$('table').prop('nodeType');
```

The second parameter to prop can be used to set the value of the property if required.

Likewise, if you want to invoke a method (or trigger an event) on a jQuery selection, you have used the following approach:

```
$("audio")[0].play();
```

This can also be written with jQuery using the trigger method:

```
$('audio').trigger('play');
```

Again, this allows you to work directly with a jQuery selection rather than obtaining a reference to the native DOM object. The trigger method name can also accept any other parameters needed by the method that will be invoked.

The following web page declares a video element without adding any controls, although it is set to autoplay. It then provides two buttons to increase or decrease volume. The volume property on a video can be set to any value between 0 and 1, and defaults to the value of 1. A value of 0 is equivalent to mute.

```
<!DOCTYPE html>
<html lang="en">
    <head>
        <meta charset="utf-8">
        <script src="jquery-2.1.1.js"></script>
    </head>
    <body>
        <video width="800" autoplay poster="poster.png">
            <source src="test.ogg" type='video/ogg; codecs="theora, vorbis"'>
            <source src="test.m4v" type="video/mp4">
Your browser does not support the video element.
        </video>
        <div id="buttons" style="padding:5px;">
            <a href="#" id="decreaseVolume">Lower volume</a>
            <a href="#" id="increaseVolume">Increase volume</a>
        </div>
        <script>
        $('#decreaseVolume').click(function(evt) {
            evt.preventDefault();
            var currentVolume = parseFloat($('video').prop('volume'));
            $('video').prop('volume', Math.max(0, currentVolume-0.1));
            });
            $('#increaseVolume').click(function(evt) {
            evt.preventDefault();
            var currentVolume = parseFloat($('video').prop('volume'));
            $('video').prop('volume', Math.min(1, currentVolume+0.1));
            });
        </script>
    </body>
</html>
```

Notice that this example is careful to keep the volume in the range 0 to 1 by using the built-in functions `Math.min` and `Math.max`. For instance, if the volume was already 1, and the user asked to increase the volume, the new volume would be set to the minimum of 1 and 1 + 0.1, which would be 1. If the volume was 0.8 and they requested to increase the volume, you would set it to the minimum of 1 and 0.8 + 0.1, which is 0.9. If you attempt to set the volume outside the 0 to 1 range, an error will be generated.

Also notice in this case that I was careful to convert the `volume` property to a number before using it with the + operator. Because attribute values are strings by default, using the + operator with a raw attribute value would perform string concatenation.

CONTROLLING PLAYBACK SPEED

Another common feature with video, which is less common with audio, is the ability to play the track at a faster or slower rate. Slower rates are used for slow motion effects, whereas faster rates are used to allow the user to visually fast-forward to a particular point in the track.

The JavaScript API provides the ability to control the playback via the `playbackRate` property. This has a default value of 1, and therefore setting this to a value of 4 makes the video play at four times its normal rate, whereas setting it to 0.5 makes it play at half its normal rate, and setting it to 0 is the equivalent of pausing playback.

In order to demonstrate this, add two more controls to the screen:

```
<a href="#" id="slowDown">Slow down</a>
<a href="#" id="speedUp">Speed up</a>
```

And add the following JavaScript to modify the `playbackRate` property:

```
$('#slowDown').click(function(evt) {
    evt.preventDefault();
    var currentRate = parseFloat($('video').prop('playbackRate'));
    $('video').prop('playbackRate', Math.max(0, currentRate-0.1));
});
$('#speedUp').click(function(evt) {
    evt.preventDefault();
    var currentRate = parseFloat($('video').prop('playbackRate'));
    $('video').prop('playbackRate', Math.min(5, currentRate+0.1));
});
```

There is no maximum playback rate, but in this example the user is prevented from setting `playbackRate` to greater than 5.

CONTROLLING VIDEO SIZE

The HTML5 specification has been extended to allow for full screen video. The video can be made full screen by invoking the `requestFullScreen` method on the `video` element.

Because the Fullscreen API is so new, most browsers do not support this method. Instead, browsers support their own variants of the method.

It is common for browsers to provide their own implementations of JavaScript APIs or CSS properties for new specifications. In such cases, the browser family will prefix the method or property name, typically:

➤ `webkit` for Chrome or Safari

➤ `moz` for Firefox

➤ `ms` for Internet Explorer

➤ `opera` for Opera

In order to see this in Chrome, add the following control:

```
<a href="#" id="fullscreen">Fullscreen</a>
```

and then add the following JavaScript:

```
$('#fullscreen').click(function(evt) {
    evt.preventDefault();
    $('video').trigger('webkitRequestFullScreen');
});
```

Notice that the method invoked is `webkitRequestFullScreen`. If you open this example in Chrome or Safari, you will be able to enter full-screen mode.

If you want to write an example that works in any browser, you need to determine which browser the page has been loaded into and invoke the correct method. The typical way of achieving this is as follows:

```
$('#fullscreen').click(function(evt) {
    evt.preventDefault();
    var video = $('video')[0];
    if (video.requestFullscreen) {
        video.requestFullscreen();
    } else if (video.mozRequestFullScreen) {
        video.mozRequestFullScreen();
    } else if (video.webkitRequestFullScreen) {
        video.webkitRequestFullScreen();
    } else if (video.msRequestFullScreen) {
        video.msRequestFullScreen();
    }
});
```

Browsers will eventually support the `requestFullscreen` method; therefore, the code first attempts to use this. If this is not provided, it tests whether the method is available under a browser-specific name. This code relies on the fact that an undefined function returns `undefined` (which is false), whereas a defined function will return the function definition (which evaluates to true).

Different browsers may also choose to add additional security around this functionality. For instance, Firefox displays the warning shown in Figure 23-1.

Browsers typically provide users with the ability to exit full-screen mode; it is, however,

FIGURE 23-1

possible to listen for a `keypress` and invoke the `exitFullscreen` method (or its browser-specific implementations).

MEDIA SOURCE EXTENSIONS

Although the video tag is sufficient for displaying video on most websites, it is not sufficient for some of the larger video providers. Websites such as Netflix and YouTube have requirements that are not covered by the functionality discussed so far.

The next three sections will briefly cover some of the more advanced standards that are emerging in the HTML5 video space.

One of the key requirements for many streaming websites is the capability to downgrade the video quality if the user's Internet connection slows down. This removes the need to freeze the video entirely while it buffers.

Additionally, a user may choose to jump to the 60-minute point of a 90-minute video. It is extremely wasteful on bandwidth if the user is still required to download the entire video file.

The Media Source API is an extension to the HTML5 `audio` and `video` tags that enables more fine-grained control over the source of media. Rather than linking to a static video file on the server, it allows JavaScript to build streams for playback from "chunks" of video. This enables techniques such as adaptive streaming and time shifting.

In order to facilitate this, the Media Source API allows a media stream to be defined in JavaScript as follows:

```
var stream = new MediaSource();
```

and its type to be defines as follows:

```
stream.addSourceBuffer('video/webm; codecs="vorbis,vp9" ');
```

It is then possible to dynamically add chunks of video to the stream:

```
stream.appendBuffer(chunkOfVideo);
```

The chunk of video will typically be requested from the server on an "as-needed" basis, and may only cover a few seconds of the overall video track. This means that when each chunk is requested, the appropriate portion of the video can be retrieved, using the appropriate bitrate for the user's connection.

ENCRYPTED MEDIA EXTENSIONS

The other main feature required by many commercial websites is the ability to stop the video from being pirated using Digital Rights Management (DRM). This has been a highly controversial area of the HTML5 specification.

The main specification for protecting video is Encrypted Media Extensions (EME). This provides an API for encrypting media streams using the `video` and `audio` tags. EME defines a standard for determining how HTML5 browsers should detect that encrypted streams are being used, and then find an appropriate Content Decryption Module (CDM) that will verify the license associated with the video. It will also perform the task of decrypting the video data.

Encrypted Media Extensions therefore provides an API that enables web applications to interact with content protection systems, to allow playback of encrypted audio and video.

EME is an optional extension to the HTML5 specification so browsers can choose not to support it. If it is not supported, websites may decide not to play video inside the browser.

WEB CRYPTOGRAPHY

The final specification being developed to support video inside the browser is the Web Cryptography API (WebCrypto). This is a JavaScript API for performing common cryptographic functions, such as encoding and decoding data using common cryptographic algorithms.

Although this API is not directly related to the other video APIs, it is one of the ingredients needed to support the EME specification.

The Web Cryptography API is large and complex and not fully supported by most browsers, but it is an important standard to watch over the coming years.

TRY IT

In this Try It, you will add a simple enhancement to the web page that has been developed during this lesson so far. If you have not been developing this throughout the lesson, it can be downloaded from the book's website (it is called `video_pre.html`).

This enhancement will allow the user to skip 10 seconds forward or backwards in the video by clicking a button.

Lesson Requirements

You need to have created the `video_pre.html` file, along with its dependent resources such as jQuery, `poster.png`, and the video files. These are all available from the book's website.

Step-by-Step

1. Start by adding two new controls to the web page called "Jump forward" and "Jump back." Assign appropriate IDs to both elements.

2. Add an event listener to the jump back button. This should start by obtaining the `currentTime` property from the video and converting it into a number.

3. Subtract 10 from the `currentTime` property, and set this as the new `currentTime`. Ensure that this does not result in a negative number by using `Math.max`.

4. Add an event listener for the jump forward button. This is essentially the same, but it needs to also access the `duration` property, and ensure that the `currentTime` is not set to a value greater than this.

   My controls looked like this:

   ```
   <a href="#" id="jumpForward">Jump forward</a>
   <a href="#" id="jumpBack">Jump back</a>
   ```

And my event listeners looked like this:

```
$('#jumpBack').click(function(evt) {
    evt.preventDefault();
    var currentTime = parseFloat($('video').prop('currentTime'));
    var newTime = currentTime-10;
    $('video').prop('currentTime', Math.max(0, newTime));
});
$('#jumpForward').click(function(evt) {
    evt.preventDefault();
    var currentTime = parseFloat($('video').prop('currentTime'));
    var duration = parseFloat($('video').prop('duration'));
    var newTime = currentTime+10;
    $('video').prop('currentTime', Math.min(duration, newTime));
});
```

> **REFERENCE** *Please go to the book's website at* www.wrox.com/go/html5jsj-query24hr *to view the video for Lesson 23, as well as download the code and resources for this lesson.*

24

Canvas: Part I

The HTML5 `canvas` element provides a canvas for capturing bitmap images. The Canvas API, on the other hand, allows you to interact with the `canvas` element using JavaScript. The canvas can be used for simple drawing, such as shapes and lines, and for more advanced features, such as animation. The `canvas` element and API provide an alternative to plugins such as Adobe Flash.

This lesson covers the basics of the Canvas API; the next lesson covers some of the advanced features. Although the features covered in this lesson appear quite basic, they can still be combined to construct complex images.

The Canvas API is, however, a reasonably low-level API. This has the benefit of making almost anything possible, but it also means that it is sometimes tedious to perform relatively simple operations.

The `canvas` element creates a bitmap (or raster) image. Essentially, this means that each pixel on the screen is represented by a position in memory that describes the color of the pixel.

> **NOTE** *Originally, bitmap images were referred to as bitmaps because each pixel could have a 0 or 1 value to denote black or white. Because the canvas supports multiple colors, it is technically a pixmap.*

The other major category of image is vector graphics. Vector graphics describe shapes as mathematical formulas, and therefore do not need to store information about every pixel. The shapes can then be assigned properties such as their fill color. Vector graphics work extremely well when the user may zoom into the image because the quality of the image remains the same regardless of how far the user zooms in.

> **NOTE** *Browsers do also support vector graphics natively, in the form of SVG, but that is beyond the scope of this book.*

In order to get started with the HTML5 canvas, you need to add a `canvas` element to the web page. In addition, it is customary to provide it with an ID to allow it to be selected:

```
<canvas width="800" height="500" id="myCanvas"></canvas>
```

Notice also that the `height` and `width` have both been specified to control the size the canvas onscreen. Because the height and width default to 0, these are mandatory, unless you use CSS to control the size of the canvas.

If you open this web page, you will see a white screen. Although the canvas is present, every pixel is colored white by default, and therefore you will not see anything.

With the canvas in place, you can start using the Canvas API to begin drawing shapes on the canvas. In order to draw a shape, you need to describe:

➤ Where on the canvas the shape should appear

➤ The type of shape you wish to draw, along with its size

➤ Any other properties associated with the shape, such as its color

I will address these needs one at a time in the sections that follow.

SIMPLE DRAWING

The Canvas API uses pixels for specifying sizes. If you wish to draw a new shape onto the canvas, you need to specify the coordinates of the shape relative to the top-left corner of the canvas. The top-left corner can be thought of as having a position of 0, 0. You can therefore specify the position of the shape, relative to this position, using x and y coordinates.

For instance, if you wanted the shape to be drawn 200 pixels from the top of the screen and 300 pixels from the left of the screen, you would use a position of 300, 200 as the top-left corner of the shape. The x-axis is always specified first, and represents the horizontal axis, while the y-axis represents the vertical axis.

Suppose you are drawing a rectangle: You would also need to specify the height and width of the rectangle.

Once you determine these properties, you can obtain a reference to the canvas's graphical context, and use the JavaScript API to draw the shape, a rectangle in this case:

```
<canvas width="800" height="500" id="myCanvas"></canvas>
<script>
    var context = $('#myCanvas')[0].getContext("2d");
    context.fillRect(300, 200, 100, 200);
</script>
```

> **NOTE** *If following along the examples in this lesson, ensure the code is placed inside an HTML5 page structure, and that the jQuery library is included in the* head *section.*

When the canvas context is requested, it must include the parameter 2d because the canvas element can also support 3D APIs, most notably WebGL. This API is outside the scope of this book and is not currently well supported.

Notice that the `fillRect` method accepts four parameters:

➤ The x-position of the rectangle

➤ The y-position of the rectangle

➤ The width of the rectangle

➤ The height of the rectangle

This code produces the shape shown in Figure 24-1.

FIGURE 24-1

By default, the rectangle will be filled with a black color, but this can easily be overridden by specifying the `fillStyle` for the canvas context:

```
<script>
    var context = $('#myCanvas')[0].getContext("2d");
    context.fillStyle = 'red';
    context.fillRect(300, 200, 100, 200);
</script>
```

Shapes can overlap on the canvas, but in this case the last shape drawn simply overwrites the pixels of the shape below it. For instance, the following code:

```
<script>
    var context = $('#myCanvas')[0].
getContext("2d");
    context.fillStyle = 'lightgrey';
    context.fillRect(300, 200, 100, 200);
    context.fillStyle = 'grey';
    context.fillRect(50, 300, 400, 100);
</script>
```

FIGURE 24-2

produces the result shown in Figure 24-2. Notice that the light-grey shape appears behind the grey shape.

It is also possible to specify the border of a rectangle without coloring the fill area. This can be achieved by using `strokeRect`, as you can see in the following example:

```
<script>
    var context = $('#myCanvas')[0].getContext("2d");
    context.fillStyle = 'lightgrey';
    context.fillRect(300, 200, 100, 200);
    context.strokeStyle = 'grey';
    context.lineWidth = 3;
    context.strokeRect(50, 300, 400, 100);
</script>
```

This produces the drawing shown in Figure 24-3.

DRAWING LINES

Rectangles can only take you so far; to draw more complex shapes you need to use lines. For instance, the API does not provide a method for drawing triangles, but it is easy to draw one as follows:

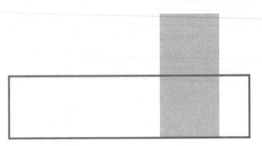

FIGURE 24-3

```
<script>
    var context = $('#myCanvas')[0].getContext("2d");
    context.beginPath();
    context.moveTo(100,20);
    context.lineTo(30,100);
    context.lineTo(170,100);
    context.fill();
</script>
```

You begin by specifying that you are beginning a path, and then use moveTo to move to the position you want to start drawing from. You then specify that you want to draw from here to another point using lineTo. You can then call lineTo as many times as necessary, each time specifying the coordinates you want the line to end up at.

In this example, you have only specified two of the three sides for the triangle, but when you call fill, the third line is implied because it is only possible to fill a closed shape. This code therefore produces the drawing shown in Figure 24-4.

It is also possible to draw the outline of the shape by using the stroke method.

FIGURE 24-4

```
<script>
    var context = $('#myCanvas')[0].getContext("2d");
    context.beginPath();
    context.moveTo(100,20);
    context.lineTo(30,100);
    context.lineTo(170,100);
    context.lineTo(100,20);
    context.stroke();
</script>
```

In this case, however, it would be necessary to specify all three lines of the triangle; alternatively, the third lineTo call could be replaced with the following line of code:

```
context.closePath();
```

CIRCLES AND CURVES

The Canvas API also provides methods for drawing curved lines and shapes such as circles. This can be achieved with the arc method, as shown in the following example:

```
<script>
    var context = $('#myCanvas')[0].getContext("2d");
    context.beginPath();
    context.arc(70, 70, 50, 0, 2 * Math.PI, true)
    context.fill();
</script>
```

The `arc` method accepts the following parameters:

➤ The x and y coordinates for the center of the circle, which have both been specified as 70.

➤ The radius of the circle in pixels.

➤ The starting angle in radians—a value of 0 is equivalent to the three o'clock position on a clock.

➤ The ending position in radians: `2 * Math.PI` is equivalent to 360 degrees, whereas `Math.PI` would be equivalent to 180 degrees.

➤ A fifth parameter is also accepted, which specifies whether the arc should be drawn clockwise or counter clockwise, with the default being false, which indicates clockwise. This is not relevant if drawing a full circle.

This example produces the circle shown in Figure 24-5.

It is also possible to draw the outline of a circle without filling it by using the `stroke` method. The following example draws an arc beginning at 0 radians, and ending at `0.5 * Math.PI`, which is equivalent to 6 o'clock. This particular example is drawn counter-clockwise, meaning the line extends 270 degrees:

FIGURE 24-5

```
<script>
    var context = $('#myCanvas')[0].getContext("2d");
    context.beginPath();
    context.arc(70, 70, 50, 0, 0.5 * Math.PI, true);
    context.stroke();
</script>
```

This code produces the line shown in Figure 24-6.

It is also possible to draw an arc between two points using the `arcTo` method. This method lets you specify the coordinates for two tangents to the curve and then define the radius of a circle that would touch those two tangents. This method is slightly more difficult to explain, but assume that you started from the coordinates of 50,50:

FIGURE 24-6

```
context.moveTo(50,50);
```

Next, you specify that the coordinates of the first tangent are 150, 20. You would therefore draw an imaginary line between 50, 50 and 150, 20. Next, you draw an imaginary line from this point to a second point specified—for example, 150, 150. You therefore have specified the imaginary lines shown in Figure 24-7.

FIGURE 24-7

Now you specify that the radius of the circle that touches these tangents is 80 pixels:

```
var context = $('#myCanvas')[0].getContext("2d");
context.beginPath();
context.moveTo(50,50);
context.arcTo(150,20,150,150,80);
context.stroke();
```

This effectively creates the imaginary circle shown in Figure 24-8, and therefore creates the arc shown in Figure 24-9.

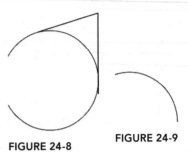

FIGURE 24-8   **FIGURE 24-9**

DRAWING TEXT

The final feature this lesson will cover is text. It is possible to draw text onto the canvas using the `fillText` method, as shown in the following example:

```
<script>
    var context = $('#myCanvas')[0].getContext("2d");
    context.font="20px Courier";
    context.fillText("Hello World!",20,50);
</script>
```

Notice that the font of the context is set, and then the `fillText` is called with the relevant text and the coordinates for the text to start at. The coordinates represent the bottom-left corner of the text; therefore, it is not possible to specify 0 for the y-axis because the text would be positioned above the canvas.

The preceding example produces the result shown in Figure 24-10.

`Hello World!`

FIGURE 24-10

Adding text to a canvas is not like adding text to an HTML document. The text will not wrap if it reaches the right-hand edge of the canvas, and there are no checks to ensure that the text displays on the canvas at all. It is possible to specify a forth parameter to `fillText`, which specifies the maximum width of the text, but this will not cause text to wrap.

To help with issues positioning text, the Canvas API does support a `measureText` method. This allows you to determine the width of an arbitrary string of text, given the current font. For example:

```
context.measureText("Hello World");
```

The Canvas API also supports a `strokeText` method. This is identical to `fillText`, except it only draws the outline of the text. For example, the following code:

```
<script>
    var context = $('#myCanvas')[0].getContext("2d");
    context.font="30px Georgia";
    context.strokeText("Hello World!",20,50);
</script>
```

Hello World!

produces the text shown in Figure 24-11.

FIGURE 24-11

TRY IT

In this Try It, you are going to create a "random walk." Random walks are often used to describe price movements of commodities, stocks, and currencies in economics, and are derived by imagining the path followed by a drunk who wakes at intermittent intervals and staggers in a random direction.

In this Try It, you will perform 10,000 random walks, each time moving 3 pixels up, down, left, or right from a given starting position. The pattern created each time you run this will be different, but Figure 24-12 shows an example I created.

FIGURE 24-12

Lesson Requirements

You will need a text editor for writing the code and the Chrome browser for running the code.

Step-by-Step

1. Start by creating a standard HTML5 web page, and include an import for jQuery.

2. Add a `canvas` element to the web page, assign it an ID, and give it a `width` and `height` of 800.

3. Start by finding the `canvas` element, and call `getContext("2d")` on it, assigning the result to a variable called `context`.

4. Call `beginPath` on the context, and then use the `moveTo` method to move to the center of the canvas.

5. Create two variables to record the current X and Y coordinates. These should be initialized to the values you passed to the `moveTo` method.

6. Create a for-loop that iterates 10,000 times. Steps 7–10 will occur inside the for-loop.

7. Start be creating a random number using `Math.random()`, and assign this to a variable.

8. Create an if-else block that has four branches depending on whether the random number is:

   ➤ Less than 0.25

   ➤ Less than 0.5

   ➤ Less than 0.75

   ➤ Less than 1

9. Within each of these four blocks, perform one of these four operations (making sure each operation is performed in one, and only one, branch):

   ➤ Subtract 3 from the current Y coordinate.

   ➤ Add 3 to the current Y coordinate.

   ➤ Subtract 3 from the current X coordinate.

   ➤ Add 3 to the current X coordinate.

10. Use the `lineTo` method to move to the new X and Y coordinates.

11. After the for-loop finishes, call `stroke` on the context.

12. You can try running the web page as many times as you like. Each time you run it, you will be surprised at how different the patterns look.

    My version of the JavaScript supporting this page looked like this:

```
<script>
    var context = $('#myCanvas')[0].getContext("2d");
    context.beginPath();
    context.moveTo(400,400);
    var currentX = 400;
    var currentY = 400;
    for (var i = 0; i < 10000; i++) {
        var r = Math.random();
        console.log(r);
        if (r < 0.25) {
            currentX = currentX-3;
        } else if (r < 0.5) {
            currentX = currentX + 3;
        } else if (r < 0.75) {
            currentY = currentY - 3;
        } else {
            currentY = currentY + 3;
        }
        console.log('Moving to ' + currentX + ' ' + currentY);
        context.lineTo(currentX, currentY);
    }
    context.stroke();
</script>
```

> **REFERENCE** *Please go to the book's website at* www.wrox.com/go/html5jsj-query24hr *to view the video for Lesson 24, as well as download the code and resources for this lesson.*

25

Canvas: Part II

In the previous lesson, you learned how to use the Canvas API to create simple two-dimensional bitmaps. This lesson will consolidate your knowledge from the previous lesson, and also look at some of the more advanced canvas features, such as animation.

LINEAR GRADIENTS

In the previous lesson, all lines and shapes used block colors. Linear gradients allow you to create colors that start with a specific color and end with another color, and gradually transform from one color to the other over the area of the feature being colored.

In order to create a linear gradient, you first need to use the `createLinearGradient` method, and specify the x and y coordinates for an imaginary line through which the color should be transformed. For example:

```
var gradient = context.createLinearGradient(50,0,350,0);
```

In this case, the gradient runs horizontally from the x-coordinate of 50 to the x-coordinate of 350. This is not coloring any feature; it is just creating a line through which features can be colored with a linear gradient.

Next, you need to specify the color at specific points along the line using the `addStopColor` method. Usually, specifying the starting and ending color is sufficient, but you can specify the color for as many points along the line as you need. The following specifies the color for the start and end of the line:

```
gradient.addColorStop(0.0, "black");
gradient.addColorStop(1.0, "white");
```

The first parameter to `addStopColor` represents the position on the line: A value of 0 represents the start of the line, while 1.0 represents the end of the line. The second parameter represents the color for that position on the line.

Once the gradient has been defined, it can be specified as the fill style of the context, and you can use any of the methods from the previous lesson to add features to the canvas:

```
context.fillStyle=gradient;
context.fillRect(50,50,350,350);
```

This will produce the result shown in Figure 25-1.

Notice that the line defined above does not actually run through the rectangle (it is above it), but it does run the entire horizontal length of the rectangle. The line defined is simply a guide for the color that should appear at specific points on the canvas, and only takes on meaning when features are added within the bounds of that line.

FIGURE 25-1

It is also possible to define more complex gradients. For example, the following starts out red, gradually becomes white and stays white for 20 percent of the length of the line, and then gradually becomes blue.

```
gradient.addColorStop(0, "red");
gradient.addColorStop(0.4, "white");
gradient.addColorStop(0.6, "white");
gradient.addColorStop(1, "blue");
```

It is naturally also possible to define vertical gradients, or gradients that run on an angle through the canvas. For instance, the following code creates a gradient that runs on an angle from top left to bottom right of the canvas:

```
var gradient = context.createLinearGradient(50,50,250,250);
gradient.addColorStop(0, "black");
gradient.addColorStop(1, "white");
context.fillStyle=gradient;
context.fillRect(50,50,200,200);
```

This produces the result shown in Figure 25-2.

SHADOWS

Another interesting color-based effect involves the use of shadows. Just like linear gradients, shadows can be applied to any of the features you have looked at so far, including text, rectangles, and arcs.

FIGURE 25-2

To begin using shadows, you first instruct the canvas context to use shadows by specifying a shadow color:

```
context.shadowColor = "#ABABAB";
```

Next, you need to specify the direction of the shadow. This is achieved by specifying how far the shadow should extend from each point on the feature in both the horizontal and vertical direction. For instance, if you want the shadow to extend 10 pixels up and 10 pixels to the right of a feature, you specify the following:

```
context.shadowOffsetX = 10;
context.shadowOffsetY = -10;
```

In order to visualize how the shadow works, think of each pixel as having a position of 0, 0. Then imagine the coordinates where the shadow should end in relation to this point.

Next, you add visual elements just as you normally would; for instance, the following adds text to the canvas in a 50-point font:

```
context.font="50px Courier";
context.fillText("Hello World!",20,50);
```

In this case, the effect shown in Figure 25-3 is created.

FIGURE 25-3

You will notice that in this case, the shadow is very crisp. It is possible to make the shadow blurry by setting the following property:

```
context.shadowBlur = 5;
```

The default value is 0, and the larger the number, the more blur is applied. For instance, a blur level of 5 creates the image shown in Figure 25-4.

FIGURE 25-4

Once you have specified a shadow color, any visual elements added after that point will have a shadow. There are several ways to stop shadows, such as setting shadowOffsetX and shadowOffsetY to 0.

There is a more general solution, however: It is possible to save the state of the context at any point and then revert back to this state in the future. For example:

```
var context = $('#myCanvas')[0].getContext("2d");
context.fillStyle = 'red';
context.save();
context.shadowColor = "#ABABAB";
context.shadowOffsetX = 10;
context.shadowOffsetY = -10;
context.font="50px Courier";
context.fillText("Hello World!",20,50);
context.restore();
context.fillRect(100,100,200,200);
```

In this example, the fillStyle is set to red, and then the context is saved. The shadow properties are then set, and the text is written to the canvas. You then revert back to the saved version of the canvas using restore, and draw a rectangle. In this case, the rectangle will have a red fill color, but will not have a shadow.

The save and restore methods are used extensively when creating complex bitmaps because they allow you to save a default set of properties, and then temporarily augment these as needed.

IMAGES

Rather than drawing on the canvas, it is possible to load an existing image directly onto the canvas. Once an image has been added, it is possible to draw over top of the image; therefore, it is often useful to use an image as the background of a canvas.

To start, create an `Image` object, and set the `src` property to the absolute or relative URL of the image:

```
var image = new Image();
image.src = "cat.jpg";
```

The image specified can be downloaded from the book's website, or you can use your own image.

A complication with adding images to the canvas is that they need to be downloaded from the web server before they can be added to the canvas. You therefore need to add an event listener to the image to listen for the download to complete; you can then add it to the canvas:

```
image.addEventListener('load', function() {
    context.drawImage(image, 20, 20, 360, 260);
});
```

The call to `drawImage` contains the following parameters:

➤   The `Image` to be drawn.

➤   The x and y coordinates to position the top-left corner of the image.

➤   The width and height of the image: These can be omitted, in which case the image will not be scaled.

The preceding code will add the image to the canvas, as shown in Figure 25-5.

FIGURE 25-5

TRANSFORMING SHAPES

Up until this point, each feature has been added with its own location and its own size. In some cases, it can be easier to repeatedly draw the same feature, while changing the way the canvas context scales, positions, or skews these features.

You can achieve this by using the `transform` method. As a very simple example of the `transform` method in action, consider the following:

```
context.fillStyle='#444444';
context.fillRect(10,10, 180,180);
context.transform(0.5, 0, 0, 0.5, 30, 30);
context.fillStyle='#CCCCCC';
context.fillRect(10,10, 180,180);
```

This example starts by drawing a rectangle in a dark grey color. Once the first rectangle is drawn, the `transform` method is called on the canvas context, and passed six parameters that control how any future features are moved, skewed, or scaled. These six parameters are:

➤ **The amount of horizontal scaling that should be applied, with 1.0 being the default:** In the previous example, the horizontal scaling is 50 percent, meaning any new features will only be half as wide as they otherwise would have been.

➤ **The amount of horizontal skew:** You will look at this parameter shortly, but it is used to angle the horizontal axis up or down.

➤ **The amount of vertical skew:** You will look at this parameter shortly, but it is used to transform the vertical axis left or right.

➤ **The amount of vertical scaling, with 1.0 being the default:** In the preceding example, the vertical scaling is 50 percent, meaning any new features will only appear at half the height specified.

➤ **The number of pixels to offset drawing by horizontally:** In this case, the offset is 30 pixels, so any drawing will occur 30 pixels to the right of where it would have otherwise. This can be a negative number to move features to the left.

➤ **The number of pixels to offset drawing by vertically:** In this case, the offset is 30 pixels, so any drawing will occur 30 pixels below where it would have otherwise. This can be a negative number to move features higher.

These six values represent the *transformation matrix* of the canvas context, and all values default to 0.

> **NOTE** *A transformation matrix is a set of nine numbers, ordered into three rows, and is used to transform a bitmap via linear algebra. The six parameters mentioned in the preceding bulleted list are listed as parameters a–f, while the last row of the matrix always has the values 0*
> *0 1:*
>
> *a c e*
> *b d f*
> *0 0 1*
>
> *It is not necessary to have an understanding of how linear algebra works, but you should understand the purpose of each parameter in the matrix.*

Once the context has been transformed, you can draw the exact same rectangle in a lighter grey, and the result will be as you see in Figure 25-6.

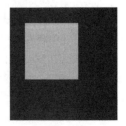

If you were to call `transform` again and draw another shape in white, the current context (which is already drawing at a 50 percent scale) would be transformed. For instance, in the following case, you will draw a third rectangle at 25 percent the size of the original.

```
context.transform(0.5, 0, 0, 0.5, 30, 30);
context.fillStyle='white';
context.fillRect(10,10, 180,180);
```

FIGURE 25-6

This produces the result shown in Figure 25-7. Notice in this case that the 30-pixel horizontal and vertical movement is also scaled.

It is also possible to use `setTransform` rather than `transform`. This method accepts identical parameters but will set the transformation matrix back to its default values before setting the requested values. This ensures that you are not transforming a transformation matrix that has already been augmented.

FIGURE 25-7

This example can also be changed to include skewing. The following code skews the squares by 0.3 horizontally, and −0.3 vertically:

```
context.fillStyle='#444444';
context.fillRect(10,10, 180,180);
context.transform(0.5, 0.3, -0.3, 0.5, 80, 30);
context.fillStyle='#CCCCCC';
context.fillRect(10,10, 180,180);
context.transform(0.5, 0.3, -0.3, 0.5, 80, 30);
context.fillStyle='white';
context.fillRect(10,10, 180,180);
```

This produces the result shown in Figure 25-8.

The values used for the skew parameters are tangents; therefore, if you know the angle you would like to skew shapes by, you can use the utility method `Math.tan`, and pass the angle as a parameter.

The horizontal skew of 0.3 lifts the bottom-left corner, creating an angle of approximately 60 degrees. The vertical skew of −0.3 pulls the bottom-left corner to the left, creating an angle of approximately 60 degrees.

FIGURE 25-8

If you want to maintain the shape of a feature, the horizontal and vertical values need to be the inverse of one another. For instance, if both values are set to 0.3, the effect in Figure 25-9 is produced.

The Canvas API provides three additional utility methods for modifying the transformation matrix. If you only need to modify the vertical and horizontal scale, you can use the `scale` method and pass it two parameters.

If, on the other hand, you only need to modify the horizontal and vertical offset, you can use the `translate` method, and pass it two parameters. You can think of the `translate` method as a mechanism for modifying where the 0, 0 coordinate appears on the canvas.

FIGURE 25-9

Finally, it is possible to use the `rotate` method to rotate the context of the canvas by a given number of radians. This does not rotate the canvas itself, but means that any features drawn onto the canvas will appear at an offset angle. You will look at this method in the Try It section.

BASIC ANIMATION

The final subject that will be introduced in this chapter is basic animation. Up until this point, all shapes, lines, and text have been static: Once they are added, they don't change. It is also possible to animate these features.

Basic animation works by redrawing the canvas, or portions of the canvas, at a specified interval. In order to perform a task at a given interval, it is common to use the built-in setInterval JavaScript function. This accepts two parameters: a function to execute, and the time in milliseconds between each execution. The function will then be invoked indefinitely at the specific interval.

> **NOTE** *There is no guarantee* setInterval *will execute at exactly the specified interval. Instead,* setInterval *places an event on a queue at the appropriate time, and JavaScript executes this when all other tasks at hand have completed.*
>
> *JavaScript is inherently single threaded, meaning it can perform only a single task at a time. The event queue is therefore a mechanism of controlling the order in which processing will occur.*

In this example, you will write an animation that shows a blue box running from the top left of the canvas to the bottom right. The canvas is assumed to be 400 by 400 pixels. Once it reaches the bottom, it will change direction and head for the top right again. The animation will update every 30 milliseconds in this example, creating a reasonably smooth animation.

The only new method that will be introduced in this example is clearRect. This is the opposite of fillRect, and this example therefore works by clearing the previously drawn rectangle and creating a new one.

```
var context = $('#myCanvas')[0].getContext("2d");
context.fillStyle='blue';
var startX = 0;
var startY = 0;
var forward = true;
setInterval(drawRectangle, 30);

function drawRectangle() {
    context.clearRect(startX,startY, 40, 40);
    if (forward && startX === 400) {
        forward = false;
    } else if (!forward && startX === 0) {
        forward = true;
    }
    if (forward) {
        startX = startX + 1;
        startY = startY + 1;
    } else {
        startX = startX - 1;
        startY = startY - 1;
    }
    context.fillRect(startX,startY, 40, 40);
}
```

As you can see, the rest of the code in this example is straightforward. You use global variables to keep track of the x-coordinate and y-coordinate, and either increase or decrease these by 1 before re-drawing the rectangle.

TRY IT

In this Try It, you are going to create an animated clock that counts the seconds as they pass. This will use a combination of the techniques covered in this lesson, and those covered in the previous lesson.

Lesson Requirements

You will need a text editor for writing the code and the Chrome browser for running the code.

Step-by-Step

1. Start by creating a standard HTML5 web page, and include an import for jQuery.

2. Create a canvas with `height` and `width` set to 400.

3. Create a script block and obtain a reference to the canvas context using the approach outlined in Lesson 24.

4. Begin by setting the `fillStyle` to blue.

5. Create a circle using an arc with a center at 200, 200. The radius should be set to 130.

6. Use the `fill` method to fill the arc.

7. Set the `lineWidth` property to 2. You will use this when you start drawing the second hand.

8. Use the `translate` method to set the offset to the center of the circle (position 200, 200).

9. Create a new function for drawing the second hand called `drawSeconds`.

10. This method should start by overwriting the second hand that was drawn previously, so set the `strokeStyle` to blue.

11. Invoke the `beginPath` method, and then use the `moveTo` method to move to position 0, 0. (This is the center of the circle as a result of the translation that occurred in Step 8.)

12. Invoke the `lineTo` method with an x-coordinate of 0, and a y-coordinate of –120. This will draw a line up from the center of the circle.

13. Invoke the `stroke` method.

14. You now want to rotate the canvas context by an amount corresponding to 1 second. The easiest way to do this is to invoke the `rotate` method (which accepts the number of radians to rotate the canvas context), and pass the parameter: `(2 * Math.PI) / 60`. Remember that `2 * Math.PI` is 360 degrees; thus, dividing this by 60 produces the number of degrees in one second.

15. Set the `strokeStyle` to white, and draw a new line using the exact same actions outlined in Steps 11–13.

16. Invoke the `setInterval` method, passing a reference to the `drawSeconds` function, and use an interval of 1000 milliseconds.

17. Load the page, and leave it open. The result should be an animated white second hand on a blue clock.

Your code should now look like this:

```
<script>
    var context = $('#myCanvas')[0].getContext("2d");
    context.fillStyle='blue';
    context.arc(200, 200, 130, 0, 2 * Math.PI, true);
    context.fill();
    context.lineWidth = 2;
    context.translate(200,200);
    setInterval(drawSeconds, 1000);

    function drawSeconds() {
        context.strokeStyle = 'blue';
        context.beginPath();
        context.moveTo(0,0);
        context.lineTo(0,-120);
        context.stroke();

        context.rotate((2 * Math.PI) / 60);
        context.beginPath();
        context.strokeStyle = 'white';
        context.moveTo(0,0);
        context.lineTo(0,-120);
        context.stroke();
    }
</script>
```

You may notice a problem with my implementation: Faint white outlines are left when the white line is overwritten. Try to find one of the many solutions for resolving this issue.

> **REFERENCE** *Please go to the book's website at* www.wrox.com/go/html5jsj-query24hr *to view the video for Lesson 25, as well as download the code and resources for this lesson.*

26

CSS3: Part I

Just like HTML, CSS is evolving over time. The latest version of CSS is called CSS3 and adds several important modules to CSS that will be explored over the next two lessons.

Nothing fundamental has changed with CSS in version 3: The language still uses selectors to identify elements and still allows a set of stylistic properties to be defined for these elements. CSS3 is important, however, because it specifies a number of new selectors style properties. Together, these selectors and properties greatly improve the expressiveness of CSS.

Unlike with HTML, you may have noticed that it is not necessary to specify which version of CSS you are using. CSS3 is entirely backwards compatible; therefore, if you want to use CSS3 features, you simply include them in your existing style sheets, and the browser will simply ignore them if it does not support them.

The next two lessons will not provide an exhaustive introduction to CSS3, but they will introduce the most interesting features, and will further help consolidate your knowledge of CSS.

SELECTORS

CSS3 provides a number of new selectors for selecting elements based on a wider set of criteria.

CSS3 includes one new operator called the tilde operator. This is used to select elements that are siblings of a specified element, and are declared anywhere after that element. For instance, in `contacts.css`, you might want to style `tfoot` elements differently if they have a sibling element of type `thead`; this could be achieved as follows:

```
thead ~ tfoot {
    font-size: 0.75em;
    text-align:right;
}
```

This will only match `tfoot` elements if a sibling that is a `thead` precedes them.

This operator is similar to the + operator introduced in CSS2, but the + operator only finds elements that are immediately preceded by the specified element, which it is not in this case.

The + operator could be used to match `tbody` elements that are preceded by `thead` elements because `tbody` is directly preceded by `thead`. Therefore, the following rule could be used in `contacts.css`:

```
thead + tbody {
```

CSS3 also greatly enhances the way selectors can interact with attribute values. Before looking at these, I will briefly examine three additional CSS2 selectors that allow CSS selections based on attributes.

To match an attribute name, the following selector can be used:

```
[required] {
```

Notice that this uses the same square bracket notation seen with jQuery. Additionally, in order to match both the attribute name and value, the following syntax can be used:

```
[name= "emailAddress"] {
```

Often, you match attribute values based on more complex rules. For instance, you may want to match any `name` attribute that has a value beginning with `email`. This can be achieved with the following selector:

```
[name^= "email"] {
```

Alternatively, you may want to match attributes with values ending in a specific value. For example, the following CSS3 rule will color two labels red (the `contactName` and `companyName` labels):

```
label[for$= "Name"] {
    background:red;
}
```

Finally, you may want to match any element that has an attribute value containing specified text. For instance, the following will select any elements that have an inline `style` attribute that contains a `display` property override:

```
[style*= "display"] {
```

Most of the other new selectors are pseudo-class and pseudo-element selectors. As you will remember from earlier in the book, pseudo-class and pseudo-element selectors directly tie CSS rules to the state of the DOM: If the DOM changes, elements will dynamically be selected or deselected based on their state.

Some of these have already been introduced earlier in the book. The remainder of the most widely used selectors are introduced in the selection listed in Table 26-1, but this is not an exhaustive list.

TABLE 26-1: CSS3 Selectors

SELECTOR	PURPOSE
:checked	Finds radio buttons or checkboxes that are checked.
:disabled	Finds input fields that are disabled, and that therefore restrict user entry. Input fields can be disabled via the disabled attribute.
:empty	Finds elements that do not have any children.
:enabled	This is the opposite of :disabled.
:invalid	As you have seen in earlier lessons, this selects elements that have failed validation.
:not	Selects elements that do not meet specific criteria. For instance, the following rule selects any elements that are not divs: :not(div).
:nth-child	Selects elements that have a specific index among their siblings. For instance, the following finds the third element within the tbody element, provided it is a tr element: tbody > tr:nth-child(3).
:nth-of-type	This is essentially the same as :nth-child, except it only looks for elements of the specified type. For example, this selector finds the third tr element that is a child of the tbody element: tbody > tr:nth-of-type(3).
:optional	Selects any input fields that are not marked as required.
:read-only	Selects any input fields that have been marked with the readonly attribute.
:read-write	Selects any input fields that are not marked as readonly or disabled.
:valid	Selects all the input fields that have passed validation, or that do not need validation.

CSS BORDERS

You have already seen numerous examples of CSS borders using the border property. Although these borders allow you to express the style of the border, the thickness of the border, and the color of the border, they are somewhat limited.

CSS3 adds three important capabilities, each of which will be explored in this section. All the examples in this section will be added to the div element shown in the following example:

```
<!DOCTYPE html>
<html lang="en">
```

```
<head>
    <meta charset="utf-8">
    <style>
        div {
            margin:50px;
            width:300px;
            height:300px;
            background:#cdcdcd;
        }
    </style>
</head>
<body>
    <div></div>
</body>
</html>
```

CSS3 allows for curved corners on borders. Curved corners are commonly used as a stylistic device to soften the impact of the border. In order to demonstrate this, you need to ensure the element already has a border, so add the following to the `div` rule:

```
border: 1px solid #555555;
```

Then simply add one additional property:

```
border-radius: 20px;
```

The value specifies how much the corners should be curved. If you open the web page, it will look like what you see in Figure 26-1.

The second addition to borders is the ability to use images for borders. This allows you to create more interesting borders because you are not limited to simple lines. Imagine that you have the photographic pattern shown in Figure 26-2, and you want to use it for a border.

FIGURE 26-1

This picture is available on the book's website, named `border.png`.
You can begin by specifying a transparent border with the required thickness:

```
border: 30px solid transparent;
```

The width of the border should be the thickness you want the photographic image to appear, in this case 30 pixels. With that in place, you can use the `border-image` property to specify the image that should be used for the border:

```
border-image:url("border.png") 30 30 30 30 stretch;
```

This property accepts the following parameters:

➤ The file that should be used.

➤ Four different values specifying how to slice the image—these will be discussed shortly. These can either be percentages or pixels. Oddly, if they are percentages, the % sign must be used, but if the values are pixels, the px suffix cannot be used.

➤ How to deal with the fact that the image may not be the same size as the border. In this case, I have specified that the image should be stretched. Other possible values are:

   ➤ `repeat`: The border image will be repeated as many times as necessary.

   ➤ `round`: The image will be repeated to fill the area, and it will ensure that there are a round number of repetitions, scaling the image if necessary.

FIGURE 26-2

This produces the effect shown in Figure 26-3.

FIGURE 26-3

The four values used (all of which were set to 30 pixels) effectively state how much of the image should be used for the top, right, bottom, and left of the border. I have specified these as the same size as the border, meaning the image does not need to be stretched in order to fit into each position.

> **NOTE** *If you are referring to images from an external CSS style sheet, it is important to realize that the file locations will be relative to the style sheet location, not the web page itself.*

The third main enhancement to borders is the ability to add shadows to elements, just as you saw with the Canvas API. This feature is not explicitly linked to borders because it is possible to add shadows to any element, regardless of whether it has a border or not.

In order to demonstrate the use of shadows, add the following property to the `div` element:

```
box-shadow: 10px -10px 10px #888888;
```

The parameters used are as follows:

➤ **The horizontal position of the shadow:** Because this is a positive number, the shadow will appear on the right side of the `div`.

➤ **The vertical position of the shadow:** Because this is a negative number, the shadow will appear above the `div`.

➤ **The amount of blur to use:** If a value of 0 is used, there is no blur at all to the shadow, whereas in this case, the blur extends for 10 pixels.

➤ **The color of the shadow.** In the example above this has been specified as a shade of grey.

This example produces the effect in Figure 26-4.

FIGURE 26-4

It is possible to place a border around the entire element using an optional parameter immediately before the color. This specifies the size of the border:

```
box-shadow: 0 0 10px 10px #888888;
```

In this case, a 10-pixel border, with 10 pixels of blur, extends around all four sides of the element. Notice that I have set the first two parameters to 0 to indicate that the border is not offset to the left, right, top, or bottom.

It is also possible to produce a shadow inside the element. This is produced by specifying `inset` as the final parameter. For example:

```
box-shadow: 0 0 10px 10px #888888 inset;
```

This produces the effect in Figure 26-5.

CUSTOM FONTS

One problem with specifying fonts is that there is no guarantee which fonts will be available inside each browser. This is the reason that fonts have been specified as follows:

```
font-family: Arial, Helvetica, sans-serif;
```

FIGURE 26-5

This allows the browser to select the best available font that matches your requirements. If Arial or Helvetica are available, they will be used; otherwise, the default browser sans-serif font will be used.

> **NOTE** *A serif is a small line attached to the end of a line on a character. Serif fonts are typically used in print books because it is argued that they are more readable. Web pages, on the other hand, tend to use sans-serif fonts.*

This approach can be problematic. As a result of the difference in size of different characters in different fonts, a web page may look quite different if an alternative font is used. In order to circumvent this problem, it is possible for a website to provide its own fonts, have the browser download them, and use them in the CSS.

One of the reasons that different browsers support different fonts is that many fonts need to be licensed from their creators. In this section, you will use the Open Sans font, which was commissioned by Google and is available for use with an open license.

> **NOTE** *The main disadvantage of using your own fonts is that the user needs to download them, and they can be several megabytes in size.*

Open Sans is an ideal font for web pages because it strives to present a neutral impression that is pleasing to the eye and easy to read.

In order to get started with Open Sans, you need to obtain a copy of the font files. These are made available in a collection of files with .ttf extensions (for true-type font). Different files are available for regular font, bold font, italic font, and bold-italic font. These can be found on the book's website.

> **NOTE** *Open Sans actually provides 10 variants, including light, semi-bold, and extra bold. If you download these and wish to use them, it is possible to indicate the variant that should be used via the* font-weight *property: Along with values such as* bold*, this can be assigned a number between 100 and 1000. 400 is the same as normal, and 700 is the same as bold; therefore, 600 will use a semi-bold font, provided that variant is supported by your chosen font.*

Once they are downloaded, you need to refer to them in your style sheet or the style section of the web page. For example:

```
@font-face {
    font-family: "Open Sans";
    src: url(OpenSans-Regular.ttf);
    font-weight: normal;
}
@font-face {
    font-family: "Open Sans";
    src: url(OpenSans-Bold.ttf);
    font-weight: bold;
}
@font-face {
    font-family: "Open Sans";
    src: url(OpenSans-BoldItalic.ttf);
    font-weight: bold;
    font-style: italic;
}
@font-face {
    font-family: "Open Sans";
    src: url(OpenSans-Italic.ttf);
    font-weight: normal;
    font-style: italic;
}
```

Notice that these are not regular CSS selectors because they do not select elements from the DOM. Instead, these rules define the name of the font and the location of the font file.

You can now add a font-family style, confident that you do not need to provide any fallback options:

```
body {
    font-family: "Open Sans";
}
```

Finally, you can add the following markup to the page to use this font:

```
<p>This is open sans</p>
<p><strong>This is open sans bold<strong></p>
<p><em>This is open sans bold<em></p>
```

> **NOTE** *Remember that the* b *and* i *tags for bold and italics have been depre-cated, but it is considered acceptable to use* strong *and* em *(short for emphasis). These tags are considered acceptable because they describe the effect that should be used, rather than exactly how this effect should be achieved.*

This will produce the web page shown in Figure 26-6.

This is open sans

This is open sans bold

This is open sans bold

FIGURE 26-6

TRY IT

In this Try It, you will create a layout that appears as tabs, using a number of the techniques learned in this lesson.

The goal is to create a set of tabs, as shown in Figure 26-7.

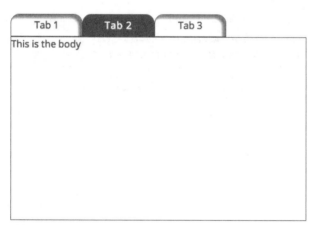

FIGURE 26-7

This Try It will only contain very general hints rather than specific steps. This lesson, together with the lessons on CSS, provides all the necessary information to implement this panel.

Lesson Requirements

You will need a text editor for writing the code and the Chrome browser for running the code.

Step-by-Step

1. Start by creating a standard HTML5 web page.

2. Create a layout for the various elements on the page. I used `div` and `a` elements: Each of the tabs is an `a` element, and the three tabs are surrounded by a `div`. I also used a `div` for the tab content and surrounded the entire structure with a `div`.

3. The font I have used is Open Sans, so import this into the style sheet, and declare that the tabs use Open Sans.

4. I have two distinct types of tabs. Active tabs use a white font and a dark background, while inactive tabs use the inverse of this.

5. The inactive tabs have a shadow around the top and right sides.

6. The tabs should have rounded corners on the top edges. The `border-radius` property can accept four sizes representing the radius of all four corners, starting in the top left. This can be used to prevent rounded corners appearing on the bottom border of the tabs.

7. The example that follows does not implement functionality for changing tabs, but you can try implementing behavior if you like: Every time the user clicks a tab, you could set it to the active tab and change the contents of the panel.

My version can be found on the book's website, and is named `tryit.html`.

> **REFERENCE** *Please go to the book's website at* www.wrox.com/go/html5jsj-query24hr *to view the video for Lesson 26, as well as download the code and resources for this lesson.*

27

CSS3: Part II

This lesson will continue where the previous lesson left off, and continue looking at CSS3 features. The features introduced in this lesson may seem somewhat familiar because many of these features were introduced with the Canvas API, such as linear gradients, transformations, and transitions.

These features have been introduced to allow browsers to natively implement complex visual effects that previously could only be achieved with images, or DOM manipulation.

> **NOTE** *Before beginning this lesson, it is worth reiterating that CSS3 is a major specification in its own right; thus, this lesson will only touch the surface of what can be achieved with these features.*

LINEAR GRADIENTS

CSS3 linear gradients have a lot in common with those introduced with the Canvas API. A line is imagined for the gradient to run through, and colors are defined for points along the line. The browser is then responsible for creating a smooth transition from one color to the next.

In order to define a linear gradient, it is necessary to use a CSS function called `linear-gradient`. Although I have not discussed CSS functions so far, you have seen them in action. For instance, in the previous lesson a URL was defined as follows:

```
url("border.png")
```

A CSS function is just like a JavaScript function: It accepts parameters and returns a value. Throughout this lesson, you will use a number of useful CSS functions, beginning with `linear-gradient`. The main difference between CSS and JavaScript functions is that you cannot create your own CSS functions.

The simplest form of the `linear-gradient` function accepts the following parameters:

➤ The angle of the line that the gradient runs through

➤ The start color

➤ The end color

For instance, after creating an HTML page with a single `div` element, add the following style to create a linear gradient that runs at a 45-degree angle through a `div`.

```
<style>
    div {
        margin:20px;
        width:250px;
        height:250px;
        background:linear-gradient(45deg, white, black);
    }
</style>
```

FIGURE 27-1

This produces the effect seen in Figure 27-1.

Rather than specifying an angle in degrees, it is possible to use one of the following shortcuts:

➤ `to top`: The gradient runs from the bottom to the top of the element. This is equivalent to 0 degrees.

➤ `to bottom`: The gradient runs from the top to the bottom of the element. This is equivalent to 180 degrees.

➤ `to left`: The gradient runs from the right to the left of the element. This is equivalent to 270 degrees.

➤ `to right`: The gradient runs from the left to the right of the element. This is equivalent to 90 degrees.

For instance, the following creates a linear gradient that changes from white to black as it progresses from left to right:

```
background: linear-gradient(to right, white, black);
```

The `linear-gradient` function accepts as many colors as required and automatically creates a linear gradient from one color to the next. For example:

```
background:linear-gradient(45deg, red, white, blue);
```

These are equivalent to color stops seen with the Canvas API, and, as with the Canvas API, it is possible to specify where each color stops based on pixels or percentages. For example:

```
background: linear-gradient(45deg, red 0%, white 20%, blue 100%);
```

CALC FUNCTION

Another useful CSS function introduced in CSS3 is the `calc` function. This allows you to specify sizes as calculations, which can be extremely useful when you need to size elements using a combination of two or more units of measure.

When laying out web pages, there are generally two ways to size elements:

➤ **As absolute sizes, for instance specifying width and height in pixels:** This approach is great for providing a consistent user experience but means content must be sized for the smallest supported browser resolution.

➤ **As percentages, specifying how much of the available space each element should use:** This is great for taking advantage of the user's entire browser but can cause issues if the browser is sized too small because there may not be enough space available for a specific element.

The `calc` function essentially provides the best of both worlds because it lets you mix and match units. For instance, imagine a case where you want a `div` to use 30 percent of the space available, minus 20 pixels. This can be specified as follows:

```
width:calc(30% - 20px);
```

The `calc` function allows you to perform calculations using any combination of addition, subtraction, division, and multiplication, and also lets you specify operator precedence. For instance:

```
width:calc((30% / 2) - 20px);
```

CSS3 also specifies two companion functions that have the potential to be even more useful. Consider a case where you want the width of an element to use 30 percent of its available space, but never be less than 200 pixels. This can be achieved with the `min` function:

```
width:min(30%, 200px);
```

Likewise, it is possible to use the `max` function to specify that the width should be the greater of two values.

Unfortunately `min` and `max` have not appeared in most browsers as yet, but expect them to be added in the near future.

TEXT EFFECTS

Although a wealth of textual information is contained in web pages, it has never been possible to control the presentation of text in web pages to the degree that is possible with other formats, such as PDF.

CSS3 has countered this problem from two angles. The first is pseudo elements, which allow you to add classes to specific portions of an element, such as the first line of a paragraph; the other is via text effects.

This section will look at the text effects that have been implemented in most browsers. CSS3 also specifies a number of other text effects that have not been adopted by any browsers but are likely to appear in the future.

To begin, let's look at text shadows. Just as it is possible to provide shadows for elements, it is possible to provide shadows for text. For instance, the following example adds a text shadow to any h1 elements on a web page:

```
h1 {
    font-family: Arial, sanf-serif;
    text-shadow: 3px 3px 5px #888888;
}
```

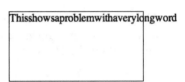

In this case, the shadow extends 3 pixels below and 3 pixels to the right of the text, and has 5 pixels of blur. This produces the effect shown in Figure 27-2.

FIGURE 27-2

A number of the other text effects introduced deal with how to handle overflowing text. Very long words can cause a particular problem to browsers because the web browser does not know how to break them, and therefore, by default, never does break them. In the example in Figure 27-3, the text is placed inside the div but overflows its boundary:

Thisshowsaproblemwithaverylongword

FIGURE 27-3

It is now possible to specify that the web browser can break the word by using the following property:

```
word-wrap:break-word;
```

This will produce the result shown in Figure 27-4.

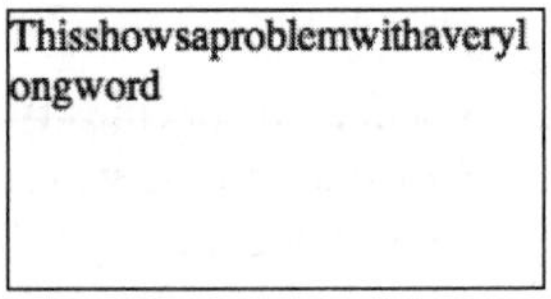

Thisshowsaproblemwithaveryl
ongword

FIGURE 27-4

Another common overflow problem occurs when text is too long for its containing element. This can be a particularly difficult problem when using relative sizing because the size available will depend on the resolution of the user's web browser. This can lead to the effect shown in Figure 27-5.

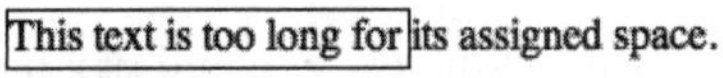

This text is too long for its assigned space.

FIGURE 27-5

You will notice in this case that the text overflows to the right rather than the bottom. The following property created this effect:

```
white-space: nowrap;
```

The nowrap value means that text does not wrap when it reaches the right-hand boundary of an element. In order to prevent the text spilling outside its boundary it is possible to use the following property:

```
overflow: hidden;
```

This presents a problem however because it simply truncates any text that overflows the element, and it not obvious that the text has been truncated. CSS3 therefore supports a more graceful alternative by adding a `text-overflow` property:

```
text-overflow:ellipsis;
```

This produces the result shown in Figure 27-6.

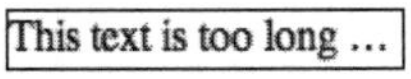

Unfortunately the technique outlined here only works when the text overflows to the right of the element, not when it overflows below an element.

This text is too long ...

FIGURE 27-6

2D TRANSFORMATIONS

The concept of a transformation matrix was introduced in Lesson 25 in relation to the Canvas API. This allowed canvas features to be scaled, skewed, or offset based on a matrix of values provided to the API. As discussed, a transformation matrix is a generic mechanism for transforming shapes.

CSS3 also introduces the concept of a transformation matrix and allows elements to be manipulated in a manner almost identical to the Canvas API. CSS3 introduces a function called `matrix` that allows the six non-constant values to be provided for the transformation matrix, but before looking at this, you will look at the functions that allow you to control the individual aspects of the transformation.

> **NOTE** *Many of the 2D Transformation functions are only supported via browser-specific prefixes. Where appropriate, the examples that follow will use* `-webkit-` *prefixes (for Chrome and Safari), but remember to also include prefixes for other browsers where appropriate:* `moz` *for Firefox and* `ms` *for Internet Explorer.*
>
> *When adding CSS properties that require prefixes, it is also best practice to also provide a non-prefixed version of the property. This will ensure that when the property is eventually supported, the CSS does not need to be changed. A typical example will look as follows:*
>
> ```
> -webkit-property=value
> -moz-property=value
> -ms-property=value
> property=value
> ```

All the examples in this section will operate on the two `div` elements defined in the following web page:

```
<!DOCTYPE html>
<html lang="en">
```

```
<head>
    <meta charset="utf-8">
    <style>
        div {
            height:200px;
            width:200px;
            border:1px solid black;
            margin:50px;
            background:#888888;
            float:left;
        }
        #div2 {
            background:#bcbcbc;
        }
    </style>
</head>
<body>
    <div id="div1"></div>
    <div id="div2"></div>
</body>
</html>
```

To begin, you will scale the `div` with the ID `div2` so that it is 50 percent the size of the other `div`. This can be achieved by adding the following rule to `#div2`:

```
transform: scale(0.5,0.5);
```

In these examples, the property name will always be `transform`, while the function names utilized will vary. The two parameters passed to the function in this case refer to the width and the height, although it is possible to use `scaleX` or `scaleY` if you only need to scale a single axis. This produces the result shown in Figure 27-7.

FIGURE 27-7

It is also possible to skew elements by using the rotate function. For example:

```
-webkit-transform: rotate(45deg);
```

You can also skew an element by defining an angle for the X and Y-axis respectively. For example:

```
-webkit-transform: skew(10deg,-45deg);
```

This produces the result shown in Figure 27-8.

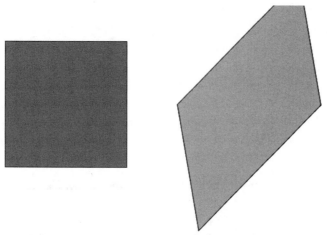

FIGURE 27-8

Finally, it is possible to move elements from where they otherwise would be placed by using the `translate` function. As with the Canvas API, the best way to think about this is that it is a mechanism for offsetting where the 0,0 coordinate would be for each element. For instance, the following code will position an element 40 pixels to the right and 40 pixels above where it otherwise would be positioned:

```
transform: translate(40px,-40px);
```

If you only want to offset the X- or Y-axis, you can use the `translateX` and `translateY` functions respectively.

If you wish to invoke more than one of the `translate` functions, you can simply list them in a space-separated manner. For example:

```
transform: translate(40px,-40px) scale(0.5,0.5);
```

Alternatively, if you are transforming more than one aspect of an element, you can use the `matrix` function. This accepts the following parameters:

➤   The scaling for the X parameter, with 1 being the default.

➤   The amount to skew the X-axis by. A value of 0.45 is equivalent to 45 degrees.

➤   The amount to skew the Y-axis by.

➤   The scaling for the Y parameter, with 1 being the default.

➤   The X-axis offset. Offsets are expressed in pixels, but the `px` suffix must be omitted.

➤   The Y-axis offset.

I hope you noticed that this list is exactly the same as with the Canvas API.

The following is an example use of the `matrix` function:

```
transform: matrix(0.5, 0.45, -0.45, 0.5, -300, 0);
```

This produces the result shown in Figure 27-9.

FIGURE 27-9

> **NOTE** *The transitions demonstrated in this section have been 2D transitions because they adjust the element in two dimensions. CSS3 also supports three-dimensional transitions. Although these are beyond the scope of this book, you may want to explore them in your own time. The CSS functions supporting this are* `translate3d`, `scale3d`, `rotate3d`, *and* `matrix3d`. *These are essentially the same as the functions demonstrated in this section, except they accept parameters representing the third dimension.*

TRANSITIONS

Earlier in the book, I introduced simple animation effects with jQuery. These effects essentially controlled the behavior as an element transitioned from one state to another, usually from hidden to visible, or vice versa.

CSS3 has also introduced a form of animation called CSS Transitions. These achieve many of the same effects as the jQuery animation libraries, but because they are implemented directly by the browser, tend to produce smoother effects.

CSS Transitions allow you to define when a transition effect will begin, how long the transition will last, and the behavior the transition will take (for instance, run at a constant speed, speed up as it nears completion, or slow down as it nears completion).

In order to see transitions in action, consider the following web page:

```
<!DOCTYPE html>
<html lang="en">
<head>
    <meta charset="utf-8">
    <style>
        div {
```

```
            height:20px;
            width:200px;
            margin:50px;
              background:black;
              color:white;
              transition:height 3s, color 2s, background 2s, border 2s;
        }
      div:hover {
            background: white;
            color:black;
            border: 1px solid black;
            height:200px;
        }
    </style>
</head>
<body>
    <div id="div1">Hover to expand</div>
</body>
</html>
```

This defines a single `div` element. The aspect of the code that allows for transition effects is the following CSS property:

```
transition:height 3s, color 2s, background 2s, border 2s;
```

This property defines how long the browser will take to transition from one state to another when various stylistic properties on the element are changed. The times are expressed in seconds, but can also be expressed in milliseconds by using the `ms` suffix.

By itself this property does not do anything. CSS Transitions rely on the stylistic properties being manipulated in some manner. In this case the styles are changed when the user hovers over the element (since the `hover` pseudo-class modifies the value of various properties), but they could be changed in other ways, such as through JavaScript manipulation of the DOM.

When a CSS property is changed, the browser checks to see whether there is a transition rule associated with that property. If there is, it applies those rules as the property is changed.

If you open this web page and hover over the element, you will notice that it takes 3 seconds for the height to change from 20 pixels to 200 pixels. Likewise, you will notice that it takes 2 seconds for the background to change from black to white, and that it changes in a linear manner, starting as a dark grey and gradually becoming lighter, until finally it is white.

In this example, the only aspect of the transition that is controlled is the time taken to complete the transition. It is also possible to control the effect that will be used and the delay that will occur before the effect begins.

As an example, you may want to specify that the effect does not begin for 1 second, and that the effect eases in and eases out:

```
transition-delay: 1s;
transition-timing-function: ease-in-out;
```

These effects can also be specified directly on the transition property, and therefore can be different for different properties. For example:

```
transition:height 3s ease-in-out, color 2s linear 1s, background 2s ease-in 2s,
border 1s ease-out 3s;
```

Combining different delays, durations, and effects is a useful way of creating a more interesting transition effect.

Naturally, not all CSS properties can be animated when their values change. For instance, it is not possible to animate changing from one font to another. The vast majority of properties that change the size or color of an element in any way can be animated, however.

TRY IT

In this Try It, you will use some of the transformation and transition techniques learned in this lesson. Begin by writing the following web page that defines a single div element:

```
<!DOCTYPE html>
<html lang="en">
<head>
    <meta charset="utf-8">
    <script src="jquery-2.1.1.js"></script>
    <style>
            div {
                height:200px;
                width:200px;
                margin:50px;
                background:green;
            }
    </style>
</head>
<body>
    <div id="div1"></div>
</body>
</html>
```

You will then add a click listener so that when the div is clicked, it transitions through four sets of colors, and rotates by 90 degrees as it changes color.

Lesson Requirements

You will need a text editor for writing the code and the Chrome browser for running the code.

Step-by-Step

1. Start by creating the web page with the div element. Be sure to import the jQuery library because this will be used to add a click listener.

2. The div CSS rule needs to be given a transition property, which needs to contain values for changes to the background color and transformation (this will be -webkit-transform because you will use the rotate function, and this uses browser prefixes), so add two sets of transition rules specifying the number of seconds the transition should take, and the effect for the transition.

3.   Create a `script` block in the web page and add an array of four colors. For example:

```
var colors = ['green', 'teal', 'indigo', 'purple'];
```

4.   Add a click listener to the `div` element. When this is clicked, perform Steps 5–7.

5.   Increment a counter variable by 1, and then use the modulus operator to determine whether this is state 0, 1, 2, or 3.

6.   Change the background color to the next value in the array, cycling back to the start when the end is reached.

7.   Use the `rotate` function to rotate the `div` by an additional 90 degrees. The easiest way to do this is to multiply 90 by 0, 1, 2, or 3.

My version of the web page can be found on the book's website, and is named `tryit.html`:

> **REFERENCE** *Please go to the book's website at* www.wrox.com/go/html5js-jquery24hr *to view the video for Lesson 27, as well as download the code and resources for this lesson.*

28

CSS3 Media Queries

You will end this section by taking a first look at CSS3 media queries. This is a subject you will return to when you look at developing web applications for mobile phones, but this lesson will introduce the fundamentals for developing web applications that render differently on different devices, and in different contexts.

It is now very common for a web application to be used on many different devices. For example:

➤ In a web browser, on a desktop or laptop

➤ Output to a printer

➤ On a small screen device, such as a smart phone

➤ On an alternative device, such as a TV

Although the basic functionality of the web application may be the same in each case, it may be necessary to reposition, hide, or augment the display of specific elements for each device.

There are several ways to solve this problem. Historically, the most common approach has been for the web server to detect the browser (or user agent) accessing the web page, and directing the user to a page created specifically for this device.

Any time a browser requests a web page, it provides a variety of information in HTTP headers. These can be can be used by the web server to reliably detect the browser and operating system. For example, Figure 28-1 shows the headers that were passed to the web server when performing a simple HTTP GET request, including the User Agent header.

There are two main problems with this approach. The first is that it does not necessarily provide the entire context of the user's web browser. For instance, if the user is using a tablet, it will not contain information on whether he or she is using landscape or portrait mode. Likewise, it cannot be used to augment the web page for printing because printing a page does not trigger a request for a new web page from the server.

FIGURE 28-1

The second problem is that it can become difficult to maintain content in this manner. There will often be large amounts of duplication across the different versions of the web pages. When a change is required to the web application, it may therefore be necessary to make the same change in many different files.

CSS3 now offers an alternative mechanism for solving this problem in the form of media queries. These queries allow a stylesheet to tell the browser how to behave in various contexts, and therefore allow the same page to render differently without changing any markup.

With media queries, it is up to the browser itself to determine whether specific stylesheets, or portions of stylesheets, are relevant for them based on a set of rules, and to render the web page appropriately.

Media queries allow a stylesheet to provide custom rules based on:

➤ The device type—for instance, screen, printer, or TV

➤ The width or height of the browser or screen

➤ Whether the orientation is landscape or portrait

➤ Whether the device is color or monochrome

This lesson will focus on the first of these bullet points and return to examine the other bullet points when you develop mobile web applications in future lessons.

ADDING MEDIA QUERIES

Imagine that you wish to add print capabilities to the CRM web application. When clicked, this will only print the contacts in the table; it will never print the editable section of the screen, even if it is present, and it will not print the `header` or the `footer`.

One way to achieve this may be to add a new class called `noprint` to every element you do not wish to print. For example:

```
<header class="noprint">Contacts</header>
```

Then, add the following rule to `contacts.css`:

```
@media print {
  .noprint {
     display: none;
  }
}
```

Notice that the rule begins with the `@media` tag. This indicates that the rule will only apply in specific contexts. The `@media` tag is followed by a query that allows the browser to determine whether the rule is applicable in specific contexts. In this case, the query is `print`, which indicates that the rule only applies if the web page is being printed.

The other common values for media queries are:

➤ `all`: Matches all device types.

➤ `screen`: Matches any screen-based device, which therefore excludes printers.

➤ `tv`: Matches when the page is viewed on a television.

➤ `handheld`: This is intended to match browsers on small screen devices such as smart phones. I don't recommend that you use this option, however, because it is not reliably supported. You will look at a more reliable alternative to this later in the book.

Next, add a print button to the screen, and also ensure that the "Add a new contact" button does not print:

```
<div class="controls noprint">
 <a href="#" id="addContact">Add a new contact</a>
 <a onClick="window.print()" href="#">Print</a>
</div>
```

I also updated the table so that the Actions column has the `noprint` class (both the `th` and `td` elements). If you now elect to print the web application, it should generate a preview, as shown in Figure 28-2.

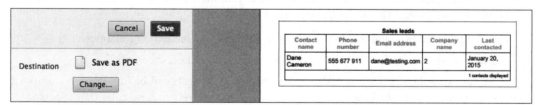

FIGURE 28-2

You will notice that only the appropriate elements are included in the print preview. You may notice, however, that the table header does not print as expected. In the web application, the header has a blue background and a white font. When browsers print web pages, they typically suppress background colors to save ink. As a result, they compensate by changing white fonts to have color.

In this case, the overall effect is not what you may want because the font is quite difficult to read. You also may choose to remove the border and white space from around the table. You can therefore add the following rules to your media query:

```
@media print {
  .noprint {
    display: none !important;
  }
  th {
      color:black;
      background:white;
  }
  #contactList {
      border: none;
      margin: none;
      padding:none;
  }
}
```

This will then generate the preview shown in Figure 28-3.

		Sales leads		
Contact name	Phone number	Email address	Company name	Last contacted
Dane Cameron	555 322 333	dane@testing.com	2	January 6, 2015
				1 contacts displayed

FIGURE 28-3

EXTERNAL STYLESHEETS

The approach outlined in the previous text involves adding device-specific rules to stylesheets. Often it is more convenient to create a base stylesheet that matches all device types, and then create device-specific stylesheets that override relevant styles.

This can be achieved by using the `media` attribute on the `link` element. For example:

```
<link rel="stylesheet" media="all" type="text/css" href="contacts.css">
```

After the base stylesheet is imported, the device-specific stylesheets can be imported. It is important that these are listed after the base stylesheet because they are likely to have rules that supersede those in the base stylesheet. For example:

```
<link rel="stylesheet" media="print" type="text/css" href="contacts_print.css">
```

Naturally, when stylesheets are imported in this manner, the stylesheets themselves do not need to contain media queries, although they still can if necessary.

It is important to realize that matches based on media queries do not have higher specificity than they would otherwise so it can also be necessary to use the `!important` modifier to ensure that media-specific styles are used.

TRY IT

In this Try It, you will introduce a print-specific stylesheet for printing. If you have not followed the example so far in this lesson, you may want to go back and implement the print functionality outlined before starting this Try It.

Lesson Requirements

You will need a text editor to write the code and the Chrome browser to run the code.

Step-by-Step

1. Start by creating a new stylesheet called `contacts_print.css` in the same folder as `contacts.css`.

2. Add the print-specific functionality to this stylesheet and remove any media queries.

3. Import the print stylesheet after the `contacts.css` stylesheet, and indicate that it is applicable for printing.

4. Add a media type to the `contacts.css` import, and indicate that it is applicable to all device types.

5. Add a new header specifically for printing; this should state "Printed from CRM."

6. Add a class called `print_only` to this element, and then add rules to both the base and print stylesheets. The base stylesheet should set the `display` to `none`. The print stylesheet should set the `display` to `initial`, which means to restore it to its default value.

7. Change the header style in the print stylesheet to use a black, 16-pixel font.

> **REFERENCE** *Please go to the book's website at www.wrox.com/go/html5jsj-query24hr to view the video for Lesson 28, as well as download the code and resources for this lesson.*

PART IV
HTML5 APIs

29

Web Servers

Up until this point in the book, you have been opening web pages in the browser directly from the file system. Obviously, if you intend your web pages to be viewed by others, you need to make them available over a network. The software used for exposing web pages over a network is a web server.

The term "web server" can either denote the hardware of the underlying server or the software running on that server. For the purposes of this lesson, the term "web server" will be used to denote the software, whereas "server" will be used to denote the hardware this software runs on.

The primary purpose of a web server is to expose a set of resources from the file system of a network enabled server via protocols such as HTTP and HTTPS. Resources are typically files such as HTML pages, images, and CSS files, to video and audio files.

> **NOTE** *This view is slightly simplistic because many resources in real-world web applications are dynamically generated and therefore do not exist on a physical file system, but you will ignore this complication for the most part.*

In this lesson, you will migrate the web application developed so far to a web server. You are doing this for two main reasons:

➤ **To give you an understanding of how a web server works:** Any web page or web application you develop will be uploaded eventually to a web server, so it is useful to gain some understanding of how they work, and how to configure one.

➤ **Many of the APIs introduced in this section need to run inside web servers:** The APIs included in this section will cover more advanced JavaScript APIs such as storing data inside the browser. These APIs therefore need a mechanism for segregating the data from different websites: Without this segregation, any website would be able to access data stored by any other website, which would obviously create a security loophole.

URLS

Before looking at web servers, this chapter will quickly cover the related topic of URLs (Uniform Resource Locators). A URL provides a unique network address for a resource (image, web page, CSS file). The "network" will often be the public Internet, but URLs can also be used to locate resources on private networks, such as your personal WiFi network at home.

The web server is responsible for parsing the URL and determining the resource that should be returned. The URL is also used by lower-level protocols, however, to determine how to route the request to the appropriate server on the network.

URLs are surprisingly complex, but the most familiar pattern is as follows:

```
http://testing.com:80/test1/test.html
```

This URL consists of the following components:

➤   `http`: The protocol that is being used to access the resource; other common protocols are `https` and `ftp`.

➤   `testing.com`: The domain name resolved by the browser to an IP address using a Domain Name Server (DNS). The IP address (for instance 192.168.199.133) in turn maps to a server running on a network.

➤   `80`: The port number of the web server. Because a single server may expose multiple services (for example, an FTP server and an HTTP server), port numbers provide a mechanism to logically differentiate them. You will not usually see the port number in URLs because 80 is the default for the HTTP protocol, and 443 is the default for the HTTPS protocol, and the port number can therefore usually be omitted.

➤   `test1`: The directory on the web server. Typically, the web server will map its root directory to a directory on the file system. In this case, there would be an assumption that this directory contains a subdirectory called `test1`.

➤   `test.html`: The name of the resource being accessed.

The two most important components used by the APIs in this section are the domain name and the port. These are referred to as the "origin" of a resource. Typically, a resource will only be able to interact with resources or information from the same origin: This is referred to as the *same origin policy*.

CHOOSING A WEB SERVER

There are many web servers available, both commercial and open source. Many factors come into play when choosing a web server, but these discussions are beyond the scope of this book. It is, however, worth mentioning that by far the most popular web server, almost since the advent of the World Wide Web, is the Apache web server.

Apache is an open source web server, and provides an excellent combination of stability, features, and performance. If you use a hosting service, they will almost certainly make the Apache web server available to you.

You will not use Apache in this book, mainly because it takes slightly more effort to install and configure than the web server you will use, but you may opt to use it if you choose. It can be accessed from `http://httpd.apache.org/`, and tutorials are available for guiding you through the installation and configuration process.

In this book, you will use the Mongoose web server (free edition). The main reason for choosing this is its simplicity: It requires either very little or no configuration and is therefore ideal during the development phase of your web application.

TRY IT

In this Try It, you install and configure the Mongoose web server. This Try It contains two sets of steps, one for Windows and one for OS X.

> **NOTE** *Linux source code is also available at:* `http://code.google.com/p/mongoose/downloads/list`. *To run this, the simplest option is to* cd *to the directory containing* `contacts.html` *and run* mongoose. *This runs in the foreground so use* ctrl-C *to stop.*

Lesson Requirements

As part of the steps outlined next, you will need to download the Mongoose web server from the site listed. This will involve agreeing to the non–commercial license agreement. You will also need the Chrome web browser to test that the web server is working.

Step-by-Step (OS X)

1. Download the Free Edition OS X installer from: `http://cesanta.com/downloads.html`. This requires you to accept the license agreement.

2. Once this has downloaded, double-click on the DMG file and drag it to Applications, just as you would when installing any other application.

3. Open the Finder and navigate to the Applications folder. Find the Mongoose application, and double-click on the icon to start the Mongoose server.

4. The Mongoose application can now be configured via the icon in the taskbar at the top of the screen, as shown in Figure 29-1.

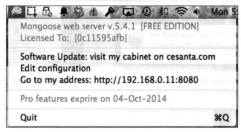

FIGURE 29-1

5.   Select the Edit configuration option. This will open a browser window with the configuration settings. Locate the document_root text field, and change the directory to the directory that contains the contacts.html file. For example /Users/dane/html5/CRM. Once entered, click "Save settings to the config file".

6.   The Mongoose server operates by default on port 8080 rather than port 80. Because it is running on your local machine, you can also use the hostname localhost. Therefore, to open the contacts page, open Chrome, and enter **http://localhost:8080/contacts.html**. This should show the main contacts web page.

Step-by-Step (Windows)

1.   Download the Free Edition OS X installer from http://cesanta.com/downloads.html. This requires you to accept the license agreement.

2.   Once the download is complete, copy the .exe file to the same directory that contains contacts.html.

3.   Double-click on the executable to start Mongoose.

4.   The Mongoose application can now be configured via the icon in the taskbar at the bottom of the screen, as shown in Figure 29-2 (although no configuration is required in this case).

FIGURE 29-2

5. The Mongoose server operates by default on port 8080 rather than port 80. Because it is running on your local machine, you can also use the hostname `localhost`. Therefore, to open the contacts page, open Chrome, and enter **http://localhost:8080/contacts.html**.

This should show the main contacts web page.

REFERENCE *Please go to the book's website at* www.wrox.com/go/html5jsj-query24hr *to view the video for Lesson 29, as well as download the code and resources for this lesson.*

30

Web Storage

When the World Wide Web was first envisioned, it was intended as a repository for static documents, primarily academic papers. The key distinguishing feature of the World Wide Web was hyperlinks, which allowed one document to provide a link to another document, and therefore allowed convenient navigation from one piece of information to another.

It wasn't long before web pages started providing more advanced features, such as online shopping. This required web pages to dynamically respond to user interaction. As you have seen, this was facilitated by technologies such as the DOM API, which allows a web page to be modified after it was loaded.

HTML and JavaScript could only take you so far, however. It still was not possible to create web pages or web applications that exhibited the features typically found in native desktop applications. For instance, web pages lacked the following capabilities:

- ➤ The ability to interact with the file system beyond the simple `file` input type.

- ➤ The ability to store large amounts of data or configuration information inside the browser (on the client).

- ➤ The ability to function without a network connection. Even if a page is cached inside a browser, it typically is not usable without a network connection.

- ➤ The ability to perform intensive processing on a background thread without impacting the user experience. Because all JavaScript processing occurs on a single thread, any intensive processing will cause the web page to "lock up."

- ➤ The ability to request additional data from a server after a page had loaded without performing a refresh of the entire web page.

You can think of these features as the services accessible to a software application. For a traditional desktop application, the operating system provides these services. Web pages cannot interact directly with the operating system; they can only interact with the browser. Therefore, unless the browser provided these services, web pages would always be constrained from achieving a higher level of sophistication.

Despite the historic limitations of HTML and JavaScript, there has been a strong push toward browser-based web applications as opposed to native applications. Browser-based web applications are enormously convenient because the same web application can be accessed on any device, from any location, at any time. This push has only intensified with the move toward cloud computing, as more and more data is pushed into globally available cloud computers.

Browser-based web applications also have the advantage that they do not need to be installed, and they can be automatically updated without any action from the user.

In order to allow web applications to achieve the same level of sophistication as native applications, the HTML5 specification provides a set of JavaScript APIs for implementing all the features just listed, along with several others. This section will cover these APIs in detail, starting with client-side storage.

CLIENT-SIDE STORAGE

The HTTP protocol used to retrieve resources from a web server was designed as a stateless protocol. It begins with the browser establishing a network connection to the web server and requesting a resource. The web server finds the resource and returns it as a response to the browser. Once the response is received, the connection between the two is closed, and no link is retained that the two ever communicated.

> **NOTE** *This is a slightly simplified view of HTTP. Because establishing connections can be time consuming, the HTTP protocol was extended early on to support a keep-alive option. This meant that multiple requests could be made on the same connection. This feature cannot be relied on in order to continue a conversation with the web server, however, because it is up to the web server to decide how long to leave the connection open for.*

This model clearly does not work well for a number of scenarios. If you consider a shopping website, the server will need to retain a shopping cart for the user as he progresses from page to page: Clearly this relies on the web server remembering each particular browser, and the history of their actions—for instance, the products they have purchased. I will refer to all the actions performed by the same browser as a session.

In order to support this, a technology was introduced called cookies. A *cookie* is simply a key/value pair that can be sent by the web server to the browser on an HTTP response. The browser will then store the information in this cookie for a configurable period of time (usually as small files on the file system). Every time the browser sends a request to the same web server in the future, it will include all the cookies that have been sent to it.

Although cookies can be used to store any textual information, typically they are used to store a unique session ID for each browser. The web server generates this session ID whenever it receives a request from a browser it has not seen before (where there is no cookie in the HTTP request), which the browser then stores, and provides automatically on future requests. The web server can then store information against this session ID, and provide that information back to the browser when required, such as when the user decides to check out.

Although cookies are great for storing small amounts of data, they do come with a number of limitations. The principle limitation is that browsers are only required to allow 20 cookies per domain name, and each cookie is limited to 4096 bytes of data. If you work through the sums, a domain may only be able to store 80 kilobytes inside the browser, which, by modern standards, is not a lot of data.

There are, however, very good reasons why a web application may want to store larger amounts of data on the client, the two main ones being:

➤ **Performance:** If the data is stored on the client, it is much faster to process and display in the browser than if it needs to be retrieved from the web server. Despite the increase in network speeds, accessing data locally is still many orders of magnitude faster.

➤ **Availability:** If the data is stored on the client, it can be accessed even when the browser is not connected to a network.

HTML5 adds not one, but three distinct APIs for storing data inside the browser:

➤ **Web storage:** This is the subject of this lesson. This is the oldest storage API and has excellent support across all browsers.

➤ **Web SQL:** This standard proposes a relational database–based API, but is not widely supported, and is unlikely to see support across all browsers in the future. Although this API has a lot to recommend it, it will be ignored in this book, because without universal browser support, the API is unlikely to find widespread adoption.

➤ **IndexedDB:** This is the subject of the next lesson. This API is considerably more complicated than the web storage API, but does offer a number of important additional features.

WEB STORAGE API

The web storage API is by far the simplest of the three data storage APIs specified in HTML5, and, as mentioned, it also has the best support across all major browser vendors.

The web storage API does come with certain limitations, however:

➤ It can only be used for storing textual data (JavaScript Strings). It is not possible to store other types of data such as JavaScript objects.

➤ Browsers may restrict a domain to 5MB of storage. Although this is a huge amount of data in comparison to cookies, it may not be feasible for all scenarios.

> **NOTE** *The 5MB limit is an even bigger constraint than it may sound. This is due to the fact that each character in a JavaScript string uses 2 bytes of storage. JavaScript uses a character encoding called UTF-16, which allows any Unicode character to be represented in 2 or more bytes. Other encodings such as UTF-8 are now far more common, and only use 1 byte for the most common Unicode characters (provided you are using a Western alphabet).*

The web storage API is remarkably simple to use; it relies on simple key/value pairs. In order to see it in action, open the `contacts.html` web page using the relevant address for your web server (for example, `localhost:8080/contacts.html`), and enter the following code in the JavaScript console:

```
> localStorage.setItem("test", "this is a test");
```

In this case, `test` is the key, and `this is a test` is the value. As you can see, the `localStorage` object provided by the browser exposes the web storage API.

> **NOTE** *The browser also exposes the web storage API via a companion object called* `sessionStorage`. *Any data stored via* `localStorage` *is retained indefinitely (or until the user deletes it), whereas data stored via* `sessionStorage` *is automatically cleared when the browser is closed. You should always be conscious of the fact that data stored via the web storage API is not encrypted; therefore, it is not appropriate for sensitive data.*

If you now open the Resources tab of the developer tools, and expand the Local Storage option, you will see that the key/value pair has been captured (see Figure 30-1).

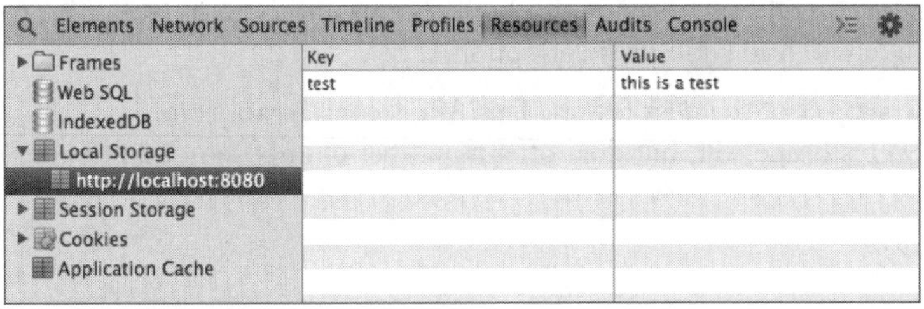

FIGURE 30-1

Notice that this data is associated with the origin `localhost:8080`. Only pages served from this origin will have access to this data.

The companion method for `setItem` is `getItem`. This allows an item to be retrieved based on a key. For example:

```
> localStorage.getItem("test");
"this is a test"
```

This method will always return a JavaScript string, or `undefined` if there is no value stored against the key specified. Two other useful methods are included in the API. The `removeItem` method can be used to remove a value based on a key. For example:

```
> localStorage.removeItem("test");
```

Finally, the `clear` method can be used to remove all data stored by the origin:

```
> localStorage.clear();
```

These simple methods are all that is required to use web storage.

STORING STRUCTURED DATA

As mentioned earlier, the web storage API can only be used for storing textual data; it cannot be used for storing structured data such as JavaScript objects. This presents a problem for your CRM web application because you would ideally like to store the JavaScript contact objects in web storage so that they are retained when the page is refreshed or the browser is closed.

> **NOTE** *The web storage API will not actually complain if you specify a JavaScript object as the value for a key; it will simply convert the object into a string by invoking its* toString *method. This will usually mean that the value persisted is* [object Object] *because this is the default value of* toString.

Fortunately, there is a simple solution to this: You can use the JSON.stringify function to convert JavaScript objects to JSON encoded strings, and then store these strings in web storage. When you need to retrieve data from web storage, you can convert it back into JavaScript objects with JSON.parse.

For instance, if you want to save a contact object, you can create the following function in contacts.js:

```
function store(contact) {
    var c = JSON.stringify(contact);
    localStorage.setItem('contacts', c);
}
```

This function adds a single contact to web storage.

Because you need to store multiple contacts, you may decide to create an array for holding the objects. Additionally, you need to retrieve the existing array from web storage before adding a new contact. The following function therefore provides the necessary functionality for storing multiple contacts:

```
function store(contact) {
    var contactsStored = localStorage.getItem('contacts');
    var contacts = [];
    if (contactsStored) {
        contacts = JSON.parse(contactsStored);
    }
    contacts.push(contact);
    localStorage.setItem('contacts', JSON.stringify(contacts));
}
```

The first line of this function extracts the existing array from web storage. If it exists, it converts it from a string into a JavaScript array. If no contacts have been saved, you simply create an empty array to hold contacts. You then push the new contact onto the array, and persist the array to web storage.

> **NOTE** *It is also possible to extract items from* localStorage *using traditional dot notation—for instance,* localStorage.contacts. *In order to use this approach, item keys must conform to the JavaScript property name standards.*

The setItem method will overwrite any existing entry for the same key; thus, every time a new contact is saved, the array stored in web storage will be entirely replaced.

The store function should be added to the contactsScreen function, immediately after the following line:

```
var initialized = false;
```

The save method should then be changed to invoke this function:

```
save: function(evt) {
    if ($(evt.target).parents('form')[0].checkValidity()) {
        var fragment = $(screen).find('#contactRow')[0].content.cloneNode(true);
        var row = $('<tr>').append(fragment);
        var contact = this.serializeForm();
        store(contact);
        row = bind(row, contact);
        $(row).find('time').setTime();
        $(screen).find('table tbody').append(row);
        $(screen).find('form :input[name]').val('');
        $(screen).find('#contactDetails').toggle( "blind" );
        this.updateTableCount();
    }
}
```

You now need to add functionality to load existing contacts when the contacts.html web page loads. This can be achieved by adding the following method to contacts.js (immediately after the save method):

```
loadContacts: function() {
    var contactsStored = localStorage.getItem('contacts');
    if (contactsStored) {
        contacts = JSON.parse(contactsStored);
        $.each(contacts, function(i, v) {
            var fragment = $(screen).find('#contactRow')[0].content.
cloneNode(true);
            var row = $('<tr>').append(fragment);
            row = bind(row, v);
            $(row).find('time').setTime();
            $(screen).find('table tbody').append(row);
        });
    }
},
```

This function is relatively straightforward; it simply extracts the contacts array from web storage, iterates through the items, and adds each one to the table onscreen using code from earlier in the book.

This function should then be invoked at the end of the init method with the following line of code:

```
        this.loadContacts();
```

If you now save a contact and re-open the `contacts.html` web page, you should see any contacts that are retained.

TRY IT

In this Try It, you will enhance the functionality added in this lesson by providing delete functionality. Currently, the delete button removes the relevant row from the table, but it does not remove the record from web storage: This means that once the page is refreshed, the contact will immediately come back.

Lesson Requirements

To complete this lesson, you will need a text editor for writing code, and Chrome for running the completed web page. It is also expected that you have completed the steps in the body of the lesson before starting this Try It.

Step-by-Step

1. Open the `contacts.js` file in your text editor. You will make a change to the saving process: When you save a new contact, you will assign it a unique ID. This will allow you to uniquely identify the contact that is being deleted. The ID you will create will be based on the current time in milliseconds. In order to achieve this, add a new line after this line:

   ```
   var contact = this.serializeForm();
   ```

   This line should set an ID property on the contact to have a value derived from the `$.now()` function call. This is another jQuery helper, and returns the current time in milliseconds (as a JavaScript number).

2. Because any existing contacts will not have `id` properties, it is important that you delete them. Use the `localStorage.clear()` method call from the command line to delete all data from web storage.

3. When contact rows are added to the table in `loadContacts`, you will add a data attribute to the `tr` element specifying the ID of the contact in the row. The delete event listener will use this to determine the ID of the contact that should be deleted. Identify the following line of code:

   ```
   var row = $('<tr>').append(fragment);
   ```

   Now, change this so that the `tr` element created has an attribute called `data-id` with the value from `v.id`. Hint: I split this into three separate lines of code.

4. The `contacts.js` file already has a `delete` method that removes a contact from the table. You need to add code before the following line to identify the `data-id` associated with the `tr`:

   ```
   $(evt.target).parents('tr').remove();
   ```

   Assign the ID to a variable called `contactId`.

5. Look up the contacts from web storage and convert it back into a JavaScript array using `JSON.parse`.

6. Use the `filter` method on the array to retain any items that do not match this ID. Assign the newly created array to a variable called `newContacts`.

7. Update the contacts in web storage so that the array stored is the newly created array. Remember to use `JSON.stringify` on the array before adding it to web storage.

> **NOTE** *You may be wondering why you needed an* `id` *to uniquely identify contacts. Typically, adding a key such as this is the easiest way to uniquely identify an object because none of the other properties on the object is guaranteed to be unique. In this case, it may have been possible to make the email address the unique key, but even this can be shared by multiple people in the real world.*

> **REFERENCE** *Please go to the book's website at* www.wrox.com/go/html5jsj-query24hr *to view the video for Lesson 30, as well as download the code and resources for this lesson.*

31

IndexedDB

As mentioned in the previous lesson, HTML5 includes specifications for three distinct APIs that allow data to be stored inside the browser. This lesson introduces the IndexedDB API.

The IndexedDB API is considerably more advanced than the web storage API. Therefore, if the web storage API meets all your needs, you may opt to skip this lesson.

The IndexedDB API does, however, offer the following benefits over the web storage API:

➤ It allows various data types to be stored rather than simple strings. For example, it is possible to store JavaScript objects directly in IndexedDB.

➤ It allows more sophisticated retrieval mechanisms. For example, it is possible to query IndexedDB for a specific record, such as a single contact, based on its unique ID.

➤ It allows create, update, and delete operations to be included in transactions. This means you can perform a set of operations and guarantee that they will either all succeed or all fail. If you are familiar with relational databases, this will be a familiar concept.

➤ It is capable of automatically generating unique keys for records. This will mean you do not need to rely on mechanisms such as the current time in milliseconds, as you saw in the previous lesson.

➤ Browsers typically allow far more data to be stored in IndexedDB as opposed to web storage.

> **NOTE** *Unlike the web storage API, the IndexedDB specification does not state how much storage space must be allocated to each domain. Browsers typically either place no limitations on IndexedDB (beyond what the hard drive will support) or place an upper limit in the gigabytes.*

Although these features can be enormously useful in some web applications, they do complicate the API. The IndexedDB API is further complicated by the fact that it relies heavily on callbacks for virtually all operations: Rather than simply invoking a method and receiving a response, the IndexedDB API relies on you to register callbacks for various scenarios. These callbacks will then be invoked when the specified event occurs.

The main reason the API relies on callbacks is to allow operations to be performed on background threads if necessary. This means that if you are performing an intensive operation, the browser may be able to perform this without impacting the user experience.

As you will see, the use of callbacks will significantly complicate the code you need to write because it will often be necessary to ensure one operation has completed before performing the next operation.

This lesson will provide an alternative implementation for the functionality added in Lesson 30. Therefore, if you want to complete the exercises in this lesson, you should start with a version of the CRM web application as it stood at the start of Lesson 30.

CREATING A DATABASE

In order to start using the IndexedDB API for the first time, you need to explicitly create a database, and tell the API the types of data you wish to store in this database. Requesting to open a non-existent database automatically creates a database.

You will add two distinct sets of data to the database. In addition to contacts, you will add a list of companies to the database, allowing the companies associated with contacts to be displayed correctly in the table (currently a number is displayed).

> **NOTE** *As you will see, IndexedDB is accessed via a browser-supplied object called* indexedDB. *In Firefox, this must currently be referenced as* mozIndexedDB, *and in IE it must be accessed via* msIndexedDB. *It is easy enough to create your own alias to this object that will work in all browsers as follows:*
>
> ```
> myIndexedDB = indexedDB || msIndexedDB || mozIndexedDB;
> ```

The code you will use for creating the database is as follows. This should be placed at the end of the init method in contacts.js to ensure it executes every time the page is loaded:

```
var request = indexedDB.open('contactsDB');
request.onsuccess = function(event) {
}
request.onupgradeneeded = function(event) {
}
```

> **NOTE** *Do not run this code yet. You need to provide implementations for these functions, or an empty database will be created.*

As you can see, you specify that you wish to open a database with a specific name, `contactsDB` in this case. If the database has already been created inside the browser (this is not the first time the user has accessed the web application), the callback function registered for the `onsuccess` event will be invoked.

If the database has not previously been created, or if you provide an optional version number as the second parameter to `open`, the function registered against `onupgradeneeded` will be invoked. It is within this function that you can define the structure of your database.

Before providing implementations for these callbacks, in order to interact with the opened database you will need a reference to it. Therefore, create a private variable called `database` as follows:

```
var initialized = false;
var database = null;
```

Now, provide the following implementations for the callback functions:

```
var request = indexedDB.open('contactsDB');
request.onsuccess = function(event) {
    database = request.result;
}
request.onupgradeneeded = function(event) {
    database = event.target.result;
    var objectStoreContacts = database.createObjectStore("contacts",
        {keyPath: "id", autoIncrement: true });

    var objectStoreCompanies = database.createObjectStore("companies",
        {keyPath: "id", autoIncrement: true });

}
```

The `onsuccess` callback is reasonably straightforward. This function simply records a reference to the database, which you will start using shortly.

The `onupgradeneeded` callback is more complicated. In this callback, you begin by obtaining a reference to the database and then create two object stores in the database. Each object store must be given a unique name, and in each case you have also specified that you would like IndexedDB to generate unique IDs for records via the `autoIncrement` property.

You have also specified that the unique ID for each record can be obtained from the `id` property, so this is the property that will be automatically generated and assigned a unique ID when records are stored.

> **NOTE** *If you are familiar with relational databases, you can think of each object store as a table. The main difference is that you do not need to specify the structure of the data that you will store; you simply need to state how each record can be uniquely identified.*

If you now open the Resources tab of the Chrome developer tools, you will see that a database has been created, and that it contains two object stores (see Figure 31-1).

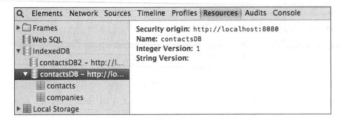

FIGURE 31-1

You can also see that the database has a version number. If you ever need to change the structure of the database, you need to open it and provide a different version number. This will ensure that the `onupgradeneeded` callback is invoked.

STORING DATA

You will begin by adding functionality to store data. Start by adding the following method to `contacts.js` just after the `save` method:

```
store: function(contact) {
    var tx = database.transaction(["contacts"], "readwrite");
    var objectStore = tx.objectStore("contacts");
    var request = objectStore.put(contact);
    request.onsuccess = function(event) {
        console.log("Added a new contact " + event.target.result);
    }
},
```

This method begins by instructing the database that you wish to create a transaction. You provide parameters specifying the object stores that will be involved in the transaction and you identify that you wish to read and write data in the transaction.

All data access with IndexedDB needs to be performed in the context of a transaction. A transaction can then consist of one or more requests. In this case, a single request is added to the transaction, and this simply adds the `contact` to the relevant object store.

> **NOTE** *IndexedDB transactions exhibit the four important properties, usually abbreviated to the acronym ACID:*
>
> **Atomic:** *Either all the operations in the transaction succeed (commits), or all the operations fail (roll back).*
>
> **Consistent:** *The database will remain in a valid state at the end of the transaction as defined by the rules of the database.*
>
> **Isolation:** *The changes made by the transaction are isolated from other transactions until all the changes have been successfully committed.*
>
> **Durable:** *Once the changes are committed, they remain committed, even if the database crashes immediately afterwards.*

As you can see, you can register an `onsuccess` callback with the request. This callback simply outputs the ID that has been assigned to the newly stored contact.

Although it is not shown here, you can also add an `onsuccess` callback to the transaction itself, and this will be invoked after all requests in the transaction have completed. It is important to note that the records added will not be available to other transactions until the transaction (rather than the individual request) has succeeded.

Additionally, it is always possible to register an `onerror` callback along with an `onsuccess` callback. This provides you with an opportunity to handle any unexpected events.

Once the `store` method has been defined, you need to invoke it during the `save` operation, just as you saw in the previous lesson. For example:

```
row = bind(row, contact);
this.store(contact);
```

If you now save a contact, the following message should be displayed in the console:

```
Added a new contact with the ID = 1
```

Additionally, you should be able to see the saved data in the Resources tab, as shown in Figure 31-2.

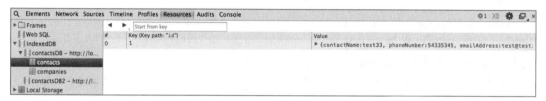

FIGURE 31-2

Each time you add a new contact, the ID automatically assigned will increase by 1.

READING DATA

Now that you have stored data, you can add functionality to read it every time the web application is opened. This functionality will perform the exact same operations as the `loadContacts` method in the previous lesson, except it will read the data from IndexedDB.

Reading data from IndexedDB introduces a new concept called a *cursor*. A cursor is a mechanism for holding a set of records. It is then possible to traverse through the cursor one record at a time and process its contents.

Start by adding the following method to `contacts.js` immediately after the `store` method:

```
loadContacts: function() {
    var tx = database.transaction("contacts");
    var objectStore = tx.objectStore("contacts");
    objectStore.openCursor().onsuccess = function(event) {
        var cursor = event.target.result;
```

```
            if (cursor) {
                var contact = cursor.value;
                var fragment = $(screen).find('#contactRow' )[0].content.
    cloneNode(true);
                var row = $('<tr>');
                row.data().id = contact.id;
                row.append(fragment);
                row = bind(row, contact);
                $(row).find('time').setTime();
                $(screen).find('table tbody').append(row);
                cursor.continue();
            }
        }
    },
```

As you can see, this method begins by specifying that you wish to create a transaction, but this time you do not specify that you need to write data. By default, transactions are always capable of reading data.

Once the transaction is created, you can simply open the relevant object store and open a cursor on the object store. By default, this cursor will provide a result set containing all the records in the object store.

You then add an onsuccess callback to the cursor. This will automatically be passed the first record in the cursor, which can be accessed from cursor.value and processed.

When you have finished processing the record, you invoke cursor.continue(). This automatically causes the onsuccess callback to be invoked again with the next record in the result set. When the value of cursor is null, you know that all the records have been processed.

You need to be careful to only invoke loadContacts after the database has been opened. In order to achieve this, add the following code to the logic that opens the database.

```
var request = indexedDB.open('contactsDB');
request.onsuccess = function(event) {
    database = request.result;
    this.loadContacts();
}.bind(this);
```

Notice that you only attempt to read data from the database after IndexedDB has confirmed it has been successfully opened.

If you wish to access a specific record from the object store, you can achieve this without processing all the records in a cursor. For instance, the following code will find the contact with the ID of 2:

```
var request = objectStore.get(2);
request.onsuccess = function(event) {
    var contact = event.target.result;
}
```

This will provide a significant performance boost as the object store increases in size because IndexedDB optimizes this operation by creating an index on the ID.

> **NOTE** *It is also possible to index any of the other properties on an object (such as* `emailAddress`*), allowing them to be searched directly and efficiently. This subject will not be discussed in this lesson, but information is available on the Internet if you wish to use this approach.*

DELETING DATA

The final subject I will cover is deleting data. You will delete data records via their `id`, which, as you will remember, is made available via a data attribute on the `tr` element.

In order to delete contacts, the `delete` method can be augmented as follows:

```
delete: function(evt) {
    var contactId = $(evt.target).parents('tr').data().id;
    $(evt.target).parents('tr').remove();
    this.updateTableCount();
    var tx = database.transaction("contacts", "readwrite");
    var objectStore = tx.objectStore("contacts");
    var request = objectStore.delete(contactId);
},
```

This code snippet begins by obtaining a reference to the `id` of the contact that is being deleted. It then performs the familiar operations of creating a transaction (which needs to be `readwrite`) and accessing the relevant object store.

Once a reference to the object store is obtained, the `delete` method can be invoked and passed the relevant `id`.

TRY IT

In this Try It, you will enhance the functionality added in this lesson by providing functionality to store a static list of companies. When a contact is stored, you will obtain a reference to the relevant company and store this against the contact. Finally, when the contact is displayed in the table, you will display the appropriate company name.

Lesson Requirements

To complete this lesson, you will need a text editor for writing code and Chrome for running the completed web page. It is also assumed that you have completed the steps in the body of the lesson before starting this Try It.

Step-by-Step

1. To begin, you will store a static list of company names in IndexedDB. You will perform this in a new method called `configureData`, so start by adding this method immediately after the init method in `contacts.js`.

2. You only need to add companies once (the first time the web application is used), so start by determining if there are any records in the companies object store. You can determine this by opening a cursor on the companies object store and determining whether event.target .result evaluates to false in the onsuccess callback. If the first record in the cursor evaluates to false, the object store is empty.

3. If there are no companies, you need to add three companies. These should be stored as objects with a single property called name. The name should be set to the following value in each record:

   ➤ ABC Incorporated

   ➤ XZY Ltd

   ➤ ACME International

   Remember that you can use a single transaction and add three requests to it in order to store these three companies. IndexedDB will automatically add id properties to these objects.

4. You need to ensure that the configureData function is only invoked after the database has initialized so invoke this immediately before the call to loadContacts.

5. Refresh the web page and ensure three contacts are created in the companies object store. Once verified, refresh the page again to ensure it does not create duplicate entries.

6. You now need to change the save operation so that it finds the company object that matches the companyName property on the saved contact.

   The code for finding the relevant company should be placed immediately after the following line:

   ```
   var contact = this.serializeForm();
   ```

   Use the IndexedDB get method to find the company object with the appropriate id, and set this as the companyName.

   Remember also to use parseInt to convert the original companyName string into a number because the get method expects a number.

7. There is now a complication: The remainder of the code in the save method needs to occur in the onsuccess callback of get. This ensures that the company is actually set on the contact before it is saved and displayed.

8. If you create a new contact now, it will display in the table as you see in Figure 31-3. This is because the bind method simply converts the company object to a string.

Sales leads					
Contact name	Phone number	Email address	Company name	Last contacted	Actions
Dane Cameron	555 333 123	dane@testing.com	[object Object]	January 6, 2015	Delete
					0 contacts displayed

FIGURE 31-3

This can be circumvented by adding additional logic to the `bind` method. One possible approach is to use "programming by convention" and assume that if a field is of `type` "object," it will have a `name` property that can act as the display value:

```
if (typeof obj[field] == "object") {
    $(val).text(obj[field].name);
} else {
    $(val).text(obj[field]);
}
```

An alternative approach would be to override the `toString` method on company objects and have this return the name field.

9. After the `loadContacts` adds contacts to the `table` you need to invoke `updateTableCount` to ensure the correct count of contacts is listed below the `table`. This will involve using the `bind` function.

> **NOTE** *Although not shown in this Try It, you may also choose to populate the options in the* `companyName` *select box from the companies stored in IndexedDB. This will ensure that if you add new companies to IndexedDB, they will automatically be available in the* `select` *box.*

> **REFERENCE** *Please go to the book's website at* www.wrox.com/go /html5jsjquery24hr *to view the video for Lesson 31, as well as download the code and resources for this lesson.*

32

Application Cache

In the previous two lessons, you learned how data can be stored inside the web browser. Although this approach meant the web application was no longer reliant on Internet connectivity to access data, the web application was still very much dependent on an Internet connection to in order to load resources such as HTML pages, JavaScript files, images, and CSS files.

For instance, if you shut down the web server and attempt to run the web application, you will receive an error message that the web page is unavailable.

There are, however, many scenarios where you might wish to use a web application without Internet connectivity. This is increasingly true now that web applications are regularly accessed from portable devices, which may not have access to networks for periods of time.

Offline-able web applications was clearly a feature that needed to be addressed in order for browser-based web applications to become a viable alternative to desktop applications; therefore HTML5 introduced a technology called the *application cache*.

The application cache is a mechanism for specifying a set of resources that should be stored inside the browser after they are accessed the first time. From this point forward they will be accessed directly from the browser, removing all reliance on Internet connectivity.

In this lesson, you will learn how to configure a web application to work with the application cache, along with approaches for interacting with the application cache via the JavaScript API.

MANIFEST FILES

The key to understanding the application cache is the manifest file. This file specifies the files that should be stored inside the browser, together with any other configuration information required.

In order to get started with the application cache, create a file called `contacts.appcache` in the same directory as the `contacts.html` web page. Within this, add the following contents:

```
CACHE MANIFEST
contacts.html
contacts_print.css
contacts.css
contacts.js
jquery-2.1.1.js
jquery-tables.js
jquery-time.js
jquery-ui.css
jquery-ui.js
images/ui-bg_highlight-soft_100_eeeeee_1x100.png

FALLBACK:

NETWORK:
*
```

The application cache consists of three sections: An empty line separates these sections from one another.

The first section is introduced with the heading CACHE MANIFEST. This section lists all the resources in the web application that need to be cached offline. As you can see, each resource is listed on a new line and can consist of a relative URL, an absolute URL, or even a URL to a resource on a different web server.

> **NOTE** *It is important to remember to include all the resources that are needed by the web page, not just those directly referenced by the web page. For instance, the last resource listed is not directly referenced by* `contacts.html`, *but is used by jQuery UI and referenced in* `jquery-ui.css`.

The (optional) second section is introduced with the heading FALLBACK. This section allows you to specify that alternative resources should be used when a resource is unavailable and has not been cached offline. For instance, the web application may display the status of the web application using an image; the fallback section may therefore appear as follows:

```
FALLBACK:
online.png offline.png
```

This configuration states that the browser should attempt to use `online.png`, but if that is not available due to network connectivity, it should resort to using `offline.png`. In this case, there is an assumption that `offline.png` is included in the application cache, thereby ensuring that it is available without network connectivity.

The final (optional) section is the NETWORK section. This section specifies the files that can be loaded from the network if they are not listed in the application cache. This is almost always set to `*`, which means any files not listed in the application cache can be loaded from the network.

Once the manifest file has been defined, the next step is to link it to an HTML page. This will ensure that when the HTML page is requested from the server the first time, the manifest file will be automatically processed, and the appropriate resources stored in the application cache.

The application cache can be linked to an HTML page via the `manifest` attribute on the `html` element. For example:

```
<html lang="en" manifest="contacts.appcache">
```

Once you have added this, open Chrome with the console open and request the `contacts.html` web page from the web server with the URL `http://localhost:8080/contacts.html`. When you do this, you should see the output shown in Figure 32-1.

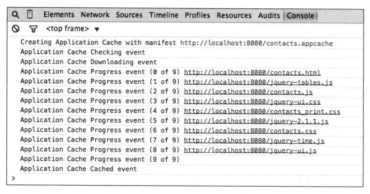

FIGURE 32-1

> **NOTE** *Even if* `contacts.html` *had not been included in the manifest, it still would have been cached because it is the web page that the manifest is referenced from.*

Chrome performs the following operations when it detects a manifest file:

➤ It first checks the manifest to see whether it has previously downloaded these resources. At this point, the browser generates a "checking" event.

➤ Once it determines that it needs to download resources, the browser generates a "downloading" event and begins downloading resources one by one into the cache, generating a "progress" event after each resource is cached.

➤ Once all the resources are downloaded, the browser generates a "cached" event.

This process is referred to as the *application cache lifecycle*.

As you will see shortly, it is possible to register callbacks to listen for these events. You can also use a special URL within Chrome to view any applications that have been cached. To see this, browse to `chrome://appcache-internals`. You should see contents similar to that in Figure 32-2:

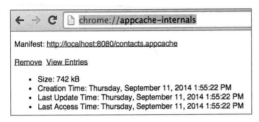

FIGURE 32-2

This page can also be used to see exactly which resources have been cached and to remove the application cache entirely.

You should now be able to shut down your web server and attempt to access the web application. The web application should load exactly the same as it would with the web server running, and the user should not notice anything different when using the web application.

There are two important points to note about the download process:

➤ If the browser cannot access one of the resources listed, it will abort the entire caching process. This means it is vitally important that if you delete a resource, you also remove it from the manifest file. It is also a good idea to check the console to ensure that the caching process is working as expected.

➤ When the web page is accessed, the resources are actually downloaded twice. They are initially downloaded for display to the user, and then, when the manifest is detected, they are downloaded again. You will look at this feature in more detail when you look at how resources are refreshed when they are modified.

UPDATING RESOURCES

With any web application, resources are likely to change over time. This presents a problem for the application cache, however, because unlike with traditional browser caching, the browser will not ever check to see whether any of the resources have been modified.

After resources are cached, they are always served from the application cache, even if the web server is accessible. The only way to cause the browser to update resources is to change something in the manifest file itself. This is simple enough if you are adding or removing resources, but presents an issue if the resources are the same but have been updated, because nothing in the manifest would change.

The typical way around this is to add a comment to the manifest and change this comment when you need a new version of the web application to be downloaded. For instance, you could add the following to the end of the manifest:

```
# version 1.1
```

The # symbol at the start of the line indicates that this is a comment and should not be processed by the browser. Despite this, a change to a comment counts as a change to the manifest.

The web browser does not behave entirely as expected when resources have changed. The behavior is as follows:

➤ The browser loads the web application using the cached resources.

➤ The manifest file is downloaded from the web server and checked to see if it has been updated.

➤ If it has been updated, all resources are downloaded whether they have changed or not.

This means that the browser will still be displaying the old version of the web application until the web page is refreshed in the browser. With a single page web application, it may be quite some time until the web page is refreshed so you will look at a workaround to this issue shortly.

> **NOTE** *It can be very frustrating to develop a web application with the application cache enabled. For this reason, I recommend that you remove the reference to the manifest when working through future lessons in this book.*

CACHE EVENTS

As mentioned earlier, it is possible to register callbacks to listen for the various events that occur during the application cache lifecycle. This can be useful for detecting the fact that a new version of the web application is available, and potentially informing the user, or automatically refreshing the web application as a result.

The basic mechanism for registering event listeners is as follows:

```
applicationCache.addEventListener('updateready', function() {
    console.log('An update is ready');
});
```

The `applicationCache` object is provided by the browser, and event listeners can be added for a variety of events via the `addEventListener` method. The most common of these events are:

➤ `downloading`: This event fires when the browser determines it needs to download resources from the web server.

➤ `progress`: This event fires every time an individual resource is downloaded.

➤ `error`: This event fires if the manifest file cannot be downloaded, or if one of the resources cannot be downloaded.

➤ `updateready`: This event fires when a new set of resources has completed downloading.

It is possible to use these events to ensure the updated version of the web application is displayed immediately after it is downloaded.

There is a general purpose JavaScript function for reloading a web page:

```
location.reload();
```

> **NOTE** *The* `location` *object is provided by the browser and also provides information about the origin of the web page.*

This means it is possible to request that the browser reload the web application as soon as a new set of resources has been downloaded and stored in the application cache:

```
applicationCache.addEventListener('updateready', function() {
    location.reload();
});
```

TRY IT

This Try It walks you through an example of updating resources in the application cache and detecting that they have updated correctly. The primary purpose of this Try It is to ensure that you fully understand the application cache lifecycle.

Lesson Requirements

To complete this lesson, you will need a text editor for writing code and Chrome for running the completed web page. It is also expected that you have completed the steps in the body of the lesson before starting this Try It.

Step-by-Step

1. Remove the line of code that will cause the application cache to reload the web page on an `updateready` event.

2. Open the contacts web application and verify that the application cache is functioning as expected by browsing to `chrome://appcache-internals`. Make a note of both the Last Update Time and the Last Access Time.

3. Click the View entries link, and verify that all the resources have downloaded.

4. Refresh the `contacts.html` page in the browser and then verify that the Last Access Time is updated in the `chrome://appcache-internals` web page. You should also notice that the Last Update Time does not change.

5. Make an obvious change to the `contacts.html` page such as displaying the text in the heading.

6. Reload the web application and verify that the change is not visible inside the browser. This demonstrates that the resource is always accessed directly from the cache.

7. Change the comment in the `contacts.appcache` file to indicate that the version has changed.

8. Open the console and refresh the web page. The console should show that new resources are being downloaded, but these should not be visible.

9. Refresh the web page one more time. This time, the application cache should determine that no updates are required, but the changes downloaded in Step 8 should finally display.

10. Browse to `chrome://appcache-internals` and verify that the Last Update Time has been updated as expected.

> **REFERENCE** *Please go to the book's website at* www.wrox.com/go/html5jsj-query24hr *to view the video for Lesson 32, as well as download the code and resources for this lesson.*

33

Web Workers

JavaScript has always been a single threaded programming language. Essentially this means that the language is only capable of performing a single operation at a time, and therefore only capable of utilizing a single CPU on the underlying hardware.

This was not a problem when JavaScript was first created because the vast majority of devices that ran browsers supported only a single CPU. Over the last 10 years there has been a major change in hardware, however, and the vast majority of devices now support multiple CPUs. Even smart phones typically support up to four CPUs.

> **NOTE** *The terms "processor" and "CPU" are essentially interchangeable and refer to the hardware responsible for executing the instructions provided by software. Many CPUs support multiple cores: A multi-core processor essentially contains multiple independent units capable of executing instructions on the same CPU. The terms "core" and "CPU" will therefore be used interchangeably in this lesson.*

A programming language is considered multi-threaded if it is capable of specifying multiple sets of instructions that can be run in parallel. Each set of instructions is encapsulated inside a thread.

The key reason that multi-threaded programming languages are important is performance. If you envisage a device with four CPUs, it is capable of executing four sets of instructions in parallel. If a programming language is not multi-threaded, however, it is only capable of using 25 percent of the overall processing power at any point in time. The same software written in a multi-threaded programming language may therefore execute up to four times faster.

> **NOTE** *Multi-threaded software can still execute on a device with a single CPU. In this case the operating system is responsible for providing each thread a share of the processor.*

There are good reasons why JavaScript does not support multiple threads. Programming with multiple threads can cause issues because two different threads may perform operations simultaneously that impact the same underlying data. This is particularly true with the DOM: If two threads were to simultaneously update the DOM it may be very difficult for the browser to determine what the outcome should be.

JAVASCRIPT EVENT MODEL

In order to adapt to the changing face of hardware, HTML5 has introduced an important API called web workers that can be used to create multi-threaded JavaScript programs.

Before looking at web workers, it is worth investigating how best to write responsive web pages within the single-threaded model. These techniques are useful because, as you will see, there are some limitations on web workers; therefore, they will not always be a viable option.

Imagine that the user presses a button onscreen, and this causes the browser to execute a set of instructions that will take 10 seconds to complete. For instance, the button may call the following function, which attempts to find the highest random number from one billion possibilities:

```
function findLargest() {
    var max = 0;
    for (var i = 0; i <= 1000000000; i++) {
        max = Math.max(max, Math.random());
    }
    console.log(max);
}
```

While this processing is occurring (which takes approximately 10 seconds on my computer) the web browser will be completely unresponsive. If the user clicks buttons, nothing appears to happen: The button will not even change appearance. This typically causes the user to click and click and click. If that was not bad enough, once the processing finishes, all those clicks will suddenly fire, which can cause havoc.

The code that is executed when the user clicks a button is wrapped in an event and placed on a queue. The JavaScript engine is then responsible for processing the code in each event in the order the events were created, not processing the next event until the previous one has completed.

In order to observe this, create the following web page or download it from the book's website (it is called longandshort.html):

```
<!DOCTYPE html>
<html lang="en">
<body>
    <a href="#" onclick="findLargest()">Long operation</a>
    <a href="#" onclick="getDate()">Short operation</a>
</body>
<script>
    function findLargest() {
        var max = 0;
        for (var i = 0; i <= 1000000000; i++) {
            max = Math.max(max, Math.random());
        }
```

```
        console.log(max);
    }
    function getDate() {
        console.log("The time is "+new Date());
    }
</script>
</html>
```

This page contains two buttons—one generates an event that runs for approximately 10 seconds, while the other generates an event that takes milliseconds. Open this page with the console open and perform the following:

1. Click the Long operation link.

2. Immediately click the Short operation link 12 times.

You should see the output shown in Figure 33-1.

FIGURE 33-1

Even if you finish clicking the Short operation link before the Long operation finishes, none of the clicks are processed until the Long operation completes.

This can create a terrible user experience. Any delay above approximately 200 milliseconds will be noticeable to users and will affect their impression of the web page.

What should you do if you need to perform processing that will take more than 200 milliseconds, and you cannot use web workers?

The ideal approach in this case is to take advantage of the `setTimeout` function. This function can be used to create an event that will execute at a defined time in the future. For instance, execute the following in the console:

```
setTimeout(function() {
    console.log('Testing');
}, 2000);
```

The will print "Testing" in the console 2 seconds after the code is executed. The first parameter is the code to execute, while the second parameter is the delay in milliseconds.

If you think about this in the context of the JavaScript event model, the function passed to `set-Timeout` becomes an event and is added to the queue of events when the specified time is reached. Just like any other event, it will not actually execute until it reaches the front of the event queue.

You can therefore split the algorithm up into separate portions and pass each to `setTimeout` in turn:

```
function findLargest() {
    var max = 0;
```

```
        var iterations = 0;
        function findLargestSub() {
            while(true) {
                iterations++;
                if (iterations === 1000000000) {
                    console.log(max);
                    break;
                } else if (iterations % 10000000 == 0) {
                    setTimeout(findLargestSub, 10);
                    break;
                } else {
                    max = Math.max(max, Math.random());
                }
            }
        }
        findLargestSub();
    }
```

The `findLargest` function now contains a sub-function called `findLargestSub`. The sub-function is essentially the same as the original function, except it processes a maximum of 10 million numbers.

If the processing has not completed after these 10 million numbers are processed, the sub-function halts and requests that it be invoked again with a 10-millisecond delay. Not only is there a delay, however, but the next portion of the algorithm will be placed at the end of the event queue, allowing any other events that have occurred a chance to complete.

If you make these changes and run the same operations again, you should notice that pressing the Short operation button produces an almost immediate response, even while the Long operation is processing in the background.

It can be difficult to write algorithms in this manner, however, which is one reason web workers are an attractive option.

WEB WORKERS

The web worker specification is part of HTML5 and is widely supported by the major browsers. The web worker API allows you to create a JavaScript file that will execute on an entirely separate thread from the JavaScript event thread. This code can, however, be passed messages from the JavaScript event thread and provide results back when it completes. Figure 33-2 shows the basic pattern used by web workers.

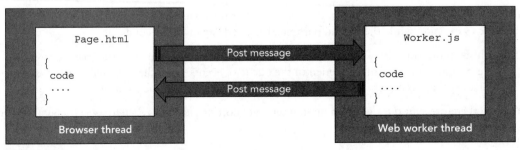

FIGURE 33-2

The two outer boxes represent two operating system threads. The browser thread is responsible for executing all the JavaScript included in the page or imported scripts, while the web worker thread is responsible for executing code in a web worker file. The two threads can only communicate via messages routed by the web worker API.

> **NOTE** *You might be wondering how web workers handle the potential issues mentioned earlier in this lesson if a web worker updates the DOM at the same time as the code in the main JavaScript thread. The web worker API has a convenient answer for that problem; it is not possible to access the* document *object from a web worker. If you need to update the DOM as a result of web worker processing, the web worker needs to pass the result back to the main JavaScript thread, which can then update the DOM.*

Web workers actually have a number of limitations. In addition to the document object, they are unable to access localStorage or sessionStorage.

In order to see the benefit of web workers, you need a piece of code that runs for an extended period of time. In order to simulate this, you will create an array of 100,000 random numbers, sort them, and display the lowest number:

```
var result = [];
for (var i = 0; i < 1000000; i++) {
    result.push(Math.random());
}
result.sort();
console.log(result[0]);
```

Depending on the speed of your computer, you may want to increase or decrease the quantity of numbers.

You will now create a web worker that accepts a parameter representing the number of random numbers to create and returns the smallest number. The code of a web worker needs to be created in a separate file so create a file called random.js (in the same folder as contacts.js so that it is available from the web server), and add the following contents:

```
self.addEventListener('message', function(msg) {
    var data = msg.data;
    var result = [];
    for (var i = 0; i < data; i++) {
        result.push(Math.random());
    }
    result.sort();
    self.postMessage(result[0]);
}, false);
```

When this web worker is loaded, it starts by adding an event listener that allows it to be notified when a message is available for it. As you will see, it does this by invoking addEventListener on an object called self.

The self object represents the global namespace, and is therefore the equivalent of the window object for conventional JavaScript code. In fact, if you type self at the console, it will return the window object. As mentioned, a web worker cannot access the window object so when it invokes self it returns its own global namespace object, which happens to be called WorkerGlobalScope.

As you can see, when the web worker receives a message, it can extract the information from the data variable on the message object—for the purposes of this example data will be a number.

The web worker then performs any processing necessary. It can use any features of the JavaScript language it needs, including built-in libraries such as Math.

Once the web worker has a result, it can return it to the main browser thread using the postMessage function.

You will now create a simple web page that allows a number to be entered into a form. When the form is submitted, the number will be passed to the web worker, and the result added to a table.

Create a web page called findnumbers.html in the same folder as contacts.html, with the following content (this is available on the book's website):

```html
<!DOCTYPE html>
<html lang="en">
<head>
    <meta charset="utf-8">
    <title>Lowest number</title>
    <link rel="stylesheet" media="all" type="text/css" href="contacts.css">
    <script src="jquery-2.1.1.js"></script>
</head>
<body>
    <header>Find the lowest number</header>
    <form method="post" style="margin:30px">
        <div class="formRow">
            <label for="contactName">Enter a number</label>
            <input required name="theNumber" type="number"
                class="validated" id="theNumber"/>
        </div>
        <div class="formRow">
            <input style="width:70px" type="submit"
                title="Find" value="Find"/>
        </div>
    </form>
    <section id="numberList" style="margin:30px">
        <table>
            <thead>
                <th>Number entered</th><th>Result</th>
            </thead>
            <tbody></tbody>
        </table>
    </section>
</body>
<script>
$('form input[type="submit"]').click(
    function(evt) {
        evt.preventDefault();
        var number = $('#theNumber').val();
        var row = $('<tr>').append('<td>'+number+'</td>'
).append('<td>'+0+'</td>');
```

```
            $('#numberList table tbody').append(row);
        });
    </script>
    </html>
```

This has not been integrated with the web worker yet, but if you open it (from the web server) and submit some numbers, it should display as you see in Figure 33-3.

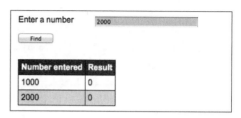

You will now add the code to construct a web worker, pass it your numbers, and listen for the result. Start by changing the JavaScript code as follows; I will then step through each new line:

FIGURE 33-3

```
$('form input[type="submit"]').click(
    function(evt) {
    evt.preventDefault();
    var number = $('#theNumber').val();
    var worker = new Worker('random.js');
    worker.addEventListener('message', function(evt) {
        var result = evt.data;
        var row = $('<tr>').append('<td>'+number+'</td>').append('<td>' +result+'</
td>');
        $('#numberList table tbody').append(row);
    }, false);
    worker.postMessage(parseInt(number));
});
```

The code starts by constructing a web worker using the following line of code:

```
var worker = new Worker('random.js');
```

Notice that this passes a reference to the script you created earlier using a relative URL. Notice also that you did not import the `random.js` script at the top of the web page: It is the reference to it here that causes the script to be downloaded from the server.

> **NOTE** *If you need the web worker to function while offline, you can also add web worker scripts to application cache manifest files.*

Once the web worker has been constructed, you register an event listener with it so that you can hear when it posts a message back to the main browser thread. In this example, this will occur when the lowest random number is identified; therefore, you also have code to process this result.

The final line of code is where you actually post a message to the web worker, causing it to begin processing. In this case, you pass the number that was extracted from the form.

You should now be able to submit numbers in the form and see them being passed to the web worker. As you post progressively larger numbers, you will notice that there is a delay before the table is updated, but despite this, it is still possible to submit another number in the form.

You can try submitting several numbers at a time and then opening Task Manager on Windows or Activity Monitor on OS X. For instance, I submitted four numbers on a machine with four cores, and saw the results shown in Figure 33-4.

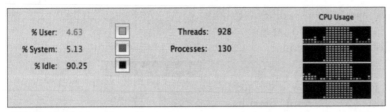

FIGURE 33-4

The four boxes on the right side show the utilization of the four CPUs over time. As you can see, as soon as I submitted four numbers, all four CPUs used 100 percent of their available resources. This ultimately meant that the task was completed four times quicker than it would have been without web workers.

You should also notice that if you submit the numbers in quick succession, they all complete in quick succession of one another, proving they processed in parallel.

It is also important to realize that even though my machine has only four cores, I could still submit 10 or 20 numbers simultaneously. In this case, each number would be processed on a separate thread, and it would be up to the operating system to provide a share of the CPUs to each thread.

TRY IT

In this Try It, you will convert the `longandshort.html` web page from earlier in this lesson to use web workers. This will ensure that it is always possible to push "Short operation" and receive immediate feedback in the console.

Lesson Requirements

To complete this lesson, you will need a text editor for writing code and Chrome for running the completed web page. You should also download `longandshort.html` from the book's website.

This example needs to execute inside a web server so the resources mentioned need to be added to the same folder as `contacts.html`, and the Mongoose web server needs to be running.

Step-by-Step

1. Create a web worker in a separate file and add code for it to listen for messages being posted to it. I have called mine `find_number.js`. The web worker will not read any data from the message, but the message will be used to signal to the web worker that it should begin processing.

2. Move the code from `findLargest` to the web worker, and when it finishes processing, post the result (the maximum number) back to the main browser thread using `postMessage`.

3. Change the logic of `findLargest` so that it constructs a web worker and posts a message to it. When the processing completes, it should receive the response from the web worker and print this to the console.

4. Ensure that the processing of the Long operation does not block the Short operation from executing immediately.

> **REFERENCE** *Please go to the book's website at* www.wrox.com/go/html5jsj-query24hr *to view the video for Lesson 33, as well as download the code and resources for this lesson.*

34

Files

Files and file systems have always been one of the most important concepts in computing because they provide a convenient mechanism for providing input to, and storing output from, computer software.

Despite this, browsers have been extremely limited in the manner they can interact with files or the file system. This interaction has been limited to the `file` input type, which can be declared as follows:

```
<input type="file" name="selectedFile"/>
```

This creates an input type that allows a file to be selected from the file system. For instance, in Chrome, the input field appears as you see in Figure 34-1, while in Firefox, the input type appears as you see in Figure 34-2.

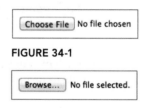

FIGURE 34-1

FIGURE 34-2

Once a file is selected, its content will be submitted to the web server when the form is submitted: The file contents can then be accessed by the web server and processed.

> **NOTE** *Some modern devices do not support the file input type because they do not expose a file system that allows files to be selected. For instance, this input type is not supported on either the iPad or iPhone.*

Despite its simplicity, the file input type is extremely important to HTML, and many of the most popular sites on the Internet could not exist without it. Any time you select a file from your computer and post it to a website, you are using this input type.

Despite this, the file input type is also very constrained. These constraints stem primarily from security concerns. For instance, imagine if the browser supported the following functionality:

➤ Add a hidden file input field to a form, programmatically select a file using JavaScript, and programmatically submit the form to the server.

> ➤ Change the appearance of the button on the file input field so it looks like a submit button, but when it is pressed, select a file from the file system, and submit the form.

Clearly these represent huge security holes because they allow a web page to access files on your device without your knowledge or permission. It is vitally important that web pages are not able to access files from your file system in this manner.

In order to ensure that the `file` input field is not misused, the following restrictions apply:

> ➤ The browser dictates the appearance of the `file` input type, and it is not possible to change this appearance with CSS or JavaScript. In addition, most browsers now prevent the user from typing a filename into a text box, and insist that the file is chosen from the operating system's file chooser.

> ➤ Browsers do not allow an initial filename to be specified, even though the `value` attribute technically supports this. This is to prevent the web page from suggesting a sensitive filename.

> ➤ It is not possible to interact with the `file` input field using JavaScript. For instance, it is not possible to read the file contents without sending the file to the web server.

> **NOTE** *There are some well-known "hacks" that allow the appearance of the file input field to be modified. These usually involve placing the* `file` *input field off the side of the screen or below another control.*

This lesson will examine an important API that overcomes some of these restrictions, in particular, allowing a file to be processed with JavaScript.

FILEREADER API

There are many reasons why it may be useful to process a file with JavaScript rather than simply submitting it to the server:

> ➤ It allows the file to be validated before it is submitted to ensure it is appropriate in terms of type, size, or contents.

> ➤ It allows the file to be pre-processed, and potentially reduces the amount of data sent to the server.

> ➤ It allows files to be processed without an Internet connection, assuming the application is loaded via the application cache.

In order to provide this functionality, the FileReader API has been introduced in HTML5. This API works with the conventional file input field, but allows you to listen for files being selected. Once the user has selected a file it is possible to read its contents via JavaScript.

It is important to realize that the FileReader API does not allow you to programmatically open files from the user's file system because this would represent a major security loophole. It is only possible to read the contents of a file once the user has explicitly selected it in some manner.

In order to demonstrate the FileReader API, you will add functionality to the CRM web application so that a file can be selected. You will assume that this file contains an array of contacts stored in JSON format, which you can then save.

In order to begin, you need to add a new section to `contacts.html` for selecting files. This can be added after the `contactList` section:

```
<section id="fileImport">
    <div class="formRow">
        <label for="importJSONFile">Import contacts</label>
        <input type="file" id="importJSONFile" name="importJSONFile">
    </div>
</section>
```

You can style this any way you like, but I added the following to `contacts.css`, which resulted in the design you see in Figure 34-3:

```
#fileImport {
    margin: 20px;
    border: 1px solid #999999;
    border-radius: 10px;
    width: 400px;
    padding: 10px 10px 0px 10px;
    background: #DAECFF;
}
```

FIGURE 34-3

There is nothing special about this `file` input field at this stage: It is identical to the `file` input fields that have been available since HTML4.

The next step is to add a change event listener to the `file` input field, just as you would with any other input field. The following code can be added to `contacts.js`:

```
$(screen).find('#importJSONFile').change(function(evt) {
    var reader = new FileReader();
    reader.onload = function(evt) {
        console.log('New file selected');
        console.log(evt.target.result);
    };
    reader.readAsText(event.target.files[0]);
});
```

The event listener starts by constructing an instance of the `FileReader` object. This object contains a set of methods supporting the reading of files that have been selected.

Next, you register an `onload` event listener with the `FileReader` that will fire when the file has been read. At this stage, you have only received a notification that a file has been selected. The file will be read asynchronously by the API when requested, and the contents passed to this event listener.

> **NOTE** *It is also possible to add an* `onerror` *callback with the* `FileReader` *to listen for any problems reading the file.*

Within the `onload` callback, the file content is available as a JavaScript string from `evt.target .result`. You will look at how the file contents are converted to a string shortly. In this example, you will simply write the contents to the console.

Finally, once the callback has been registered, you request the API to read the file with the following line of code:

```
reader.readAsText(event.target.files[0]);
```

This will cause the file contents to be read into a JavaScript string, and will then invoke the `onload` callback function.

As you can see, the selected file is available from the `files` property of the input field. Because the `file` input field supports the selection of multiple files, the `files` property contains an array of files. In this case, I have assumed that the user has only selected a single file, but obviously it would be trivial to loop through the array and read each file selected.

In this case, I have also assumed that the file contains textual contents, and that it makes sense to read the contents into a JavaScript string. The `FileReader` object also supports methods such as `readAsArrayBuffer` and `readAsBinaryString` when dealing with binary files.

In order to use this API, create a file called `contacts.txt` that should contain three contacts encoded in JSON format. This file is available from the book's website, or you can create it yourself:

```
[{"contactName":"James Cook","phoneNumber":"55521882", "emailAddress":"james@testing
.com", "companyName":"2","notes":"This is a note","lastContacted":"09/18/2014"},
{"contactName":"William Pitt","phoneNumber":"555919911","emailAddress":"william@
testing.com", "companyName":"3","notes":"Test","lastContacted":"09/01/2014"},
{"contactName":"Dane Cameron","phoneNumber":"555291111","emailAddress":"dane@
testing.com", "companyName":"3","notes":"My note","lastContacted":"09/18/2014"}]
```

Once the file is created, ensure that you can read it with the file input field and that its contents are printed to the console.

In addition, if you place a breakpoint on the line that reads the file, you can access information about the file, as you can see in Figure 34-4.

```
> event.target.files[0].name
< "contacts.txt"
> event.target.files[0].type
< "text/plain"
> event.target.files[0].lastModifiedDate
< Sat Sep 20 2014 12:15:28 GMT+1200 (NZST)
> event.target.files[0].size
< 476
```

FIGURE 34-4

This metadata can be very useful when determining how to read the file, or even if you should read the file.

The final step is to save the contacts in the file using your existing `store` method. This can be achieved as follows:

```
$(screen).find('#importJSONFile').change(function(evt) {
    var reader = new FileReader();
    reader.onload = function(evt) {
        var contacts = JSON.parse(evt.target.result);
        for (var i = 0; i < contacts.length; i++) {
            this.store(contacts[i]);
        }
        location.reload();
    }.bind(this);
    reader.readAsText(event.target.files[0]);
}.bind(this));
```

There are a couple of points to note about this code. The first is that it contains a callback within a callback. In both cases, the callback function is bound to `this`, which means that the call to `this` .`store` works as expected.

Second, note that instead of updating the table as each contact is added, you simply call `reload` on the web page once all the contacts are saved.

> **NOTE** *There is a potential problem with this approach: IndexedDB may not have finished storing the contacts when reload is called. Try to think of an approach for solving this problem; you could either use setTimeout to delay the reloading or a callback to listen for the storing process to complete.*

If you load the `contacts.txt` file, it should result in the three contacts being added to the table.

OTHER FILE-RELATED APIS

The FileReader API is the most widely supported of the file related APIs introduced in HTML5, but it is not the only API to deal with files and file systems.

The most ambitious of the file-related APIs is the FileSystem API. This API not only allows files to be read, but it also allows them to be created, and provides access to a full range of file system functions such as creating directories and deleting files.

This may sound like a very dangerous idea because clearly you do not want a web page deleting files or creating enormous files without your permission. For this reason, the FileSystem API does not allow the web page to access the operating system's file system; it provides the domain access to a sandboxed file system that is kept entirely separate from other domains and the underlying operating system.

For this reason, the FileSystemAPI does not provide much functionality that cannot be implemented using the other storage APIs demonstrated earlier in the book, but you may wish to investigate it further if you are writing a web application that deals extensively with files.

The biggest problem with the FileSystem API, however, is that it is not widely supported. Support currently limited to Chrome and Opera.

TRY IT

In this Try It, you look at how it is possible to select files via drag and drop. This section therefore ties together two topics: the ability to use the drag-and-drop API and the ability to read the contents of a file selected in this manner.

Using drag and drop for selecting files has become increasingly common and provides a more intuitive interface for many users.

Lesson Requirements

In this lesson, you will create a standalone web page for reading files selected via drag and drop. The web page will be based on the `dropfile.html` web page available from the book's website.

You will need a text editor and Chrome to complete this Try It.

Step-by-Step

1. Open the `dropfile.html` file from the book's website in your text editor.

2. The function that you are required to implement is the `drop` function. This will be invoked whenever a file is dropped onto the rectangle with the dashed border.

3. Recall from Lesson 9 the way in which the `dataTransfer` object can be accessed. This will contain an additional property called `files`, which will contain an array of the files selected. Assign the first element in this array to a variable called `file`.

4. Construct a new `FileReader` object and add an `onload` callback. Within the callback, extract the contents of the file using the techniques outlined earlier in this lesson, and set them as the text for the element with the ID `fileContents`.

5. Use the `readAsText` method on the `FileReader` to initiate the loading of the file stored in the `file` variable.

6. Access the `name` of the file, and set this as the text for the element with the ID `fileDetails`.

Figure 34-5 shows the result of dragging the `contacts.txt` file onto the drop zone.

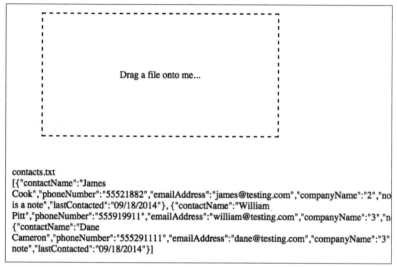

Drag a file onto me...

contacts.txt
[{"contactName":"James
Cook","phoneNumber":"55521882","emailAddress":"james@testing.com","companyName":"2","no
is a note","lastContacted":"09/18/2014"}, {"contactName":"William
Pitt","phoneNumber":"555919911","emailAddress":"william@testing.com","companyName":"3","n
{"contactName":"Dane
Cameron","phoneNumber":"555291111","emailAddress":"dane@testing.com","companyName":"3"
note","lastContacted":"09/18/2014"}]

FIGURE 34-5

REFERENCE *Please go to the book's website at* www.wrox.com/go/html5jsj-query24hr *to view the video for Lesson 34, as well as download the code and resources for this lesson.*

35

AJAX

The web was designed to operate with the HTTP protocol. As mentioned previously, the HTTP protocol is a simple request/response protocol: The browser requests a resource, and a response is received and rendered.

This model worked well for document-centric websites because a document (an HTML page) or image could be requested and the response rendered directly in the browser. This model does not work so well for dynamic web applications.

A common requirement for web applications is to request additional information after a page has loaded. For instance, a browser-based chat application will constantly check for new messages and display them immediately via DOM manipulation. Without this functionality, the user is required to constantly refresh the entire web page to check for new messages.

Although it is possible to automatically refresh an entire web page at periodic intervals, the refresh process will not only cause a very noticeable delay but it will interrupt whatever the user is doing. For instance, if the user was halfway through typing a message, this message would be cleared out and lost.

In order to support web applications such as a chat application, Microsoft introduced a JavaScript feature into Internet Explorer called the XMLHttpRequest object all the way back in 1999. This allowed HTTP requests to be performed using JavaScript after the web page had loaded, and the response to be processed and incorporated directly into the DOM.

XMLHttpRequest was eventually reverse engineered into other browsers, and this approach has come to be called AJAX. Although AJAX predates HTML5, the technology behind it has been standardized as part of the HTML5 standards process.

> **NOTE** *The term AJAX was only popularized once the* XMLHttpRequest *object began to be widely adopted in web applications such as Google's Gmail.*

Although it was slow to catch on, AJAX was potentially the most important technology leading to the widespread adoption of HTML-based web applications because it was finally possible to create *truly* dynamic web applications. A truly dynamic web application not only changes in response to user input, but it changes in response to new information received from external sources.

AJAX stands for Asynchronous JavaScript with XML:

➤ It is *asynchronous* because the HTTP request does not block the browser thread; instead, the HTTP response can be processed via a browser callback. This is an extremely important feature because it means the browser does not freeze while an HTTP request is in-flight.

If AJAX were not asynchronous, the user of the imaginary chat application would not be able to continue typing a message while the browser was checking for new messages.

➤ AJAX is based on a *JavaScript* object called XMLHttpRequest. As you will see, however, AJAX is typically used via libraries such as jQuery because XMLHttpRequest does not have the most intuitive API.

➤ AJAX was originally used primarily with the *XML* data format. AJAX is now more often coupled with the JSON data format. Essentially, you can use any data format you want with AJAX.

> **NOTE** *The technologies associated with AJAX are particularly misleading. Not only is it not inherently linked to XML, but AJAX requests do not need to be asynchronous, although they typically are. Likewise, the* XMLHttpRequest *is not inherently linked to either XML or HTTP: It is possible to use alternative protocols if required, although this also is not common.*

This lesson will introduce AJAX and the jQuery functions that can be used to simplify server interactions. AJAX is different from the other technologies that you have looked at so far, however, because it also assumes code will be deployed to the web server to dynamically generate responses to requests.

Server-side technologies are beyond the scope of this book; therefore, the examples that you will look at will be based on static JSON responses. If you would like to learn more about creating server-side services for responding to AJAX requests, you may might want to look at technologies such as PHP or Node.js.

> **NOTE** *Node.js is a server-side technology based on JavaScript. This means it allows you to leverage much of the knowledge you have gained throughout this book.*

AJAX REQUESTS

In this section, you will request data from the web server, and the web server will return a response from a static file. In order to make this available, take the contacts.txt file from the previous lesson (or from the book's website), rename it contacts.json, and copy it to the same directory as `contacts.html`. Once you have completed these steps, verify that it can be accessed from `http://localhost:8080/contacts.json`.

You can now write code for requesting this data from the web server after the web page has loaded. In this case, you will envisage a web application where many different clients can save contact information to a central repository. You can then synchronize with this central repository on request and save a copy of any contacts returned.

Begin by adding a new section to `contacts.html`, below the section added in the previous lesson:

```
<section id="serverImport">
    <div class="formRow">
        <a id="importFromServer" href="#">Import from server</a>
    </div>
</section>
```

Change the CSS in `contacts.css` so that this section uses the same styles as the `fileImport` section.

You will now add an event listener to this hyperlink in the `init` method of `contacts.js`, and add code to invoke the server:

```
$(screen).find('#importFromServer').click(function(evt) {
    $.get("contacts.json", function( data ) {
        console.log(data)
    });
});
```

With this code in place, open the console and press Import from server. Immediately after clicking this, the console should print out the result shown in Figure 35-1. This shows that three contact objects have been received in an array from the server.

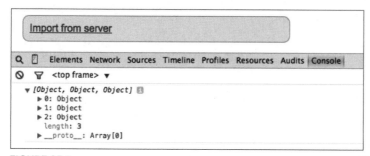

FIGURE 35-1

> **NOTE** *You can choose to implement functionality to store these contacts in offline storage using the code developed in the previous lesson if you wish.*

The simplicity of this code hides the complexity of the operations that are being performed in the background:

➤ An HTTP GET request is sent to the server requesting a resource called `contacts.json`. This is triggered by the invocation of `$.get`, which accepts the relevant URL as its first parameter.

➤ A callback function is registered to listen for a response from the server. This is provided as a second parameter to `$.get`.

➤ The jQuery library receives an HTTP response. It detects that the response conforms to the JSON format and automatically parses the response into an array of contact objects.

➤ The parsed response is passed to the registered callback.

> **NOTE** *It is only possible to request services from the same origin as the underlying HTML page. This is referred to as the* single-origin policy, *and is familiar from many of the APIs you have looked at in this book. If you are interested, there is a competing approach called JSONP that uses a "hack" to circumvent this restriction. Alternatively, a newer technology called Web Sockets is emerging and is specifically designed to remove this restriction.*

The beauty of libraries such as jQuery is that they abstract complex functionality behind a simple façade.

jQuery also supports an alternative function called `$.ajax`. This provides you more control over the underlying request and response, but is not necessary in most situations. For example, the previous example could be replaced with the following:

```
$.ajax({
    url: "contacts.json",
    dataType: "json",
    cache : false,
    type : "GET",
    timeout: 5000,
    success : function(data) {
        console.log(data);
    },
    error: function(jqXHR, textStatus, errorThrown ) {
        console.log(errorThrown);

    }
});
```

As you can see, this method allows you to specify:

➤ The URL of the request.

➤ The data format of the response. As you have seen, jQuery can usually determine this without it being specified.

➤ Whether the browser cache should be bypassed. Typically, you do want to avoid caching when requesting data from the server because the same request may result in a different response.

➤ The HTTP method to use: typically either GET or POST.

➤ The maximum time (in milliseconds) to wait for a response before the request times out.

➤ The success and error callbacks.

In the previous example, the response contained JSON-encoded data. It is also common for an AJAX response to contain HTML-encoded data, which can then be injected directly into the DOM at the appropriate location.

In order to demonstrate this, create a resource in the same directory as contacts.html called notifications.html. Add the following HTML fragment to this file:

```
<p style="color:red;font-weight:bold;margin-left:20px;">
The web server will be shutdown for scheduled maintenance in 5 minutes.
</p>
```

Notice that this is only a fragment of HTML, not intended to be loaded directly into a browser.

Now, add the following section to contacts.html:

```
<section id="notifications">
</section>
```

This is an empty section that will be populated after the web page has loaded.

You can now reload the web page and execute the following into the console:

```
$('#notifications').load('notifications.html');
```

As soon as you execute this, the notifications.html resource will be loaded from the web server and populated into the element with the ID notifications, resulting in the effect shown in Figure 35-2.

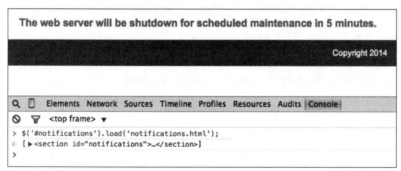

FIGURE 35-2

You will notice in this case that you have not even registered a callback for loading the markup; the load method automatically assumes that when the response is received it should be loaded directly into the element selected.

On a side note, you can also use the Network tab of the developer tools to analyze the underlying HTTP request and response. For example, Figure 35-3 shows the request sent in the previous example.

FIGURE 35-3

In most web applications, the HTML code fragment will be automatically generated based on specific criteria rather than a static block of HTML. In order to facilitate this, the second parameter to `load` can be an object or string that will be sent to the server along with the request. For example:

```
$('#notifications').load('notifications.html', {name:'dane'});
```

Typically, whenever the browser needs to send data to the web server, the underlying HTTP method used will be POST rather than GET. If you execute this call, you should be able to confirm in the Network tab that the `load` method has automatically switched to POST and automatically encoded the properties from the object into the form data.

> **NOTE** *As mentioned earlier in the book,* GET *requests can contain parameters as name value pairs. These are embedded directly in the URL. Typically, the* POST *method will be used once data extends beyond a handful of parameters.*

jQuery also provides a general purpose method called `$.post` that can be used for sending data to the server on a request and processing the response in any manner required.

TRY IT

This Try It looks at how you can create different themes for the web application so that users can choose the color scheme that suits them. In this case, themes will be developed as JavaScript files, and these will be dynamically loaded and executed via AJAX when selected by the user.

If a website supported many themes, it would be a waste of bandwidth to download all the themes for users because they are likely to use only one or two. It therefore makes far more sense to download themes "on-demand."

The book's website contains three sample theme files:

➤ `orange_theme.js`

➤ `red_theme.js`

➤ `purple_theme.js`

You can either use these or create your own. Each theme simply uses the jQuery `css` method to manipulate the background of elements, but you can choose to add more interesting effects if you like.

The theme files provided conform to the following format, but with different colors in each case:

```
$('header, footer').css('background', 'linear-gradient(to top, #C644FC ,
#5856D6)');
$('thead').css('background', 'linear-gradient(to top, #C644FC , #5856D6)');
$('#fileImport, #serverImport, #chooseTheme').css('background', '#DEDDF7');
```

Lesson Requirements

In this lesson, you will need a set of theme files, which can be downloaded from the book's website. You will need a text editor and Chrome to complete this Try It.

Step-by-Step

1. Open `contacts.html`, `contacts.js`, and `contacts.css` in your text editor. Attempt to create the section shown in Figure 35-4 for selecting themes. This can be created using the knowledge techniques learned earlier in the book.

    Each square should be represented by a hyperlink element. The background of each square should be the dominant color in the theme. Each square should also be given a data attribute specifying its related JavaScript theme file. My version can be found at the end of this lesson, and produces the design seen in Figure 35-4:

    FIGURE 35-4

2. Add a click listener to the squares created in Step 1. Start by extracting the relevant script file from the element's data attribute.

    This code should be added in the `init` method of `contacts.js`.

3. Use the jQuery `$.getScript` method to load and execute the relevant script from the server. The URL of the script should be passed as the first parameter to `$.getScript`.

4. Use the optional second parameter of `$.getScript` to register a callback method. Inside this, set a property in web storage indicating the theme file that the user has selected. This will allow you to remember the user's preferred theme when the page is reloaded.

5. When the web page is loaded, check to see whether a theme has been saved in web storage. If it has, use `$.getScript` to load this theme. This code can be placed in the `$(document).ready` callback of `contacts.html`.

The following are the HTML changes I added for the themes section:

```
<section id="chooseTheme">
    <div class="formRow">Choose a theme
        <a class="theme" href="#" style="background:#C644FC" data-theme-
file="purple_theme.js"></a>
        <a class="theme" href="#" style="background: #FF5E3A" data-theme-file="red_
theme.js"></a>
        <a class="theme" href="#" style="background:#FF9500" data-theme-
file="orange_theme.js"></a>
    </div>
</section>
```

The relevant CSS changes were as follows:

```
#fileImport, #serverImport, #chooseTheme {
    margin: 20px;
    border: 1px solid #999999;
    border-radius: 10px;
    width: 400px;
    padding: 10px 10px 0px 10px;
    background: #DAECFF;
}

.theme {
    width: 20px;
    height: 20px;
    display: inline-block;
    border: 1px solid #999999;
    border-radius: 3px;
}
```

I then added the following to `contacts.js` to listen for the user selecting a theme:

```
$(screen).find('.theme').click(function(evt) {
    var url = $(evt.target).data().themeFile;
    $.getScript(url, function() {
        localStorage.setItem('theme', url);
    });
});
```

Finally, I added the following to the `$(document).ready` section:

```
if (localStorage.theme) {
    $.getScript(localStorage.theme);
}
```

> **REFERENCE** *Please go to the book's website at* www.wrox.com/go/ html5jsjquery24hr *to view the video for Lesson 35, as well as download the code and resources for this lesson.*

36

Promises

Throughout this book, you have made extensive use of callback functions. You have used callback functions:

➤ To register event listeners that fire when specific events occur

➤ To listen for the completion of `IndexedDB` operations, such as the insertion of data or the opening of the database

➤ When using the JavaScript `filter`, `map`, and `reduce` functions to process arrays

➤ When listening for messages from web workers

➤ When waiting for AJAX responses

As you can see, callback-based programming is enormously important to many JavaScript APIs, and it is impossible to gain a solid understanding of JavaScript without understanding callback functions.

Although callback-based APIs are enormously popular, they do bring their own set of problems. These problems are often referred to as "Callback hell" and stem largely from the following issues:

➤ It is often necessary to nest callbacks inside other callbacks, and this nesting can extend to several levels. As this happens, code can become difficult to read because it is not always obvious where each level of nesting ends.

➤ It is difficult to determine the behavior of an application because it is not possible to logically follow code with your eye.

➤ Data scoping can become difficult with callbacks. You can see this primarily in relation to the identity of `this` and the corresponding necessity to use `bind` on each callback to ensure the correct `this` instance was set.

This lesson examines an alternative mechanism for implementing callback functions called promises. Promises do not alleviate all of the problems mentioned, but they do help make callbacks more manageable and add other useful functionality in the process.

This lesson is optional because it is always possible to write code without promises, as you have seen so far in this book. It is, however, recommended that you complete this lesson because promises are likely to gain greater attention as more and more APIs are designed to work with them.

WORKING WITH PROMISES

This book has used several asynchronous APIs. You may have noticed, however, that asynchronous function calls still return a synchronous response. For instance, the following code invokes an asynchronous AJAX operation:

```
$.get('contacts.json')
```

Despite this, it returns the synchronous response shown in Figure 36-1.

```
> $.get('contacts.json')
< ▼ Object {readyState: 1, getResponseHeader: function,
    ▶ abort: function ( statusText ) {
    ▶ always: function () {
    ▶ complete: function () {
    ▶ done: function () {
    ▶ error: function () {
    ▶ fail: function () {
    ▶ getAllResponseHeaders: function () {
    ▶ getResponseHeader: function ( key ) {
    ▶ overrideMimeType: function ( type ) {
```

FIGURE 36-1

Clearly, this response cannot be the response from the web server because it was not received asynchronously, so you may be wondering what this object is.

This object is referred to as a "promise."

> **NOTE** *Not all asynchronous APIs have been modified to generate promises. For this reason, this lesson will focus on the jQuery AJAX library that was retrofitted to operate with promises.*

Promises provide a mechanism for interacting with an asynchronous process because they model the flow of the underlying operation through its lifecycle. Promises always start with a status of `pending`. From this they will transition to one of two other statuses:

➤ `resolved`: The underlying process has completed successfully.

➤ `rejected`: The underlying process has failed.

Once a promise has moved into the state `resolved` or `rejected`, it is considered `settled`, and will not change state again.

Once you have a reference to a promise, you can request to be notified when the promise enters a specific state. For instance, consider the following code:

```
var promise = $.get('contacts.json');
promise.done(function(data) {
    console.log('First callback invoked');
});
promise.done(function(data) {
    console.log('Second callback invoked');
});
```

This code requests `contacts.json` and then registers two callbacks that will be invoked when the promise is resolved. If you run this code, you will notice that both callback functions are executed, one after the other.

This code immediately highlights one advantage of promises: It is possible to register more than one callback for each state

It is also possible to add multiple `fail` callbacks:

```
var promise = $.get('unknown.json');
promise.fail(function(data) {
    console.log('First callback invoked');
});
promise.fail(function(data) {
    console.log('Second callback invoked');
});
```

This code requests a non-existent file; therefore, it enters the `rejected` state and invokes all the failure callbacks.

It is also possible to create an explicit pipeline of operations that should be performed on a response via the `then` method. This is useful because it allows the response to be modified as it flows through the pipeline.

For instance, in the following scenario, the first callback filters the response so that it contains only contacts with a `companyName` value of 3. It then returns this modified response, which is then passed automatically to other callbacks in the pipeline:

```
$.get('contacts.json').then(function(data) {
    console.log('First callback invoked with ' + data.length + ' contacts');
    data = data.filter(function(c) {
        return c.companyName == '3';
    });
    return data;
}).then(function(data) {
    console.log('Callback invoked with ' + data.length + ' contacts');
});
```

In this case, the second callback does not know or care that the data it is receiving has already been processed by another callback. This therefore provides a convenient mechanism for pre-processing data.

This code prints the following:

```
First callback invoked with 3 contacts
Callback invoked with 2 contacts
```

One final benefit of working with promises is that it is possible to register callbacks that are invoked when more than one promise reaches a specific state. In order to demonstrate this, create a new file called `contacts2.json` and add a different set of contacts to it.

You can now write code that performs two separate requests for these two separate resources, and invokes the callback only if both requests succeed via the `$.when` function:

```
var promise1 = $.get('contacts.json');
var promise2 = $.get('contacts2.json');
$.when(promise1, promise2).done(function(data1, data2) {
    console.log('data1 contains ' + data1.length + ' contacts');
    console.log('data2 contains ' + data2.length + ' contacts');
});
```

This can be extremely useful if the two sets of data contain interdependencies. Without callbacks, it would typically be necessary to place the second request in the success callback of the first request.

CREATING PROMISES

Not only can you use promises created by other libraries, but you can write your own APIs that generate promises. This allows the clients of these APIs to use all the techniques outlined in the previous section, and it effectively means that your API gains extra capabilities without your having to do anything.

Promises are a useful addition to any API that performs operations that are (or can be) asynchronous.

> **NOTE** *The client of an API is any code that invokes its functions or methods; in many cases, this will be your own code. If you are developing libraries, on the other hand, you may have no idea who will be the clients of your code.*

In this section, you will create a function call for reading contacts from the web server. This function will have a catch, however. It will only invoke the server the first time it is invoked; from then on it will simply return the response that it received on the first invocation.

This approach is referred to as *caching* and is often used to improve the performance of a web application.

This functionality is interesting because it only needs to behave asynchronously the first time it is invoked. On subsequent invocations it will have a response that can be returned immediately. As you will see, promises are an excellent candidate for implementing this functionality.

Because your code needs to remember state (the contacts read from the server on the first invocation), you will create a new module in a new JavaScript file called `find.contacts.js` with the following basic structure:

```
findContacts = function() {
    var contacts = null;
    return function() {
        console.log('this is where the logic goes');
    }
}();
```

The outer anonymous function is executed as soon as this code is loaded via the `()` on the final line. Therefore, as soon as this code is loaded, the `findContacts` variable contains a reference to a function, which in turn can access the `contacts` variable via a closure.

You can now add the following implementation:

```
findContacts = function() {
    var contacts = null;
    return function() {
        var deferred = $.Deferred();
        if (contacts) {
            console.log('Returning data from the cache');
            deferred.resolve(contacts);
            return deferred.promise();
        } else {
            var promise = $.get('contacts.json');
            console.log('Returning data from the server');
            promise.done(function(data) {
                contacts = data;
                deferred.resolve(contacts);
            });
            return deferred.promise();
        }
    }
}();
```

The code always begins by creating an instance of a deferred object:

```
var deferred = $.Deferred();
```

It is this object that allows you to not only create promises, but also control the lifecycle of these promises by transitioning them from one state to another.

The preceding code contains two blocks. The first block will execute if you have already read the list of contacts from the server. In this case, any promises can be set to `resolved` immediately; therefore, you invoke `resolve` on the `deferred` object and pass it the cached list of contacts:

```
deferred.resolve(contacts);
```

On the next line of code, you generate a promise from the `deferred` object, and return this from the function. Notice that in this case the promise will already be fulfilled:

```
return deferred.promise();
```

The second block of code begins by invoking the server and registering a callback to listen for the response, but in this case you also return a promise from the function. Unlike the first block, the promise is not resolved until a response is received from the server.

Because the server will respond very quickly, it is useful to simulate a slower server to appreciate the benefit of this functionality. Therefore, change the AJAX response processing to include a 5 second delay:

```
promise.done(function(data) {
    setTimeout(function() {
        contacts = data;
        deferred.resolve(contacts);
    }, 5000);
});
```

You can now use this function. Begin by importing the JavaScript file into `contacts.html`, ensuring that it is not imported before the jQuery library.

```
<script src="find.contacts.js"></script>
```

You can now change the event listener associated with the Import from the server button in `contacts.js`, as follows:

```
$(screen).find('#importFromServer').click(function(evt) {
    var promise = findContacts();
    promise.done(function(data) {
        console.log('Data has been retrieved');
        console.log(data);
    });
});
```

Notice that the event listener does not know how the `findContacts` function operates; it only cares that it produces a promise. The code then registers a callback for when this promise reaches its `resolved` state.

If you now refresh the web page and open the console, you can try out the functionality. The first time you press the button, you should see the following immediately printed to the console:

```
Returning data from the server
```

After a further 5 seconds, you should see the following:

```
Data has been retrieved
```

If you then press the button again, you should see the following lines printed immediately:

```
Returning data from the cache
Data has been retrieved
```

Notice in this case that you have registered a callback with a promise that has already been fulfilled. When you do this, your callback simply executes immediately. It is even possible to register additional callbacks with promises that are `fulfilled` or `rejected`, and these are simply invoked immediately.

TRY IT

In this Try It, you will create a generic function for reading files and implement it so that it is compatible with promises. Although the `FileReader` object operates asynchronously, it does not produce a promise; therefore, it is not possible to use it with other utility functions such as `$.when`.

Lesson Requirements

You will need a text editor and Chrome to complete this Try It.

Step-by-Step

1. Open `contacts.js`, and start by adding a global function called `readFileWithPromise` immediately below the `bind` function. This should accept a single parameter, which is the file to read.

2. Create an instance of `$.Deferred` and assign it to a variable called `deferred`.

3. Create an instance of `FileReader` and register an `onload` callback. Inside this callback, you should resolve the deferred object and pass it the contents of `event.target.result`.

4. Read the file specified as the parameter using `readAsText`. Remember that this will cause the `onload` callback to be invoked when it completes, and will pass the contents of the file as a JavaScript string.

5. Return a promise from the function.

6. Change the event listener invoked when a file is selected so that it invokes `readFileWith-Promise` and assigns the result to a variable called `promise`.

7. Add a success listener to the promise and accept a single parameter, which will be the textual content of the file.

8. Modify the code of the callback so that the text is parsed and processed as it was previously.

    My version of `readFileWithPromise` looks like this:

    ```
    function readFileWithPromise(file) {
        var deferred = $.Deferred();
        var reader = new FileReader();
        reader.onload = function(evt) {
            deferred.resolve(evt.target.result);
        }
        reader.readAsText(file);
        return deferred.promise();
    }
    ```

    My callback listener looks like this:

    ```
    $(screen).find('#importJSONFile').change(function(evt) {
        var promise = readFileWithPromise(event.target.files[0]);
    ```

```
            promise.done(function(data) {
                var contacts = JSON.parse(data);
                for (var i = 0; i < contacts.length; i++) {
                    this.store(contacts[i]);
                }
                location.reload();
            }.bind(this));
        }.bind(this));
```

> **REFERENCE** *Please go to the book's website at* www.wrox.com/go/ html5jsjquery24hr *to view the video for Lesson 36, as well as download the code and resources for this lesson.*

PART V
Mobile

37

Responsive Web Design

Web users now expect every website they access to be available not only on a desktop or laptop, but also on tablets and mobile phones. Although the browsers on mobile phones and tablets support most of the features examined in this book, it is not always easy to write HTML and CSS that provide an optimal experience on all devices because of their obvious differences in screen resolution.

This lesson will investigate a series of techniques and technologies that can be leveraged in order to create truly cross-device web pages. These techniques and technologies are often grouped under the umbrella term *responsive web design*, or RWD for short.

Responsive web design encourages designers to create a single set of resources for all devices, rather than creating specialized websites for different devices. This is becoming increasingly important as screen sizes diverge even within the same class of devices.

Responsive web design addresses the screen resolution problem from three angles:

➤ The techniques that can be used to construct HTML that automatically adjusts to different screen resolutions and creates the best possible user experience regardless of the screen resolution. These techniques present all the same information regardless of the screen resolution, but the manner in which content is sized and placed on screen will differ depending on resolution.

➤ The use of flexibly sized images and video that takes into account the overall width and height of the screen. This means ensuring that a resource does not use more space than that allocated by the design, ensuring it scales appropriately, and also ensuring that other elements adapt to the space taken by the resource as the screen resolution changes.

➤ The technologies that can be used for changing the content displayed on a web page based on screen resolution. For instance, it may be necessary to hide specific elements on small resolution devices. This can be achieved via a version of the CSS3 media queries you encountered earlier in the book.

TESTING SCREEN RESOLUTION

It is usually possible to test the way in which your design will react to changes in screen resolution by simply resizing the browser window. You can then determine the resolution of the browser window (or viewport) using the JavaScript commands `window.innerWidth` and `window.innerHeight`.

As you change the browser size, the web page will automatically adjust the content to adapt to the new screen resolution. This is the same basic process that is performed by the browser when the DOM is manipulated and involves calculating the position and size of each element.

Chrome also provides a helpful utility for emulating other devices. Selecting the mobile phone icon in the developer tools will activate this.

Once enabled, you can choose from a variety of devices, or enter a custom screen resolution, as shown in Figure 37-1.

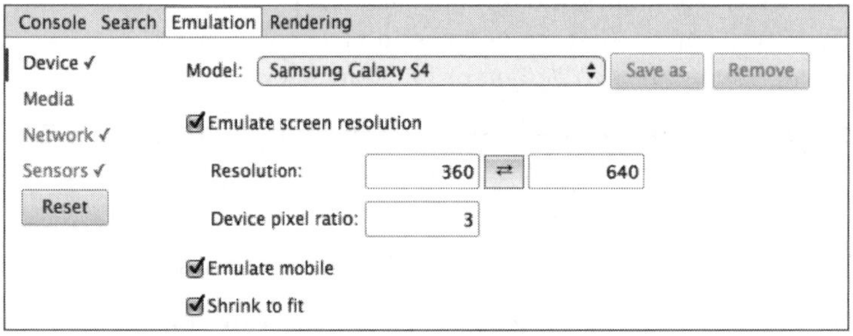

FIGURE 37-1

This allows you to see how a web page will render with various different screen resolutions.

Although useful, unfortunately the emulator does not always accurately reflect the user experience. This is primarily because mobile browsers have adapted to the fact that websites are not mobile friendly and use numerous techniques to adjust. The emulator, by comparison, does not do this. For instance, when viewed on the phone itself the web page displays very differently than the emulator suggests. Figure 37-2 shows that an actual Galaxy S4 will resize elements so that they all fit on screen:

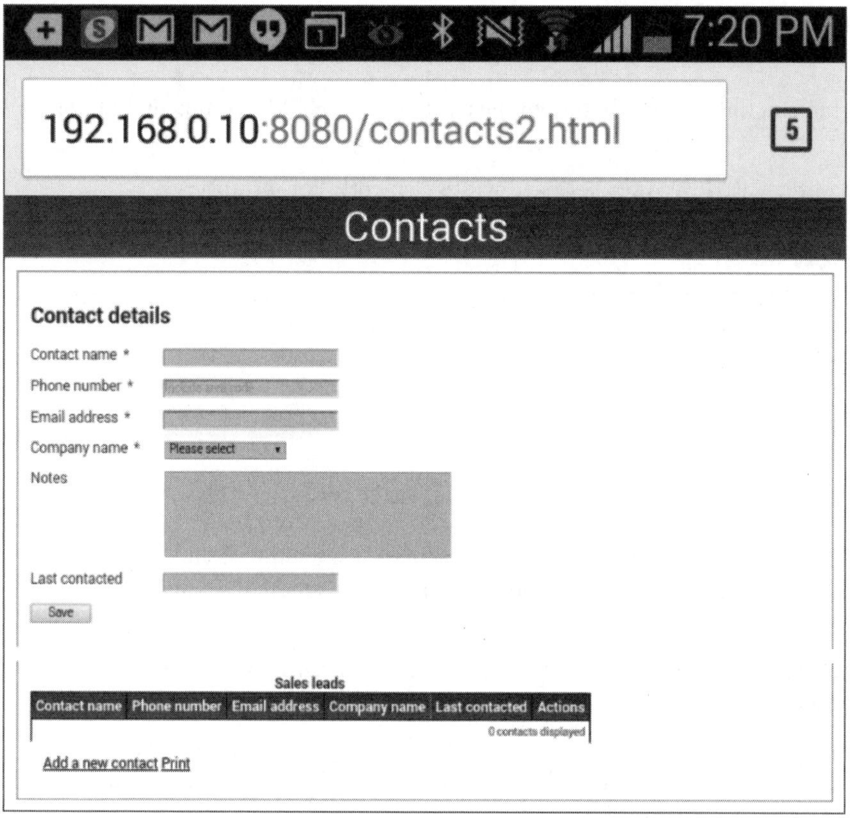

FIGURE 37-2

Although this is generally a useful feature, if you are building a truly responsive website, you generally want to disable this feature. This feature can be disabled via the following meta tag in the head section of the web page:

```
<meta name="viewport" content="width=device-width, initial-scale=1">
```

This tells the browser that it should not try to scale the website; it should just assume it has been designed for the default width of the browser viewport. With this set, the Chrome emulator will accurately reflect the actual user experience for each screen resolution.

FLEXIBLE GRIDS

Responsive web design encourages the use of flexible (or fluid) grids for laying out components. Before beginning the exercise of converting the web application to use a flexible grid, let's comment out the table section. This element is naturally too wide for many devices, so we will address it separately in the next section when you look at media queries. To comment out the table, add the following to the opening table tag:

```
<!--table>
```

and this to the closing tag:

```
</table-->
```

This will leave the table in the markup, but it will be treated as an HTML comment and not displayed.

The current design of the CRM website uses fixed width elements. For instance:

```
input {
    width:200px;
}

label {
    width:150px;
    display: inline-block;
    vertical-align: top;
}
```

Although it is very easy to lay out components with fixed widths and sizes, this can make it impossible for some devices to render them. For instance, the combined width of the label and input fields in the preceding code is 350 pixels. Once margins, paddings, and borders are taken into account, the total width of the label and input field is more than many devices support.

It is generally only advisable to use pixel-based sizing if you are targeting a single screen resolution, and, as outlined earlier, such a move would go against the principles of responsive web design.

A flexible grid layout is capable of adapting automatically to changes and differences in screen resolution. The grids themselves are created with flexible units, such as percentages and em units, and avoid fixed-width units such as pixels.

> **NOTE** *The grid system you will create is considerably simpler than many of the grid systems openly available on the Internet. As always, you are encouraged to explore openly available resources before crafting your own.*

Your design will be based on grid cells that occupy either half or one-quarter of the available width:

```
.grid_quarter {
    display:inline-block;
    vertical-align: top;
    width:23%;
    min-width:15em;
    max-width:25em;
}

.grid_half {
    display:inline-block;
    vertical-align: top;
    width:47%;
```

```
    min-width:15em;
    max-width:50em;
}
```

A minimum and maximum size for grid cells is also specified. This ensures that grid cells remain within sensible bounds.

The `width` properties have also be reduced slightly to allow for margins and borders. This means that four `grid_quarter` elements should be able to be placed side by side—assuming the screen resolution is greater than `60em`.

> **NOTE** *A common variation on this pattern is to change the overall percentage width of cells as the screen resolution decreases. This can be achieved via the media queries that will be introduced in the next lesson, and you will use a variation of this technique in the Try It at the end of the lesson.*

You can now place your input fields and labels inside these grids, using the most appropriate grid size for each element:

```html
<form method="post">
    <div class="formRow">
        <div class="grid_quarter">
            <label for="contactName">Contact name</label>
            <input required autofocus autocomplete="off" name="contactName"
type="text" class="validated" id="contactName" pattern=".{5,100}"/>
        </div>
        <div class="grid_quarter">
            <label for="phoneNumber">Phone number</label>
            <input required pattern="[0-9() ]{5,15}" placeholder="Include area
code" name="phoneNumber" type="tel"   id="phoneNumber" class="validated" />
        </div>
        <div class="grid_quarter">
            <label for="emailAddress">Email address</label>
            <input required name="emailAddress" id="emailAddress" type="email"
class="validated"/>
        </div>
        <div class="grid_quarter">
            <label for="companyName">Company name</label>
            <select required name="companyName" class="validated">
                <option value="">Please select</option>
                <option value="1">ABC Incorporated</option>
                <option value="2">XZY Ltd</option>
                <option value="3">ACME International</option>
            </select>
        </div>
    </div>
    <div class="formRow">
        <div class="grid_half">
            <label for="notes">Notes</label>
```

```
                    <textarea cols="40" rows="6" name="notes" class="validated"
maxlength="1000"></textarea>
                    <div class="textCount"></div>
                </div>
                <div class="grid_quarter">
                    <label for="lastContacted">Last contacted</label>
                    <input name="lastContacted" type="text" class="validated"/>
                </div>
            </div>
            <div class="formRow">
                <input style="width:70px" type="submit" title="Save" value="Save"/>
            </div>
        </form>
```

Notice that this design places each pairing of label and input field in its own grid element. These grid elements are then placed within your existing `formRow` elements.

This design will also rearrange the way labels and input fields are positioned in relation to one another. With a grid-based design, it is often advisable to place labels above input fields to prevent large discrepancies in size between the label and input field. To achieve this, the CSS rules associated with these elements have been changed as follows:

```
input, select, textarea {
        width:90%;
}
label {
    display: block;
}
```

With this in place, you can examine how the web page adjusts to changes in screen resolution. On a display with high resolution, the form appears as you see in Figure 37-3.

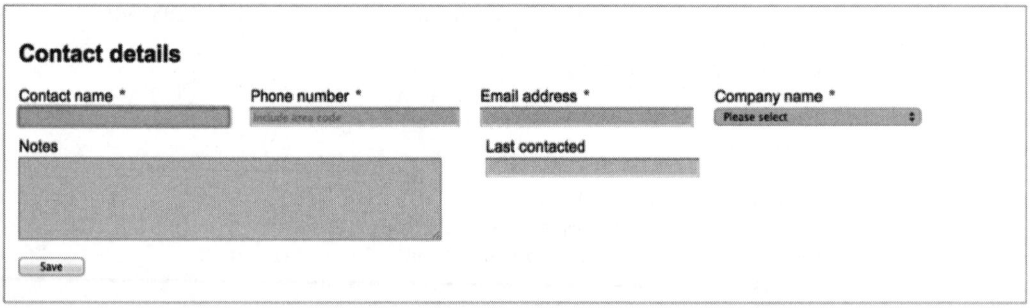

FIGURE 37-3

As the resolution is decreased, the grid elements naturally flow onto new lines, as you will see if you slowly reduce the width of the browser. Once the screen resolution is decreased to that of a typical mobile phone, it appears as you see in Figure 37-4.

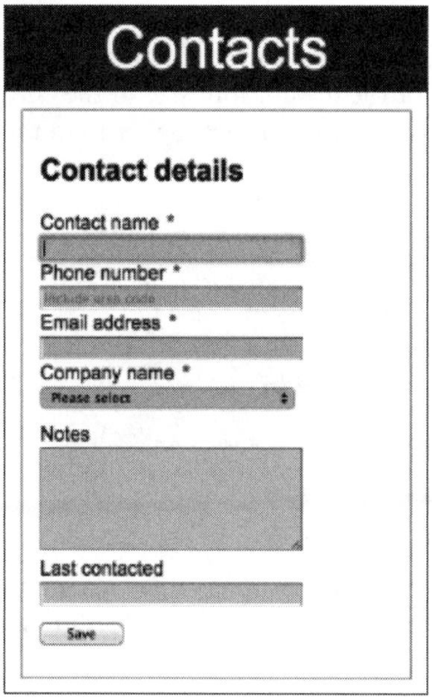

FIGURE 37-4

This design is taking advantage of the manner in which inline elements (the grid elements) flow within a block element (the form rows). You can imagine them flowing exactly the same as text does within a paragraph: When the text reaches the edge of the screen, it simply wraps onto the next line.

It is also worth examining the percentages that have been used on input fields. These have been set to 90 percent, which may sound unusual. Percentages are always specified in relation to the total space allocated to the containing element. Therefore, if an `input` is placed inside a `grid_quarter` element, it will use 90 percent of the 23 percent of the screen allocated to the grid cell, or approximately 20 percent of the total width.

I have also changed header and footer elements to use `em` units to control their height:

```
header {
        background: #3056A0;
        color: white;
        text-align:center;
        line-height: 2em;
        font-size: 3em;
}
footer {
        line-height:2em;
        background: #3056A0;
        color: white;
        text-align:center;
        font-size: 0.8em;
}
```

You will notice that although both `header` and `footer` are set to a `line-height` of 2em, the two elements have very different heights. This seeming discrepancy exists because the `em` unit type expresses sizes in relation to the font size of the element itself, not the default font size of the entire page. Because the `header` font is 3em, the height of the `header` is over three times higher than the `footer`, which has a font size of 0.8em.

> **NOTE** *The fact that the `em` units relate to the element they are defined in can sometimes be a problem. For instance, if a single font size is changed, this may be picked up by many elements, and a variety of element sizes will change as a result. In order to counter this, CSS3 introduces a new unit called `rem`. This unit allows sizes to be defined in relation to a font size defined on the `html` element itself.*

Most of the other changes made to the design involve changing pixels to `em` units and ensuring that elements always have appropriate minimum widths. For instance, the following two rules eliminate fixed sizes entirely:

```
#fileImport, #serverImport, #chooseTheme {
    margin: 2em;
    border: 1px solid #999999;
    border-radius: 1em;
    width: 50%;
    min-width:12em;
    padding: 1em 1em 0 1em;
    background: #DAECFF;
}
.theme {
    width: 1.5em;
    height: 1.5em;
    display: inline-block;
    border: 1px solid #999999;
    border-radius: 0.2em;
}
```

The one exception where pixel sizing is retained is with border sizes. This is usually considered acceptable because it is common to need finer control over the size of borders to stop them from becoming overpowering.

If you look through `contacts.css` on the book's website, you will see a number of other minor changes. The end result is that the web page can adjust to screen widths as low as 275 pixels, and it would be trivial to change it to function on even smaller screen resolutions.

MEDIA QUERIES

Using a flexible grid should always be your starting point when creating a responsive design, but often it is not sufficient for all your needs. Sometimes changes to screen resolution mean that you need to make fundamental changes to your design.

This section will demonstrate how media queries can be used to detect screen resolution and will provide specific rules to suit this resolution.

Before beginning, uncomment the `table` in `contacts.html` because you will investigate how this can be modified with media queries to ensure it displays appropriately at all screen devices.

The table in the `contactList` section is a problem: There is no way that a six-column table will render on a small screen device such as a mobile phone. Although it is possible to add horizontal scrolling, this typically annoys users. You will therefore change the CSS to dynamically hide columns as the screen width shrinks.

Begin by adding three rules to `contacts.css`:

```
@media (max-width: 600px) {
  .medium-suppressed {
    display: none;
  }
}
@media (max-width: 450px) {
  .small-suppressed {
    display: none;
  }
}
@media (max-width: 300px) {
  .tiny-suppressed {
    display: none;
  }
}
```

These rules specify three new classes:

➤ `medium-suppressed`: Can be used to hide elements on screens smaller than 600 pixels

➤ `small-suppressed`: Can be used to hide elements on screens smaller than 450 pixels

➤ `tiny-suppressed`: Can be used to hide elements on screens smaller than 300 pixels

These classes can then be applied to cells in the table header:

```
<thead>
    <th>Contact name</th>
    <th class="medium-suppressed">Phone number</th>
    <th class="small-suppressed">Email address</th>
    <th class="small-suppressed">Company name</th>
    <th class="tiny-suppressed">Last contacted</th>
    <th class="noprint">Actions</th>
</thead>
```

and in the template that creates table rows:

```
<template id="contactRow">
    <td data-property-name="contactName"></td>
    <td class="medium-suppressed" data-property-name="phoneNumber"></td>
    <td class="small-suppressed" data-property-name="emailAddress"></td>
    <td class="small-suppressed" data-property-name="companyName"></td>
    <td class="tiny-suppressed">
```

```
            <time data-property-name="lastContacted"></time>
            <div data-property-name="notes" class="overlay">
            </div>
        </td>
        <td class="noprint"><a href="#" data-delete-button>Delete</a></td>
    </template>
```

If you now reload `contacts.html`, and progressively shrink the screen resolution, columns will automatically disappear. For instance, at a width of 600 pixels, the web page appears as you see in Figure 37-5.

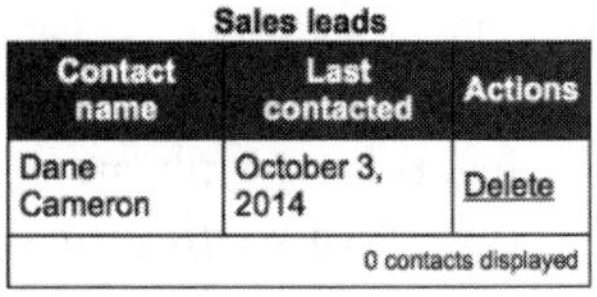

If the user turns his or her phone into landscape mode (with a screen width of 640 pixels), however, the web page automatically adjusts as you can see in Figure 37-6.

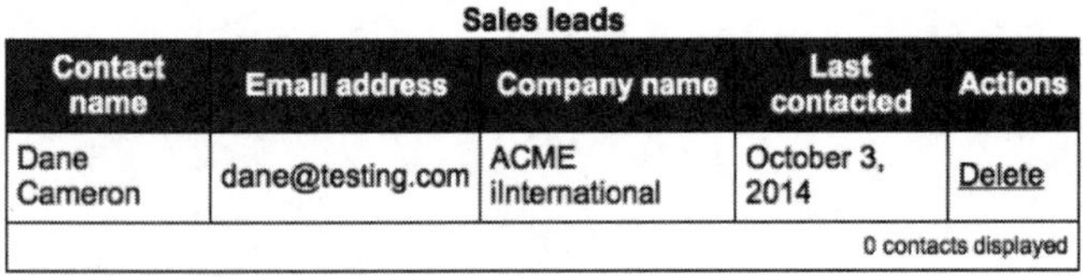

Sales leads

Contact name	Last contacted	Actions
Dane Cameron	October 3, 2014	Delete
		0 contacts displayed

FIGURE 37-5

Sales leads

Contact name	Email address	Company name	Last contacted	Actions
Dane Cameron	dane@testing.com	ACME iInternational	October 3, 2014	Delete
				0 contacts displayed

FIGURE 37-6

You now need an alternative approach for displaying the information that has been suppressed. For the sake of the example here, you will take advantage of the overlay that already displays notes.

Start by defining three classes that are the inverse of those created earlier: They hide elements as the screen resolution reaches a minimum width. This is achieved with the `min-width` property:

```
@media (min-width: 650px) {
  .medium-displayed {
    display:none;
  }
}
@media (min-width: 450px) {
  .small-displayed {
    display:none;
  }
}
@media (min-width: 300px) {
  .tiny-displayed {
    display:none;
  }
}
```

You can now rearrange the overlay so that it includes the various columns that may be hidden:

```
<div class="overlay">
    <div class="medium-displayed" data-property-name="phoneNumber"></div>
    <div class="small-displayed" data-property-name="emailAddress"></div>
    <div class="small-displayed" data-property-name="companyName"></div>
```

38

Location API

Developing web applications for mobile phones can simply mean utilizing the techniques and technologies associated with responsive web design and ensuring that the user receives the best possible experience regardless of the screen resolution.

It can also open up a whole world of possibilities, however, by taking advantage of the features and services that are unique to mobile devices. For instance, mobile devices typically provide a variety of services that can be used in applications:

> ➤ The ability to detect the location of the device

> ➤ The ability to detect motion—for instance, the user moving the device side to side

> ➤ The ability to know which direction the device is facing

> ➤ The ability to take photos and videos

> ➤ The ability to connect to periphery devices using wireless technologies such as Bluetooth

> ➤ The ability to receive and generate notifications

Unfortunately it is not currently possible to interact with most of these services via JavaScript because they are only made available with native APIs, and these vary across platforms.

One API that is available in JavaScript, however, is the Geolocation API. This lesson looks at how you can take advantage of this API to create a web application that tracks a user's motion.

The Geolocation API is available in JavaScript via the `navigator.geolocation` object. This API is available in all the most common browsers, regardless of the device the browser is running on.

Despite the fact that the Geolocation API is available on all devices, it has obvious uses on mobile devices because these change location on a regular basis, and the user is more likely to perform actions in relation to his or her current location. These devices also typically have more accurate mechanisms for determining location, such as GPS.

In order to see the Geolocation API in action, open `contacts.html` via the web server, open the console and enter the following:

```
> navigator.geolocation.getCurrentPosition(function(location) {
    console.log('Latitude: '+ location.coords.latitude);
    console.log('Longitude: '+ location.coords.longitude);
    console.log('Altitude: '+ location.coords.altitude);
    console.log('Accuracy: '+ location.coords.accuracy);
});
```

When you enter this code, Chrome adds a message at the top of the screen, as shown in Figure 38-1.

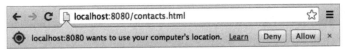

FIGURE 38-1

The Geolocation API specification states that the browser must obtain permission before providing access to the user's location. This is similar to the approach taken with mobile phone apps when they are installed, and it prevents websites from accessing a user's location against the user's will.

Browsers employ a variety of approaches to ask for this permission, and most will either remember the decision made by the user or provide you with an option for this decision to be remembered.

One consequence of this approach is that you can only use the Geolocation API in a web page downloaded from a web server, not from a web page loaded directly from the file system. This is because the permission is associated with your origin—`localhost:8080` in this case—and pages loaded from the file system do not have an origin.

Once you click Allow, your coordinates will be printed to the console. For example:

```
Latitude: -41.22799199999996
Longitude: 174.88613729999998
Altitude: null
Accuracy: 25
```

The latitude and longitude are expressed as numbers. For latitude, a positive number indicates North, a negative number indicates South, and a value of 0 indicates the equator. The numbers will always be in the range –90 through to 90.

For longitude, a positive value indicates East, while a negative value indicates West. The value 0 indicates Greenwich, London, while all other locations have a value in the range –180 through to 180.

The Geolocation API also provides altitude information. This will typically only be available if the location information is obtained via GPS, or an in-built altimeter, but when available represents the number of meters the device is above sea level.

Finally, the API provides information regarding how accurate the location information is. As you can see, in my case Chrome was capable of finding my location within 25 meters.

Devices have a variety of mechanisms for determining your location:

➤ The most accurate form of location information is via GPS. Later in the lesson, you see how you can specifically request the device to provide information via GPS, where supported.

➤ Where GPS information is not available, the device will typically attempt to calculate its location based on the WiFi access points that are within range and their relative strengths. This is how my location was obtained in the previous example and proves reasonably accurate.

➤ Where a device has access to cellular networks, it may also try to triangulate its location from the signal strength of cellular towers that are within range. This will typically only be accurate to within a few hundred meters.

➤ Where no other information is available, the device may need to determine its location based solely on IP address. This is likely to be an approximation at best, and could be wrong by an enormous amount.

Different devices will determine location using different approaches, but the main lesson to understand is that location information will not always be accurate, and you must take this inaccuracy into account when designing web applications.

MONITOR MOVEMENT

In this section, you will use the Geolocation API to monitor the distance traveled by a user, along with their current speed. In order to implement this, your web application will sample the user's location intermittently, and record the user's location at each point in time. By comparing two points in terms of both location and time, you can determine the speed that the user is traveling.

In order to implement this web application, you need a mechanism for determining the distance between two points. Although you could write this functionality yourself, it makes sense to reuse existing code where available. You will use a library created by Google, which is available on the book's website (google.geometry.js). You can also download it from the following URL:

```
http://maps.google.com/maps/api/js?sensor=true&libraries=geometry
```

Start by creating the following web page, and name it locate.html:

```
<!DOCTYPE html>
<html lang="en">
<head>
    <meta charset="utf-8">
    <meta name="viewport" content="width=device-width, initial-scale=1">
    <script src="google.geometry.js"></script>
```

```
        <script src="jquery-2.1.1.js"></script>
        <style>
            body {
                    font-family: Arial, Helvetica, sans-serif;
                    margin: 2em;
                    font-size: 2em color: #333333;
                    background:#E6DEDC;
            }
            #summary {
                width:80%; min-height: 4em;
                border: 1px solid #e2e2e2;
                margin: 1em 0 1em 0;max-width: 20em;
            }
            .button {
                font-size:2em;font-weight:bold;
                color:white;background:#1BA61B;
                width:7em; text-align:center;
                text-decoration:none;line-height:2em;
                display: inline-block;
            }
            .row {
                padding:0.5em;
            }
            .row label {
                width:9em;display: inline-block;
            }
        </style>
</head>
<body>
    <h1>Track movement</h1>
    <div id="summary">
      <div class="row">
          <label>Current speed:</label>
          <span id="currentSpeed"></span>
      </div>
      <div class="row">
          <label>Total distance:</label>
          <span id="distance"></span>
      </div>
      <div class="row">
          <label>Altitude:</label>
          <span id="altitude"></span>
      </div>
      <div class="row message"></div>
      </div>
      <a href="#" class="button" id="activate">Start</a>
</body>
<script>
</script>
</html>
```

This will produce the output shown in Figure 38-2.

FIGURE 38-2

The web page has been created according to the the principles of responsive web design, as outlined in lesson 37, and therefore will function on small or large screens.

The screen consists of a button for starting the tracking and an area for displaying output. Notice that it also imports the jQuery library, which you will use to add dynamic functionality.

The functionality will be implemented as a module with a single public method. Add the following to the `script` block:

```
locationModule = function locationModule() {
    var lastPosition = null;
    var totalDistance = 0;
    var id = null;
    function updateLocation(position) {
    }
    return {
        toggleState: function(evt) {
            if (lastPosition) {
                lastPosition = null;
                lastPositionTime = null;
                totalDistance = 0;
                navigator.geolocation.clearWatch(id);
                $(evt.target).text('Start');
            } else {
                startTime = $.now();
                id = navigator.geolocation.watchPosition(updateLocation,
                function(error) {console.log(error)},
                {maximumAge: 3000, timeout: 20000,
                    enableHighAccuracy: true });
                $(evt.target).text('Stop');
            }
        }
    }
}();
$('#activate').click(locationModule.toggleState);
```

This has been implemented as a module because it needs to store state as the web application executes. The state includes the total distance covered and the last position recorded. Using a module allows this state to be stored as private variables that cannot be manipulated by other code.

The method exposed by the module is called toggleState. This method either starts or stops the tracking, depending on its current state. The application is considered to be running if it has a lastPosition; otherwise, it is considered stopped. As you can see, this method is invoked when the button with the ID activate is clicked.

This application needs to sample the user's position at regular intervals. Obviously, you could use a combination of setInterval and getCurrentPosition for this, but the Geolocation API provides a specific method for this purpose called watchPosition, which accepts the following parameters:

➤ **A success callback:** Identical to the one used with getCurrentPosition.

➤ **An optional error callback:** Invoked if it is not possible to obtain the user's location.

➤ **An optional set of options that act as hints to the API:** In this case, you have specified that you would like an accurate location if possible (using GPS), that you would like to be informed of the user's location every 3 seconds (maximumAge), and that you would like to be notified of the user's location no later than 20 seconds after watchPosition is invoked (timeout). If the device cannot obtain a location in accordance with this contract, the error callback will be invoked.

These three parameters are also accepted by the getCurrentPosition method.

The call to watchPosition returns a number. This needs to be stored by the application because it needs to be provided if you wish to cancel the tracking. You can see this in the following line of code:

```
navigator.geolocation.clearWatch(id);
```

You can now implement the updateLocation callback, which is currently an empty function:

```
var lastPosition = null;
var totalDistance = 0;
var id = null
function updateLocation(position) {
    var updateDate = new Date(position.timestamp);
    $('.message').text('Last updated at ' +updateDate.getHours() +
        ':'+ updateDate.getMinutes()+':'+updateDate.getSeconds());
    if (lastPosition) {
        // time in milliseconds since last reading
        var timeSinceLastReading = position.timestamp-lastPosition.timestamp;
        // distance travelled in meters
        var distance = google.maps.geometry.spherical.computeDistanceBetween
          (new google.maps.LatLng(position.coords.latitude,
              position.coords.longitude),
          new google.maps.LatLng(lastPosition.coords.latitude,
              lastPosition.coords.longitude));
        totalDistance = totalDistance + distance;
        if (timeSinceLastReading / 1000 > 0) {
            var metersPerMinute = distance / (timeSinceLastReading
                / 60 / 1000);
            $('#currentSpeed').text(Math.round(metersPerMinute) +
                ' meters per minute');
        }
}
```

```
        $('#distance').text(Math.round(totalDistance) + ' meters travelled');
        if (position.coords.altitude) {
            $('#altitude').text(Math.round(position.coords.altitude) +
                ' meters above sea level');
        }
    }
    lastPosition = position;
}
```

You always need two positions in order to determine movement, so the first time this callback is invoked, it will simply update a message onscreen stating the last time a reading was obtained, and set the lastPosition variable to the location retrieved.

On subsequent invocations, this function will compare the new location to the previous location in both time and distance.

To determine the time between two invocations, you can use the timestamp property. This contains information on the exact timestamp (time in milliseconds) the user was in this location, not the time that the callback function was invoked.

In order to determine the distance between two locations, you utilize the computeDistanceBetween method from the Google API. To use this, you need to transform the coordinates you receive into instances of the google.maps.LatLng class.

Once you know the time and distance traveled, you can compute the speed at which the user is traveling. For the purposes of this exercise, you will only make this computation if the two readings have different timestamps; otherwise, you would be dividing by zero.

You need to calculate the meters traveled per minute. Therefore, you divide the total distance traveled by the time since the last reading, then 60, then 1000. For instance, if the user had traveled 20 meters, and there were 10,000 milliseconds between the readings, you would calculate:

distance = 20 / (10,000 / 1000/60)

distance = 20 / (10 / 60)

distance = 20 / 0.16666

distance = 120

If the user traveled 20 meters in 10 seconds, he is likely to travel 120 meters in a minute, so this is the expected answer.

You will also update a message onscreen for the total distance covered, and the current altitude if it is available.

LOADING THE APPLICATION

Although you can use this web application from your desktop or laptop, it makes far more sense to try it with a mobile device. To use this application on a mobile device, you first need to make it available via your web server.

In order for your mobile device to connect to your web server, you will need to ensure the port is "open" and also find the appropriate IP address to connect to. These instructions will then explain how to request web pages from within your local network—for instance, your home WiFi network on both Windows and OS X.

These instructions assume that your mobile device and the computer running your web server are both attached to the same WiFi network.

Windows Instructions

You will need to ensure that your computer firewall is either turned off or configured to allow Mongoose to accept inbound connections. This can be configured via the New Inbound Rule Wizard and involves opening port 8080, as shown in Figures 38-3 and 38-4.

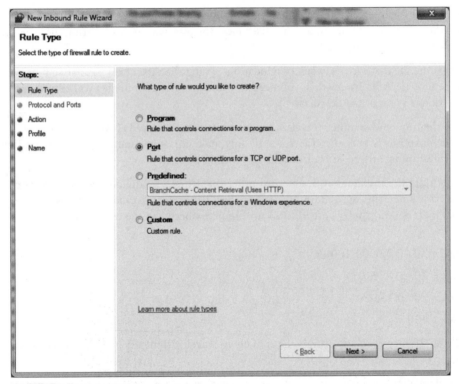

FIGURE 38-3

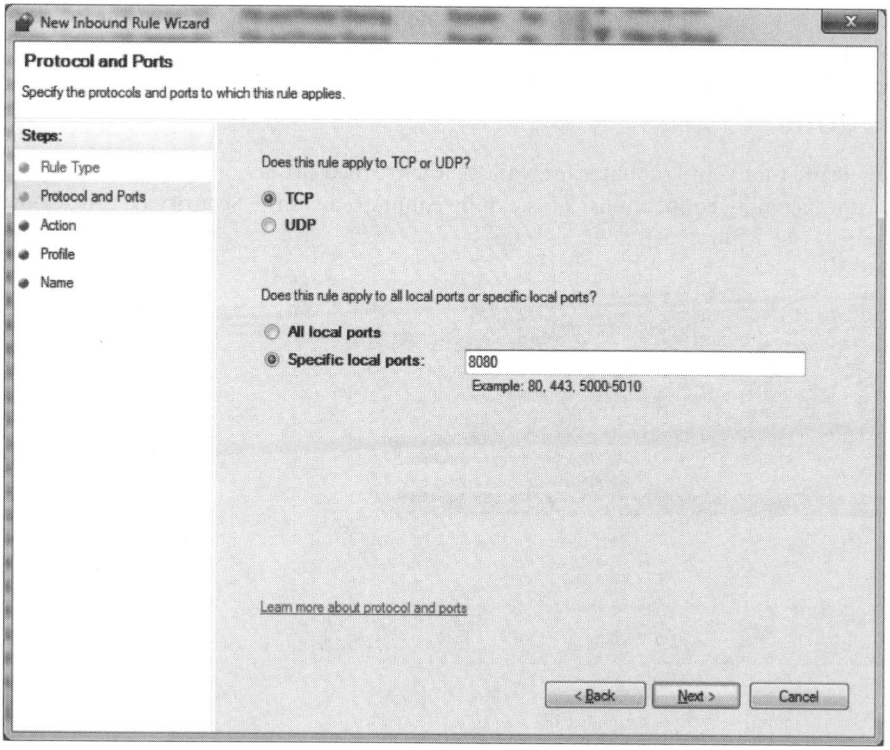

FIGURE 38-4

You will then need to determine the IP address of the computer hosting the web server. There are many ways to do this, but the easiest is to open a command prompt and type `ipconfig`. Your IP address will be listed as IPv4 Address, as you can see in Figure 38-5.

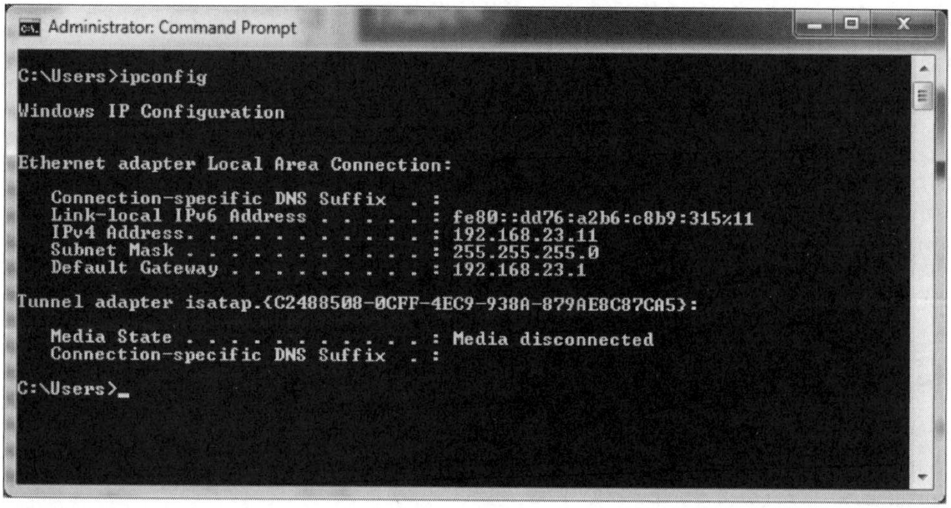

FIGURE 38-5

You should now be able to load the web page from your mobile device using the relevant IP address, and the port used by Mongoose—for example, `http://192.168.23.11:8080/locate.html`.

OS X Instructions

You will need to ensure that your computer firewall is either turned off or configured to allow Mongoose to accept incoming connections. This can be configured via the Security & Privacy menu in System Preferences (see Figure 38-6).

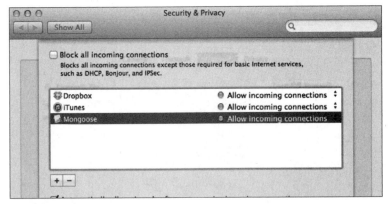

FIGURE 38-6

You will then need to determine the IP address of your computer. This can be found in the Network options of System Preferences, as Figure 38-7 illustrates.

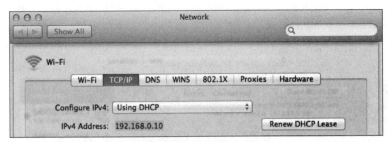

FIGURE 38-7

You should now be able to load the web page from your mobile device using the relevant IP address and the port used by Mongoose—for instance, `http://192.168.0.10:8080/locate.html`.

Using the Application

Once the web application is loaded on your mobile phone, you can begin using it by pressing the Start button. As you start walking, you should see the screen update with your distance traveled.

Because the web page is being loaded from your web server on your WiFi network, you will not be able to reload the web page once you are outside the range of your WiFi network. You could, however, choose to configure an application cache to make this web application available offline, as outlined in lesson 32.

TRY IT

In this Try It, you will enhance the capabilities of the web application developed in this lesson:

➤ You will display to the user the direction they are heading in.

➤ You will smooth variations in the user's speed per minute by averaging the last five recordings (assuming five are available).

Lesson Requirements

In this lesson, you will need the `locate.html` page, which can be downloaded from the book's website if you have not created it. You will also need two libraries used by this web page (jQuery and Google geometry), which are also available from the book's website.

Step-by-Step

1. Open `locate.html` in your text editor and in Chrome.

2. Start by adding a new `div` to the summary section for displaying the user's heading or direction. This should follow the same pattern as the other headings.

3. The user's heading can be calculated in the same manner as her distance traveled by using the `computeHeading` method. Invoke this with the current and previous `LatLng` objects and store the result in a variable.

4. The heading represents the degrees from true North. Round this to a whole number, and output it onscreen.

5. Create a private array in the module for storing the last five calculations of `metersPerMinute`.

6. After `metersPerMinute` is calculated, add it to the array using the `push` method.

7. If the array contains more than five members, remove one using the `shift` method. This approach ensures that the array uses a last in, first out (LIFO) strategy.

8. Create a private function for averaging the contents of an array. Try to use the `reduce` method to calculate the sum of the members in the array, and then divide this by the length of the array.

9. Set the `currentSpeed` to the average of the last five readings.

Your finished version will look something like Figure 38-8.

FIGURE 38-8

jQuery Mobile: Part I

I began this section of the book by looking at how a web application can be designed for mobile devices using the techniques and technologies associated with responsive web design. Responsive web design encourages the use of a single set of resources while ensuring the content dynamically adjusts to all relevant screen resolutions.

Although responsive web design is increasingly popular, there is an alternative school of thought that says large-screen devices and small-screen devices are fundamentally different, and their respective needs can only be met by creating two different web applications.

The following are the main arguments in favor of mobile-specific versions of web applications:

➤ Mobile devices support a different set of events from traditional desktop devices. This stems primarily from the fact that the user is holding the device in her hands, meaning it is possible to respond to touch- and motion-based events, such as the user swiping the screen, tapping and holding, or rotating the screen.

➤ Mobile applications typically approach navigation in a different manner than desktop applications. Rather than providing a single page with a diverse set of information, they provide information in bite-sized pages, and make it possible to quickly navigate from one page to another.

Users of web applications on desktops and laptops, by comparison, typically become frustrated by websites that require excessive navigation, even though this is a popular technique used to increase advertising revenue on many sites.

➤ Mobile devices are often connected to slower connections than networked devices such as desktops, and users typically pay far more money for their mobile data. The fact that a typical home page on a website is now over 1MB in size, and can be far larger, can have a major impact on usability for mobile users, both in terms of time and money.

A mobile-specific web application will therefore ensure that a minimal set of resources is downloaded on page load and that subsequent resources are loaded on-demand.

The next two lessons will look at how the jQuery Mobile library can be used to create a mobile-specific web application. This will involve creating a new set of resources for the CRM web application while retaining the majority of the JavaScript code.

> **NOTE** *The main disadvantage of this approach is that there will be two versions of the web application that need to be supported. Not only does this add extra effort, but it is also very easy to introduce inconsistencies between the two versions of the web application. It is therefore essential to weigh the tradeoffs before beginning a mobile-specific web application.*

This lesson will focus on the way in which a mobile web application can be structured into a set of pages and the manner in which the user can navigate between these pages. The next lesson will then focus on mobile-specific UI components and mobile-specific events.

UNDERSTANDING JQUERY MOBILE

Despite the fact that it has jQuery in its name, jQuery mobile encourages a very different form of programming from what you have seen up until this point in the book.

jQuery Mobile is a *framework* for developing mobile web applications. In order to use jQuery Mobile, you are responsible for describing the style and behavior of each element, but jQuery Mobile—for the most part—is responsible for implementing this.

For example, consider the following hyperlink, which will form part of your web application:

```
<a href="#settingsPage" data-role="button" data-icon="gear" class="ui-btn-right"
data-transition="slideup">Settings</a>
```

As you can see, this hyperlink contains three data attributes and a class, all of which have special meaning to jQuery Mobile. Some of these describe the way the hyperlink should appear:

➤ It should be styled as a button.

➤ It should appear on the right side of its container.

➤ It has an icon provided by jQuery Mobile called "gear."

Other data attributes describe the behaviors of this hyperlink when clicked; for example, it transitions using a "slide-up" effect.

With these attributes and classes in place, simply importing the jQuery Mobile library and style sheet is sufficient to create the button shown in Figure 39-1 and provide its "click" functionality:

jQuery Mobile supports well over a hundred data attributes, all with their own specific purpose and set of values. Although this lesson focuses on only a small number of these, once you understand the basic approach, it is straightforward to discover a whole world of functionality by browsing the demos and APIs at `jquerymobile.com`.

FIGURE 39-1

> **NOTE** *Using a framework like jQuery Mobile requires a mind-shift. You need to be prepared to hand over more control to the framework and also to live within its constraints to some extent. In return, you potentially need to write considerably less CSS and JavaScript than you would otherwise.*

Importing jQuery Mobile

To begin your mobile web application, create a file called `mobile_contacts.html` in the same folder as `contacts.html`.

You will use version 1.4.4 of jQuery Mobile in this lesson. As with most JavaScript libraries, you have the choice of using a CDN-hosted version or downloading and hosting your own copy of this library. In this lesson, you will host your own version of the library.

jQuery Mobile can be downloaded from the jQuery Mobile website at `jquerymobile.com`, or it is available on the book's website. The download consists of a zip file containing a set of JavaScript files, CSS files, and images.

> **NOTE** *If you download the library yourself, it is also possible to construct a version of jQuery Mobile conforming to your preferred themes. This process will then construct a set of CSS files conforming to your required color scheme.*

Once downloaded, extract the zip file into the folder containing `mobile_contacts.html`, creating a sub-folder called `jquery.mobile`. You should then import the relevant resources in the `head` section of `mobile_contacts.html` (ensuring that the jQuery Mobile library is imported after the main jQuery library). Your HTML page should begin like this:

```
<!DOCTYPE html>
<html lang="en">
    <head>
        <meta charset="utf-8">
        <meta name="viewport" content="width=device-width, initial-scale=1">
        <title>Contacts</title>
        <script src="jquery-2.1.1.js"></script>
        <script src="jquery-ui.js"></script>
        <script src="contacts.js"></script>
        <script src="jquery-time.js"></script>
        <script src="jquery-tables.js"></script>
        <script src="find.contacts.js"></script>
        <link rel="stylesheet" type="text/css" href="jquery-ui.css">
        <link rel="stylesheet" href="jquery.mobile/jquery.mobile-1.4.4.min.css" />
        <script src="jquery.mobile/jquery.mobile-1.4.4.min.js"></script>
    </head>
    <body>
        <main id="contactScreen">
        </main>
    </body>
</html>
```

Notice that you also set the viewport `width` and `initial-scale`, and that you have imported any other relevant files such as `contacts.js`. You do not import `contacts.css`, however, because jQuery Mobile includes its own style sheets, and these will meet most of your needs.

Mobile Design

Your first task in designing your web application is to determine the pages that will make up the web application, and the flow a user will follow as he navigates from one page to another.

This web application will consist of four logical pages:

➤ A page containing a list of saved contacts. This will be the default page presented to users when the web application loads.

➤ A page for entering details for a new contact. Users can navigate to or from this page via the list page.

➤ A page for viewing details and any notes relating to a contact: This has been implemented as an overlay in the current web application but makes sense to implement as a page in your mobile web application. This user will navigate to this page from the list view.

➤ A page for any settings or utilities such as file upload and server download functions. This user will navigate to this page from the list view.

JQUERY MOBILE PAGES

A page in a jQuery Mobile web application does not need to be realized by an HTML file. Instead, it is possible to group together many mobile pages in the same HTML page, and use jQuery Mobile to navigate from one page to another.

jQuery Mobile achieves this via DOM manipulation: It simply hides the logical pages that are not visible and transitions from one page to another through a combination of DOM manipulation and animated transitions.

In order to indicate that an element in the web page represents a logical page, you tag it with the attribute `data-role="page"`, and provide an `id` to uniquely identify the page.

Although it is common to use `div` elements as the container for pages, it is possible to use any block-based element, such as a `section`. For instance, the following represents a page for displaying a list of contacts. Read through the code first, and I will then walk you through each relevant element and attribute:

```
<section id="contactListPage" data-role="page">
    <div data-role="header">
        <h1>Contact list</h1>
        <a href="#settingsPage" data-role="button" data-icon="gear" class="ui-btn-
right" data-transition="slideup">Settings</a>
    </div>
    <div data-role="content">
        <table data-role="table" data-mode="columntoggle"
            class="ui-responsive ui-table">
            <thead>
                <tr>
```

```
                <th data-priority="1">Contact name</th>
                <th data-priority="1">Phone number</th>
                <th data-priority="1">Actions</th>
            </tr>
        </thead>
        <tfoot>
            <tr>
                <td colspan="3">0 contacts displayed</td>
            </tr>
        </tfoot>
        <tbody>
        </tbody>
    </table>
</div>
<div data-role="footer" class="ui-bar" data-position="fixed">
    <a href="#contactDetailsPage" id="addContact" data-role="button" data-
transition="slide" data-icon="plus">Add</a>
</div>
</section>
```

The page itself has been broken into three sections, each of which consists of a div with a data-role attribute:

➤ The top div defines the header of the page; in mobile web applications, it is typical for this to describe the content of the web page and to offer navigation links to other pages.

➤ The middle div contains an area for the main content of the page.

➤ The bottom div contains the footer of the page. It is conventional for this area to contain a toolbar for invoking actions on the page.

In this particular example, the footer has a property data-position="fixed": This will ensure that the footer always appears fixed at the bottom of the screen, even if the table contains a large number of contacts and requires scroll bars.

Within this basic structure, you begin adding content. For instance, the content area of the screen contains the table of contacts. You will notice that this table has been defined with the following attributes: data-role="table" data-mode="columntoggle".

The first of these attributes is used to tell jQuery Mobile that it needs to customize this table for mobile devices, while the second attribute tells it what strategy to use for this customization.

jQuery Mobile supports two basic modes or strategy of table. These two modes are both intended to allow the table to respond to varying screen resolutions, but each does so in its own unique way.

> **NOTE** As you will see in the next lesson, adding data attributes to many elements not only alters the way they look, but it causes them to be converted into fully fledged UI components complete with their own set of methods and properties.

The default table mode is reflow: In this mode, the table is displayed in a conventional manner where space permits, but when the resolution becomes too low, the columns are displayed vertically rather than horizontally, as Figure 39-2 shows.

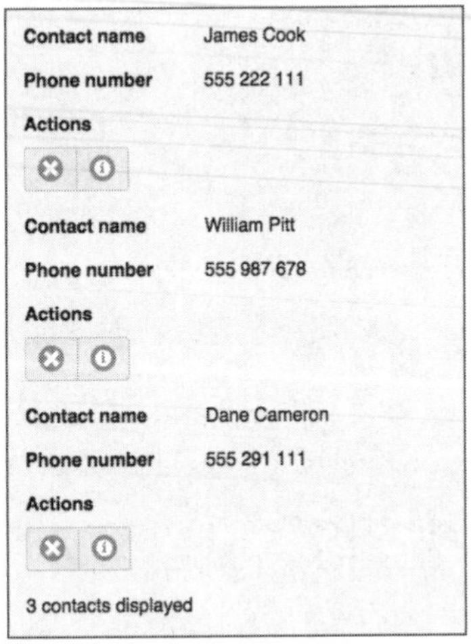

FIGURE 39-2

For the example here, you will use the `columntoggle` mode. This mode will mean that a button is automatically added to the screen to allow users to hide or show columns as required. In addition, this mode allows `th` cells to be marked with the `data-priority` attribute: If the table contains too many columns to fit the screen resolution, jQuery Mobile will start excluding columns that have the lowest priority (the highest number). In this particular case, it will mean hiding the phone number column. This produces the table shown in Figure 39-3.

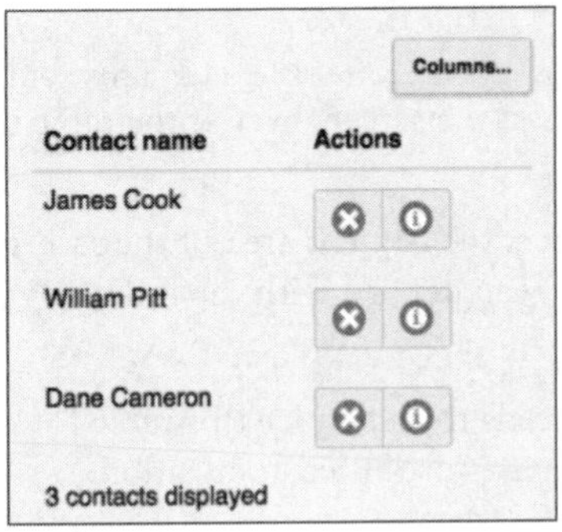

FIGURE 39-3

You will continue to use a template to add contacts to the web page so add the following to the web page before the closing `main` tag. It is not necessary to add the `data-priority` attribute to the cells in the body of the table:

```
<template id="contactRow">
    <td data-property-name="contactName"></td>
    <td data-property-name="phoneNumber"></td>
    <td>
        <div data-role="controlgroup" data-type="horizontal" class="ui-mini">
            <a href="#" data-role="button" data-icon="delete" data-iconpos="notext"
style="height: 18px;" data-delete-button></a>
```

```
            <a href="#" data-role="button" data-icon="info" data-iconpos="notext"
style="height: 18px;" data-notes-button></a>
        </div>
    </td>
</template>
```

This is essentially the same as the template in `contacts.html`, except it contains fewer columns and one additional button for displaying the notes for the contacts.

Because two buttons are being displayed side-by-side in single columns, they have been contained within a `div` defined with `data-role="controlgroup"`: This control can be used wherever buttons need to be grouped together, such as a menu. In this example, you have also specified that the buttons should be displayed horizontally, while the class `ui-mini` ensures that small icons are used.

You will also notice that you are taking advantage of more jQuery Mobile icons for these buttons: `delete` and `info`. jQuery Mobile provides approximately 50 icons that will meet most of your development needs; these are documented fully on the jQuery Mobile website.

> **NOTE** *One other change you will notice if you look at the JavaScript provided for this lesson is that after rows are dynamically added to the table, it is necessary to refresh the table and control groups because jQuery Mobile converts many elements into UI components or widgets, and this only happens at page load by default. This process is explored further in the next lesson.*

Once you have contacts loaded into the mobile web application, it will display as you see in Figure 39-4.

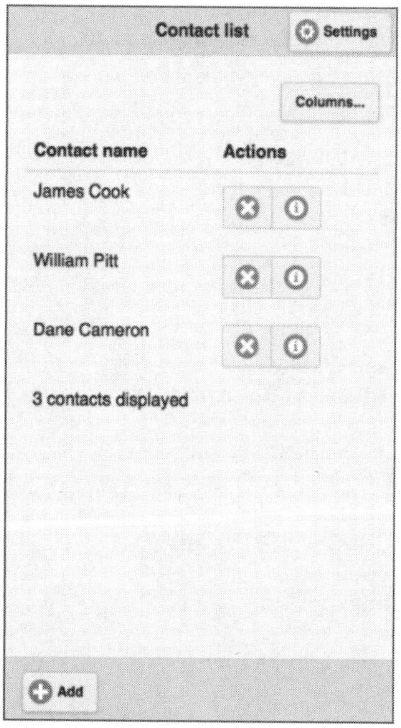

FIGURE 39-4

> **NOTE** *A single jQuery Mobile can support up to 26 color swatches (labeled a through z) defining a specific color palette for different elements. The jQuery Mobile Theme Roller feature lets you specify these, but even the default download contains five color swatches. You can try these out by adding attributes such as* `data-theme="b"` *to elements such as headers and footers.*

Notice that you did not invoke a single line of JavaScript or define a single CSS rule, yet jQuery Mobile has constructed a mobile website conforming to the conventions of mobile applications.

Form-Based Pages

You can now add the second page to your web application: This will be used for capturing information about a new contact. To create this page, add the following code, immediately after the page created earlier.

```
<section data-role="page" id="contactDetailsPage">
    <form method="post">
        <div data-role="header">
            <h1>Enter details</h1>
            <a href="#contactListPage" data-role="button" data-icon="home"
class="ui-btn-right">Home</a>
        </div>
        <div data-role="content">
            <div class="ui-field-contain">
                <label for="contactName">Contact name</label>
                <input required autofocus autocomplete="off"
                    name="contactName" type="text"class="validated"
                    id="contactName" pattern=".{5,100}" />
            </div>
            <div class="ui-field-contain">
                <label for="phoneNumber">Phone number</label>
                <input required pattern="[0-9() ]{5,15}"
                        placeholder="Include area code"
                        name="phoneNumber" type="tel"
                        id="phoneNumber" class="validated" />
            </div>
            <div class="ui-field-contain">
                <label for="emailAddress">Email address</label>
                <input required name="emailAddress" id="emailAddress"
                        type="email" class="validated" />
            </div>
            <div class="ui-field-contain">
                <label for="companyName">Company name</label>
                <select required name="companyName" class="validated">
                    <option value="">Please select</option>
                    <option value="1">ABC Incorporated</option>
                    <option value="2">XZY Ltd</option>
                    <option value="3">ACME iInternational</option>
                </select>
            </div>
```

```
            <div class="ui-field-contain">
                <label for="notes">Notes</label>
                <textarea cols="40" rows="6" name="notes" class="validated"
                    maxlength="1000"></textarea>
                <div class="textCount"></div>
            </div>
            <div class="ui-field-contain">
                <label for="lastContacted">Last contacted</label>
                <input name="lastContacted" type="text" class="validated" />
            </div>
        </div>
        <div data-role="footer" class="ui-bar" data-position="fixed">
            <input data-role="button" class="ui-btn-right"
                data-inline="true" data-icon="check" type="submit"
                title="Save" value="Save" />
        </div>
    </form>
</section>
```

The basic structure of this page is exactly the same as the contact list page; it contains header, footer, and content sections. The most interesting aspect of the form, however, is that each label/form field pair is placed inside the following construct:

```
<div class="ui-field-contain">
```

The `ui-field-contain` class is responsible for determining the best way to lay out a label alongside a form field. If space allows, the label will be placed to the left of the form field; otherwise, it will be placed above it. This means that you can simply add fields without concerning yourself with how they will be displayed.

When a jQuery Mobile web application is loaded, the first page defined in the HTML will be displayed by default. In order to display the Create contact page, you therefore need to define a transition. This was already provided in the footer of the Contacts list page:

```
<a href="#contactDetailsPage" id="addContact" data-role="button" data-
transition="slide" data-icon="plus">Add</a>
```

Notice that the `href` contains a hash and then the ID of the page that is being transitioned to? When clicked, this link will request the resource `mobile_contacts.html#contactDetailsPage`. The hash character has special meaning within a hyperlink: It is called a fragment identifier, and indicates that the browser should navigate to a specific location defined within the page—in this case, a specific location within `mobile_contacts.html`.

> **NOTE** *The fragment identifier is interesting because it is the only portion of the URL that is interpreted by the browser rather than the web server. This means that if the only thing that changes about a URL is the fragment identifier, it is not necessary to reload the page from the web server.*

This is typically achieved by adding a link with a `name` attribute within the web page:

```
<a name="section1"></a>
```

These are referred to as *named anchors*. It is then possible to link directly to this position with either relative or absolute URLs—for instance:

```
<a href="#section2">Go to section 2</a>
```

or

```
<a href="http://page1.html#section2">Go to section 2</a>
```

With jQuery Mobile, you are only responsible for ensuring that the text after the hash matches the `id` of a page: jQuery Mobile will take care of the rest.

Also notice that it is possible to define transitions using the `data-transition` attribute: In this case, we have defined a "slide" transition from one page to the other. Other supported transitions are `slideup`, `slidedown`, `pop`, `fade`, or `flip`. It is also possible to reverse the direction of a transition with `data-direction="reverse"`.

> **NOTE** *jQuery Mobile makes it trivial to implement single page web applications. One complication of single-page web applications that I have not addressed, however, is how to handle the browser's Back button. Naturally, you would like this to return the user to the last "logical" page she visited, not the last "physical" page she visited.*
>
> *Fortunately, as a user changes pages, the hash-value will change at the top of the browser window, and this generates an HTML5 event called a* `hashchange`. *Although you can listen for these events yourself and keep a history of page changes, an object called* `window.history` *is keeping track of these changes for you. This object provides methods such as* `window.history.back()` *to return to the previous page, and* `window.history.go(-2)` *to return back two pages.*
>
> *When writing single-page web applications, you can choose to manage this state yourself using two other methods on the history API called* `pushState` *and* `pop-State`. *These methods allow you fine-grained control over page navigation, even if users are not physically changing pages.*

Although the jQuery Mobile CSS files meet most of your needs, you will also add a small number of styles at this point for specific functionality required by your web application. These can simply be added in a `style` tag in the `head` section:

```
<style>
thead th {
  border-bottom: 1px solid #dedede;
}
.validated:invalid {
        background:#FAC3C9;
}

.validated:valid {
        background:#BDF0A8;
}
```

```
    .requiredMarker {
        color: red;
        padding-left:0.3em;
    }
    </style>
```

If you reload the web page and click the Add button in the footer, you should see the page shown in Figure 39-5 displayed.

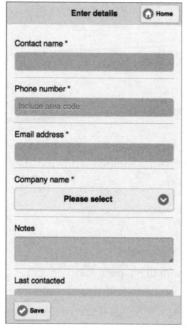

FIGURE 39-5

JavaScript

The final change you need to make is to ensure that the relevant code in contacts.js is initialized. This presents a minor problem because you do not need some of the functionality in contacts.js, but you want to reuse 90 percent of the code.

In order to deal with this, you will pass a parameter to the contact's controller indicating whether this is a mobile web application; therefore, you should add the following to the end of the web page:

```
    <script>
        $('[name="lastContacted"]').datepicker({
            minDate : "-6m",
            maxDate : 0
        });
        $(document).ready(function(evt) {
            var mainElement = document.getElementById('contactScreen');
            var screen = contactsScreen(mainElement, true);
```

```
            screen.init();
    });
</script>
```

A version of `contacts.js` that implements the necessary changes is available from the book's website. This version of the code has also reverted to the web storage API as opposed to Indexed DB. This is primarily because mobile browser support of APIs is typically behind desktop browsers, and IndexedDB is not as widely supported.

TRY IT

In this Try It, you will enhance the mobile web application by adding the capability to view notes for a contact.

Lesson Requirements

In this lesson, you will need the `mobile_contacts.html` page, which can be downloaded from the book's website if you have not followed along with this lesson. You should also download `contacts.js` from the book's website.

Step-by-Step

1. Open `mobile_contacts.html` in your text editor and in Chrome.

2. Start by adding a new page to the web application. This should have an `id` of `contactNotePage`.

3. Add a header to the page, and include in this a description of the page (for example, "Contact notes"), and a home button for returning to the List contacts page.

4. Add a content section to the page.

5. Within the contact section, add an `h2` element for the contact name. You will use the `bind` method to populate this (and the other fields that you will add) to add a `data-property-name` attribute with the value `contactName`.

6. Add four more `div` elements with `data-property-name` attributes for `phoneNumber`, `emailAddress`, `notes`, and `lastContacted`.

7. The buttons the user will press to view the notes have the data attribute `data-notes-button`. Within `contacts.js`, add click listeners for these buttons.

8. The click listener first needs to determine the contact that has been clicked on by finding the parent `tr` element, and the `contactId` data attribute that has been set on this (if you need a hint, look at what you did with the delete functionality).

9. Find the relevant contact in `localStorage` based on the ID found in Step 8. This will involve parsing the contacts into an array and looping through until you find the contact with the matching ID.

10. Invoke the `bind` function, passing it a reference to the `contactNotePage` and the contact found in Step 9. This will populate the fields in the page with the appropriate values.

11. You now need to programmatically change pages. In order to do this, you first find the page container using `$(":mobile-pagecontainer")`; in our case this will return the `main` element because that is the parent of all the pages. The `pagecontainer` method can then be invoked on this element and passed three parameters:

➤ `"change"`: Indicates that the page should be changed.

➤ `"#contactNotePage"`: This is the page that should be displayed.

➤ `{transition: 'slide'}`: This object accepts any optional parameters; for your purposes here, you only need to specify the transition effect.

You should now be able to reload the web application and click the information button next to any contact to display the notes recorded, as shown in Figure 39-6.

FIGURE 39-6

> **REFERENCE** *Please go to the book's website at* www.wrox.com/go/html5jsj-query24hr *to view the video for Lesson 39, as well as download the code and resources for this lesson.*

40

jQuery Mobile: Part II

In this lesson, you will continue with the creation of a jQuery Mobile web application but shift your focus away from pages and navigation and toward mobile-specific UI components and mobile-based events. As mentioned in the previous lesson, mobile devices naturally lend themselves to different approaches from traditional desktops and laptops, and this can impact both the UI components used and the event listeners registered.

UI COMPONENTS

Mobile phone platforms such as iOS and Android each support a toolkit of UI components (commonly referred to as widgets). Many of these, such as text fields, mirror HTML elements extremely closely. Several others, however, are intended to address the unique needs of mobile devices and do not match corresponding HTML elements.

In order to address this discrepancy, the jQuery Mobile library provides a wide variety of UI components that match those commonly found in native toolkits. You have already encountered several of these in the previous lesson: This included buttons, control groups, pages, tables, headers and footers, and you will continue looking at several others in this section.

The components you have seen so far have all been based on conventional HTML elements such as the `table` or `select` elements, but have been transformed into components by jQuery Mobile based on their data attributes and CSS classes.

In fact, in many cases you are using jQuery Mobile components even without realizing it. If you view the Add contact page, you will notice that the `select` element has been customized specifically for mobile devices, as shown in Figure 40-1.
This looks similar to the components you will see in native mobile applications, and follows the same basic design philosophy.

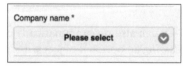

FIGURE 40-1

You will also notice that the appearance of this component has been significantly modified from the native Chrome select element, as shown in Figure 40-2, despite the fact that no jQuery Mobile specific attributes or classes were provided.

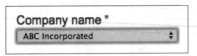

FIGURE 40-2

If you inspect the HTML for the web page, you will see that jQuery Mobile has achieved this partly via CSS classes, but more importantly, it has added a whole new set of elements to the DOM, as you can see in Figure 40-3.

```
▼<div class="ui-select">
  ▼<div id="select-24-button" class="ui-btn ui-icon-carat-d ui-btn-icon-right ui-corner-all ui-shadow">
    <span class="validated">Please select</span>
  ▼<select required name="companyName" class="validated">
    <option value>Please select</option>
    <option value="1">ABC Incorporated</option>
    <option value="2">XZY Ltd</option>
    <option value="3">ACME International</option>
  </select>
  ::after
  </div>
</div>
::after
```

FIGURE 40-3

The top two div elements shown in Figure 40-3 have been added by jQuery Mobile itself and provide a way of modifying the appearance and behavior of the select element contained within it.

Not only does this approach allow jQuery Mobile to create more mobile-friendly components that are easier to interact with using your finger, it means that you can maintain a consistent look and feel across different mobile browsers and platforms.

All jQuery Mobile components, even those based on conventional HTML elements, support a wide array of properties and methods, and therefore act more like the feature-rich UI components found in native frameworks.

For instance, if you open the Add contact screen and type the following:

```
$('select' ).selectmenu('disable');
```

the select component will be immediately disabled.

Each UI component is associated with a jQuery Mobile method. As you can see, select boxes are associated with the selectmenu method, and this line of code therefore invokes a method called disable on a selectmenu component.

Conversely, you can convert a jQuery Mobile component back into a conventional HTML component by invoking destroy on it:

```
$('select').selectmenu('destroy')
```

You can also programmatically construct components by invoking the relevant method on them and passing an optional object with any options:

```
$('select').selectmenu({'icon': 'star'});
```

The options passed can almost always also be provided via the data attributes investigated in the previous lesson, but there are times when it makes sense to programmatically construct components, particularly when they are added to the page after the page has loaded. In fact, because the contacts are loaded into the main table after jQuery Mobile had initialized, it was necessary to manually initialize the components inside the table body with the following code:

```
$(screen).find('table').table("refresh");
$(screen).find('[data-role="controlgroup"]').controlgroup();
```

> **NOTE** *The full list of options and methods supported by the various jQuery Mobile components is beyond the scope of this book, but be sure to browse the jQuery Mobile documentation at* api.jquerymobile.com *to gain a greater understanding of the power and flexibility of these UI components.*

Collapsible Components

Let's begin this look at new components by adding a final page to the web application. This page will be used to contain any settings or configuration tools required by the web application. The code for this page is as follows:

```
<div id="settingsPage" data-role="page">
    <div data-role="header">
        <h1>Settings</h1>
            <a href="#contactListPage" data-role="button" data-icon="home" data-transition="slidedown" class="ui-btn-right">Home</a>
    </div>
    <div data-role="content">
        <div data-role="collapsible-set">
            <div data-role="collapsible" data-collapsed="false">
                <h3>Import contacts</h3>
                <p>
                    <label for="importJSONFile">Import contacts</label>
                    <input type="file" id="importJSONFile" name="importJSONFile">
                </p>
            </div>
            <div data-role="collapsible">
                <h3>Import from server</h3>
                <p>
                    <a id="importFromServer" data-role="button"
                    href="#">Import from server</a>
                </p>
            </div>
        </div>
    </div>
</div>
```

The structure and heading of this page should look very familiar, but the content contains a new type of component called a collapsible set. This component functions like a set of vertical tabs: Each entry in the set is assigned a header (indicated by an h3 tag) and a details section (indicated by a p tag), and when a header is selected, its detail section is displayed, as shown in Figure 40-4.

This component is ideal for mobile web applications because it allows various options to be presented on the same page without the detail of each option distracting the user. Notice also that jQuery Mobile automatically takes care of assigning appropriate icons to each option: The plus icon indicates that the details can be shown, whereas the minus icon indicates that the option is currently selected.

It is also possible to use `collapsible` components outside the `collapsible-set` component. In this case, the component functions identically to the `summary` and `details` elements you encountered earlier in the book, but has the advantage of working consistently across all browsers.

FIGURE 40-4

Popups

An alternative way of implementing the Settings screen would be as a popup. A popup leaves the user in the context of the current page, and means users do not need to navigate back to where they came from once they complete their action.

In order to implement a page as a popup, you need to start by changing the `data-role` of the `div` from `page` to `popup`:

```
<div id="settingsPage" data-role="popup">
```

It is also necessary to move the markup for the page so that it sits inside the `contactListPage` element, preferably just before the closing `section` tag.

You will also remove the header from the Settings page when it appears as a popup, and replace it with a Close button on the right-hand side of the popup. This can be achieved by replacing the header with the following:

```
<a href="#" data-rel="back" data-role="button" data-icon="delete" data-
iconpos="notext" class="ui-btn-right">Close</a>
```

The final change is to add `data-rel="popup"` to the link that opens the settings page so that the page opens as a popup:

```
<a href="#settingsPage" data-rel="popup" data-role="button" data-icon="gear"
class="ui-btn-right" data-transition="slideup">Settings</a>
```

If you reload the web page and press the Settings button, the page will be displayed as a popup over top of the current page.

Selection

jQuery Mobile also supports a widely used mobile component called a list. This provides a mechanism for the user to select a single option from a list of options, usually with the intention of viewing additional information.

This component could have provided an additional mechanism for arranging the Contact list screen. For instance, the contacts could be arranged in a list as follows:

```
<div data-role="content">
    <ul data-role="listview">
        <li><a href="#" data-contact-id="1">Dane Cameron</a></li>
        <li><a href="#" data-contact-id="2">James Cook</a></li>
        <li><a href="#" data-contact-id="3">William Pitt</a></li>
    </ul>
</div>
```

This is a conventional unordered list, as encountered earlier in the book, except the `ul` element has been tagged with the `data-role="listview"` attribute, and each list item contains a link to the relevant contact. When viewed, this appears as you see in Figure 40-5.

Each element in the list could then be clicked to load the details and notes of the contact. Because it is only possible to select a single action per row, the delete functionality would need to be managed in an alternative manner, such as a button on the Contacts Notes screen.

Lists are often used as an alternative to tables in mobile web applications because they tend to adjust more easily to small resolutions.

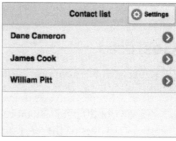

FIGURE 40-5

Flip-Switch

The final component we will address is a called a flip-switch. A flip-switch is used for selecting between two possible states, and is therefore similar to the checkboxes commonly used in HTML forms. In order to demonstrate this, add the following to the form on the Add contact screen:

```
<div class="ui-field-contain">
    <label for="followUp"Follow up required</label>
    <input name="followUp" id="followUp" type="checkbox" data-role="flipswitch" />
</div>
```

This component is modeled as a conventional checkbox, but assigned the attribute `data-role="flipswitch"`. This constructs the component shown in Figure 40-6.

Like many of these components, the main reason flip-switches are preferred over checkboxes is that they are more "touch-friendly." It feels more intuitive for a finger to slide a switch and see its state toggled because the action mirrors real-world switches such as light and socket switches. Pressing your finger inside a square and seeing a check appear, by contrast, does not mirror a real-world activity.

FIGURE 40-6

EVENTS

Our mobile web application now resembles a native mobile application in many ways, but there is still one core feature to add: mobile events.

The events generated by mobile devices are fundamentally different from traditional desktops in three basic ways:

➤ The user is holding the device; therefore they can convey meaning by moving the device. For instance, shaking an iOS-enabled device triggers an undo operation.

➤ The device (usually) supports touch screen; therefore the user can interact with the device by touching it with his or her fingers, and using "gestures."

➤ As you have seen, navigation is typically implemented differently in mobile web applications; therefore, mobile devices support a class of events linked to navigation.

Unfortunately, it is not possible to respond to the first class of events with mobile web applications because the API is only available to native web applications, but the next lesson looks at a work-around. This section addresses the other two classes of events.

Gestures

jQuery Mobile supports event listeners for four special types of events:

➤ **Swipe:** The `swipe` event involves the user moving a finger horizontally across the screen for 30 pixels or more within a time-range of 1 second. It is possible to listen for any swipe, swipes to the left (`swipeleft`), or swipes to the right (`swiperight`).

➤ **Tap:** The `tap` event is triggered by the user quickly touching the screen with a single finger. This event type is very similar to (and often confused with) a `click` event, and, in fact, mobile browsers will generate click events when the user taps the screen.

You may be wondering why you need to specifically listen for tap events when click events are generated automatically. The main reason is performance: There is often a significant lag between when the tap event is generated and when the click event is generated so if you want to create a responsive web application, you need to ensure you register tap event listeners.

If you are supporting mobile and non-mobile devices, you also need to ensure you register click listeners, of course. In order to make this process easier, jQuery Mobile supports a special event type called `vclick` (virtual click), which ensures the appropriate event listener is registered for the device.

➤ **Tap hold:** The `taphold` event is triggered when the user taps an area of the screen with one finger, and holds his finger in that spot for a sustained period (750 milliseconds by default). This event type is commonly used as an alternative to right-mouse clicks in mobile applications, and commonly produces a popup menu listing possible options from the context of the click.

Although this event has its uses, the main drawback of it is that the user may not be aware the functionality behind this event exists.

➤ **Scroll:** jQuery Mobile supports two scroll-based events: `scrollstart` and `scrollstop`. These events fire as the user scrolls a page with her finger.

jQuery Mobile event listeners are registered in an identical manner to conventional jQuery events. For instance, consider a case where you want a swipe on the Add contact screen to take the user back to the Contact list screen. This can be achieved with the following event listener:

```
$('#contactDetailsPage').on('swipe', function(evt) {
    $(":mobile-pagecontainer").pagecontainer("change", "#contactListPage", {
transition: 'slide', direction: 'reverse' });
    });
```

The event listener itself is registered on the entire page, meaning that the user can swipe anywhere on the screen, and the event will be captured.

Lifecycle Events

The other major class of event is related to jQuery Mobile lifecycle and page navigation. Because the user changes pages without loading a new HTML page, it is sometimes necessary to ensure a page is initialized appropriately when a user navigates to it for the first time, or that it is refreshed when the user navigates to it on subsequent occasions.

Just as jQuery supports a `ready` event, jQuery Mobile supports a `mobileinit` event: This method is invoked once per page refresh and indicates that jQuery Mobile has completed its initialization of the page. This event listener should be registered directly on the document—for instance:

```
$( document ).on( "mobileinit", function() {});
```

Just as the entire mobile web application is initialized, each page is also initialized once, on demand when the user first navigates to it. It is at this point that jQuery Mobile constructs the relevant UI components required by the page. It is possible to register an event listener that will be fired when this process completes. For instance, if you want to execute specific code after the Settings page is constructed, you can register the following event listener:

```
$(document).on('pagecreate','#settingsPage', function(){
    console.log('Settings page is being created');
});
```

Most of the other events are navigation related and therefore relate specifically to the `pagecontainer` component, which is the container holding all other pages. These events follow the lifecycle that occurs in jQuery Mobile as a page change is completed:

➤   An event is fired on the page that will be hidden, but while it is still visible.

➤   An event will be fired on the page that will be displayed, but before it is visible.

➤   An event is fired on the page that has been hidden, after it has been hidden.

➤   An event will be fired on the new page displayed, once it is visible.

Event listeners can be registered with this component as follows:

```
$(document).on("pagecontainerbeforechange", function( event, ui ) {
    console.log('Before change event fired');
});
```

The event listener is always passed two objects: The first is the event object you are familiar with from jQuery. In this particular case, because the page change has not occurred yet, you are afforded the opportunity to veto the page change by invoking `event.preventDefault()`.

The second object provides context about the UI event. For instance, it contains a `toPage` property indicating the page that the user is navigating to, and a `prevPage` property indicating the current page.

The other events that occur during the page navigation lifecycle are (in order):

➤ `pagecontainerbeforeshow`

➤ `pagecontainerhide`

➤ `pagecontainerload`

It is also possible to register an event listener that simply fires whenever a page transition completes; this can be accomplished by registering a listener with the `pagecontainertransition` event.

TRY IT

When developing mobile web applications, it is essential to have a fast turnaround between making code changes and seeing the results on a mobile device.

In order to ease this process, it is common to turn to mobile phone emulators. As you have seen, Chrome comes built in with a simple emulator, but in this Try It, you will install and use a more complex emulator called Ripple.

Lesson Requirements

In this lesson, you will need the Chrome web browser and a version of the CRM mobile web applications you have developed in this lesson.

Step-by-Step

1. Open the Chrome browser and browse to `chrome://apps`. From here, click the Web Store link at the bottom of the page.

2. Change the Types filter to "Extensions," and search for "Ripple." The result should return the app shown in Figure 40-7.

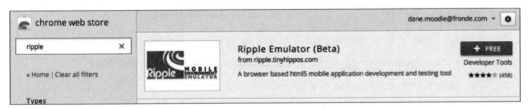

FIGURE 40-7

3. Select to install the Ripple application by clicking the + FREE button. The application will automatically be installed without a restart.

4. Open the `mobile_contacts.html` page through your web server. You will notice a small green button to the right of the toolbar, as shown in Figure 40-8. Click this, and then select Enable.

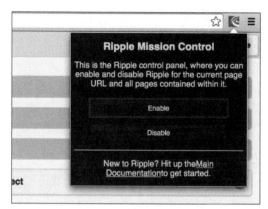

FIGURE 40-8

5. You will be prompted with a list of platforms that you wish to emulate; choose Mobile web (default).

6. You will be presented with a full screen emulator. Not only does this allow you to see how the mobile web application will look in various devices, but it allows you to manually set features such as the current location and the angle the phone is pointing.

7. In the top-left hand corner, select Devices and choose HTC Legend. The emulation should immediately change to show how the web application would appear in this particular phone.

8. Select to change the orientation of the phone to landscape mode.

9. Select the Platforms option and choose WebWorks. Press the Change Platform button. This will now show you how your web application will appear on a BlackBerry.

> **REFERENCE** *Please go to the book's website at* www.wrox.com/go/html5jsj-query24hr *to view the video for Lesson 40, as well as download the code and resources for this lesson.*

INDEX